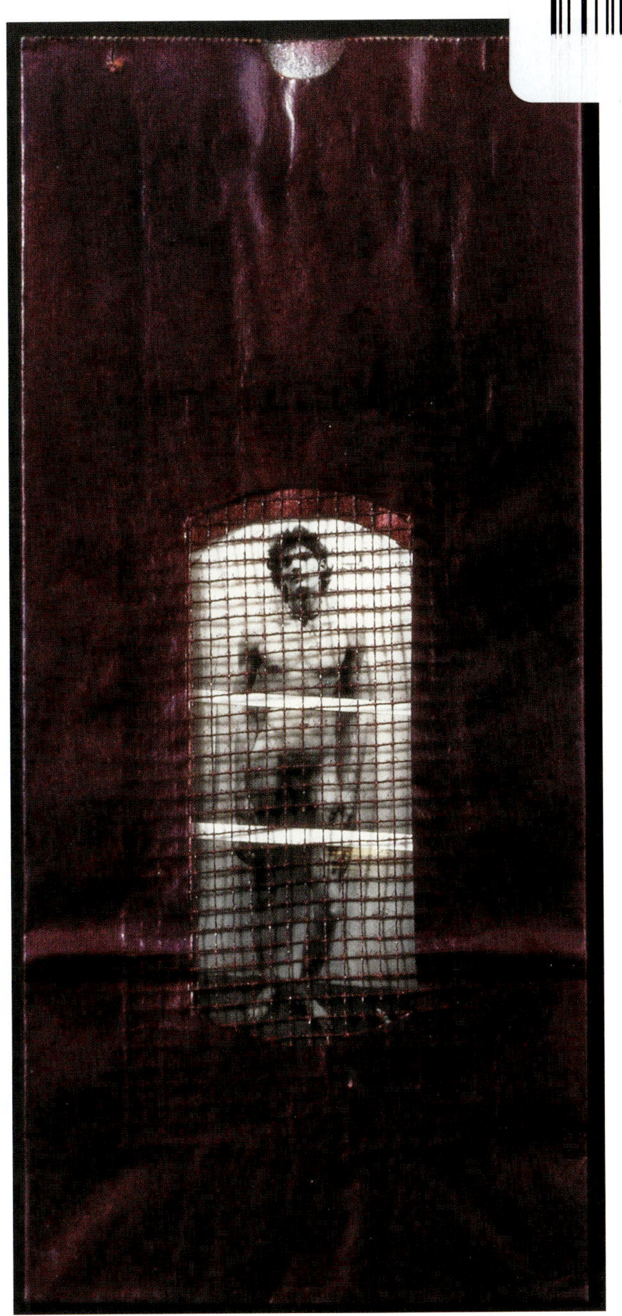

Plate 1. *Untitled (self-portrait)*. 1971

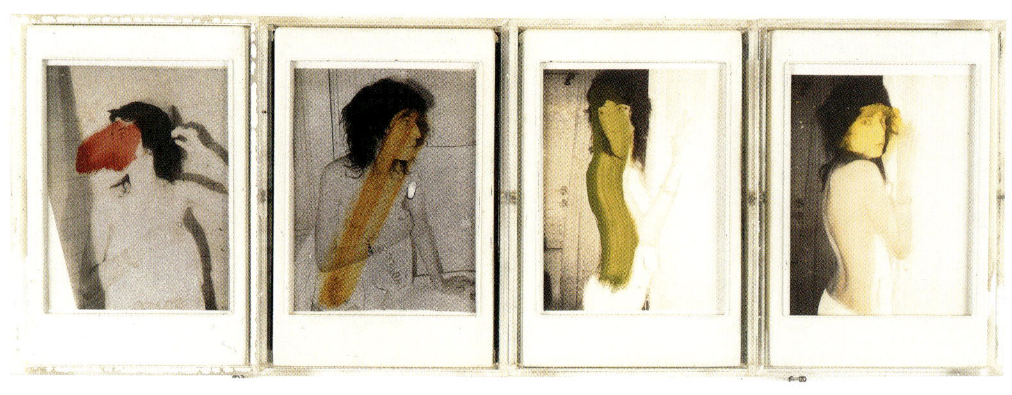

Plate 2. *Untitled (Patti Smith)*. 1970

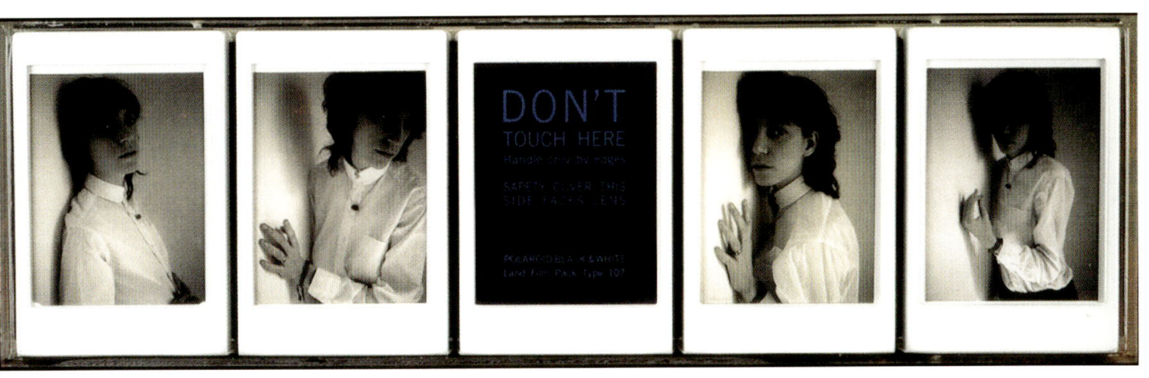

Plate 3. *Patti Smith (Don't Touch Here)*. 1973

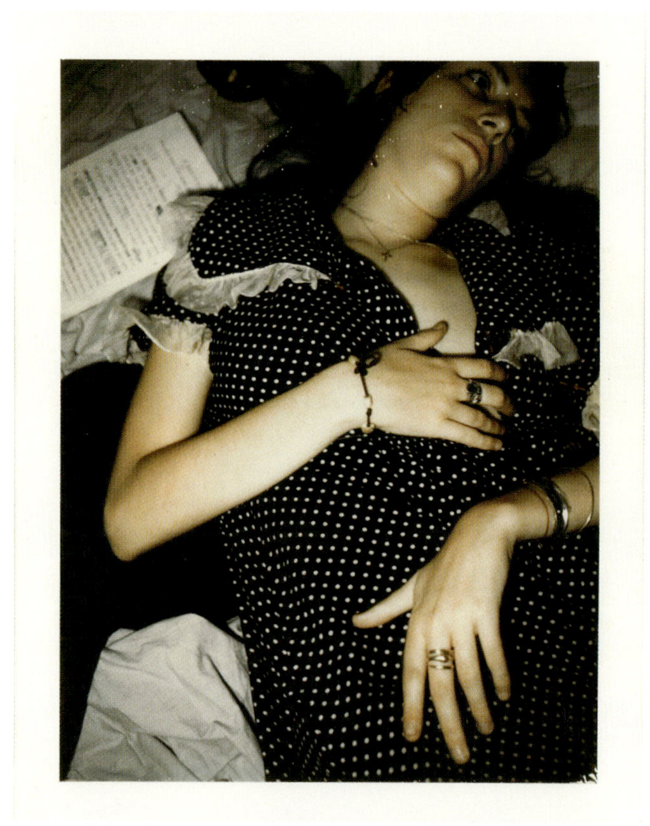

Plate 4. *Untitled (Patti Smith)*. 1971

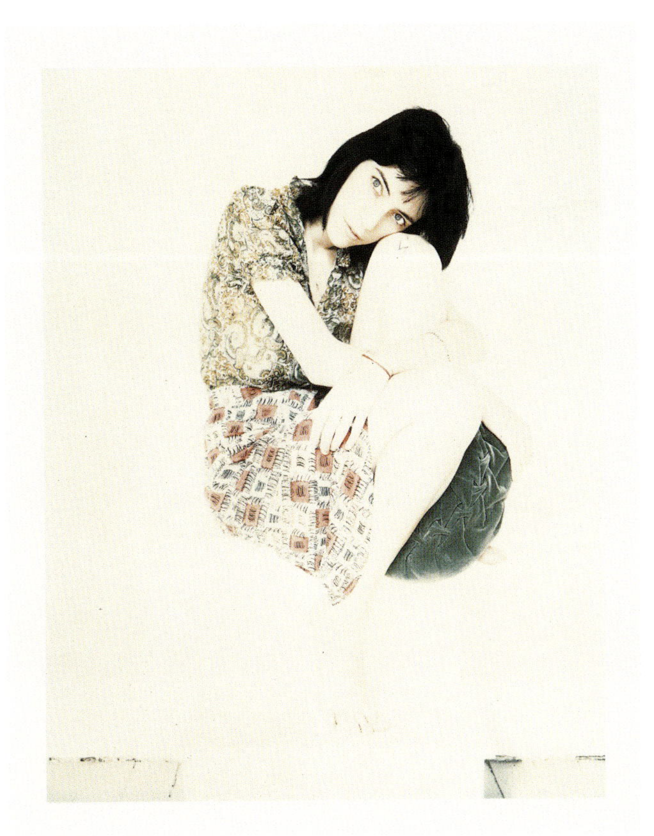

Plate 5. *Untitled (Patti Smith)*. 1971/73

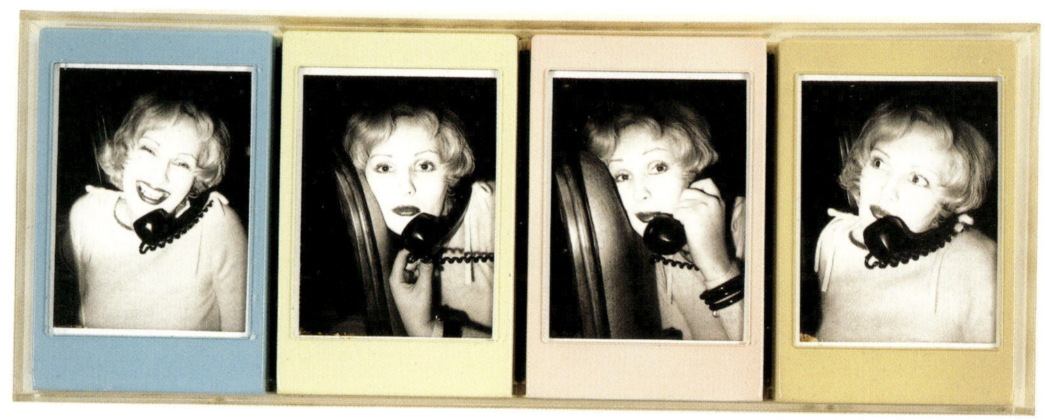

Plate 6. *Candy Darling.* 1973

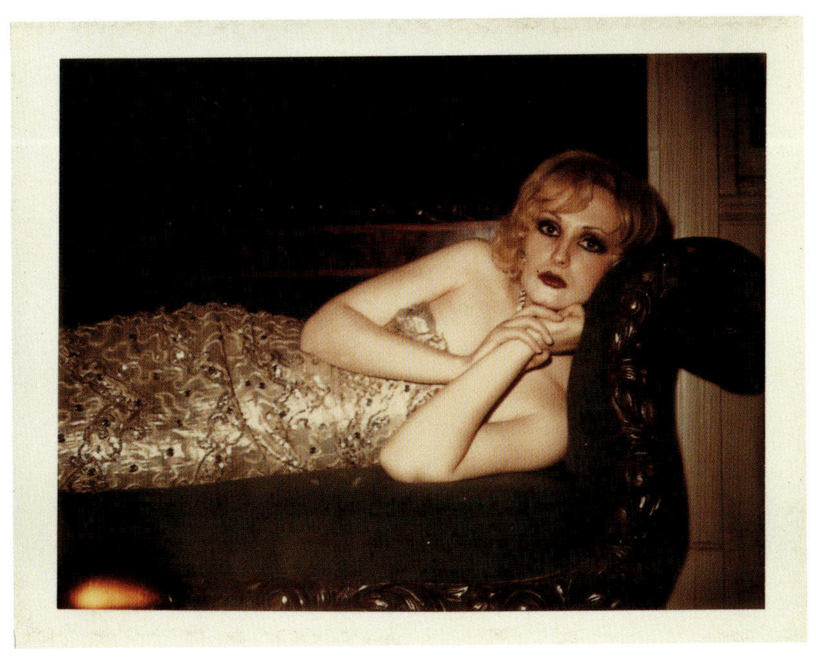

Plate 7. *Candy Darling*. 1971/73

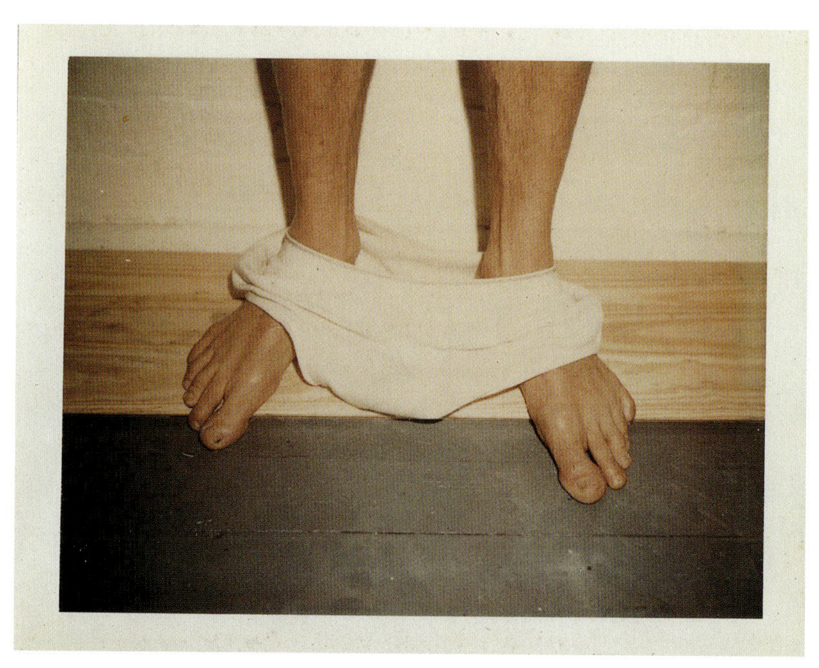

Plate 8. *Untitled (Sam Wagstaff)*. 1972/73

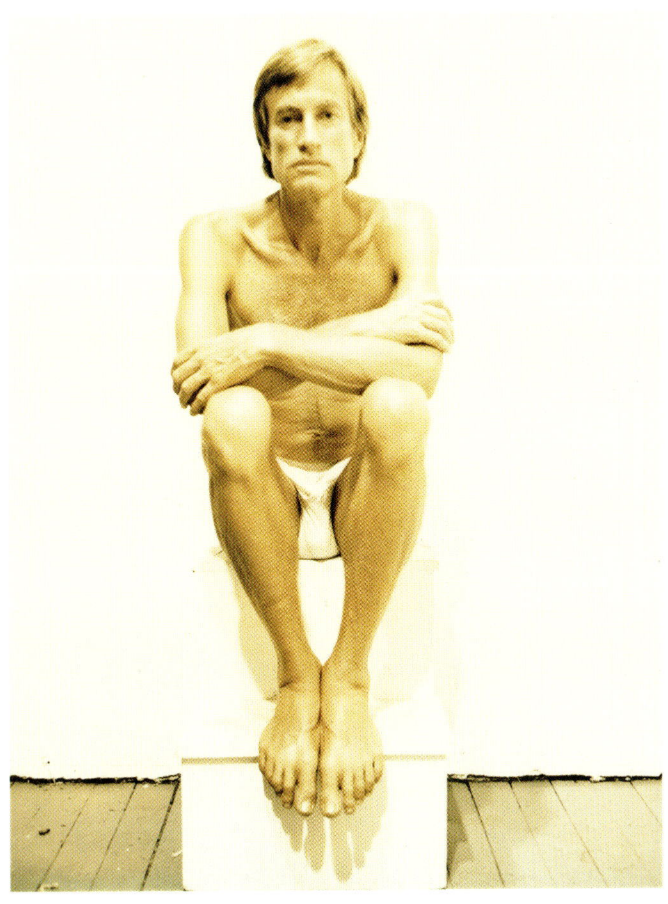

Plate 9. *Untitled (Sam Wagstaff)*. 1973/75

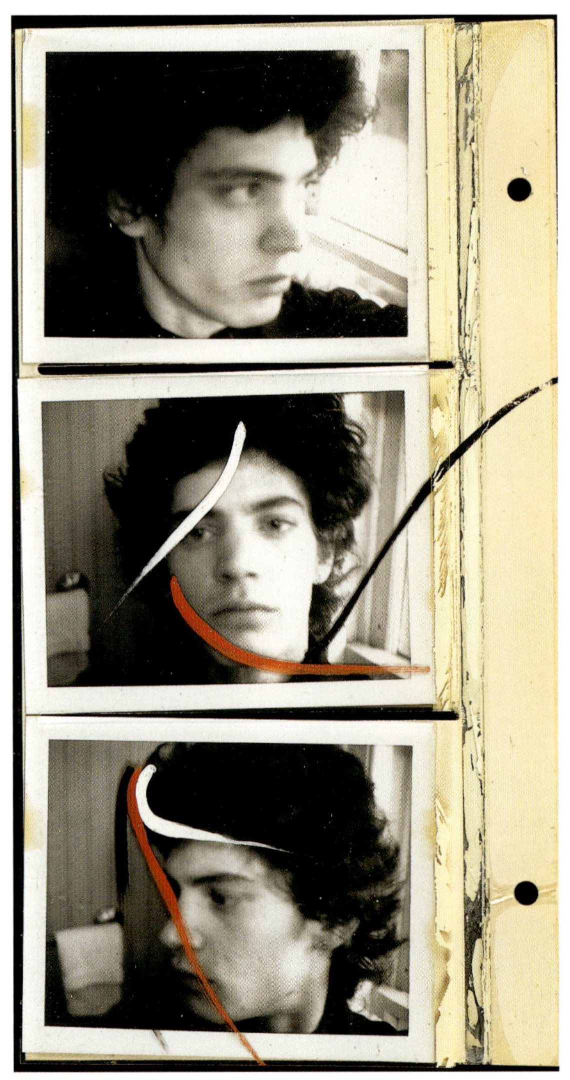

Plate 10. *Untitled (self-portrait)*. 1970/73

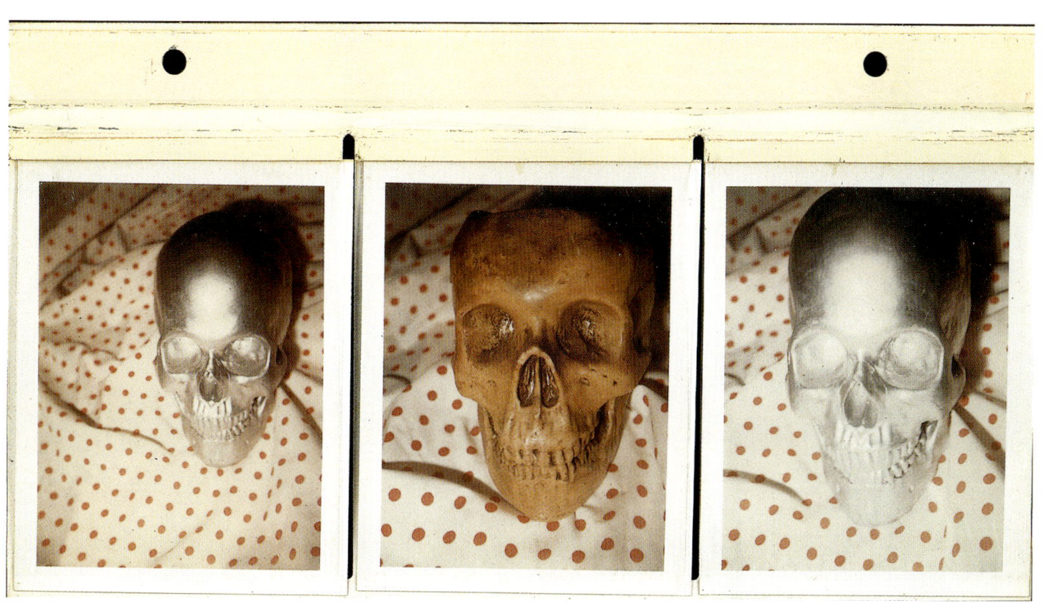

Plate 11. *Untitled*. 1970/73

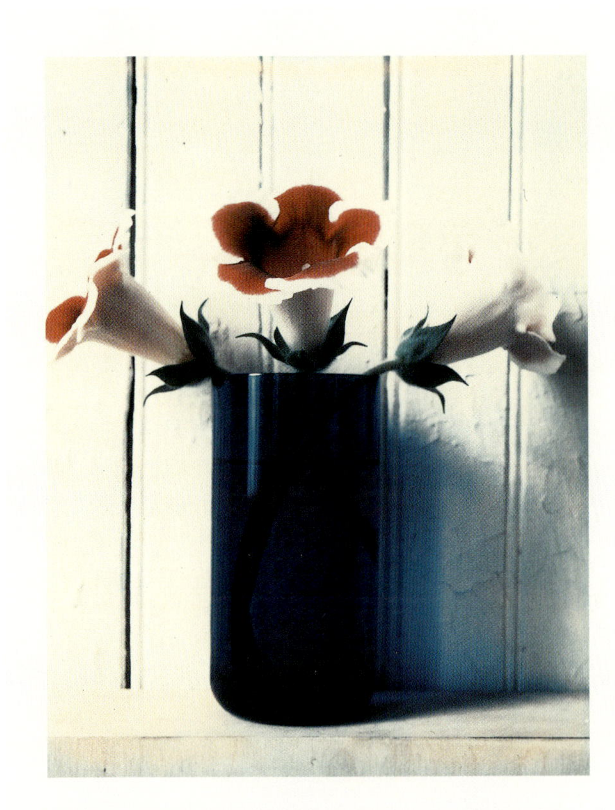

Plate 12. *Untitled*. 1970/73

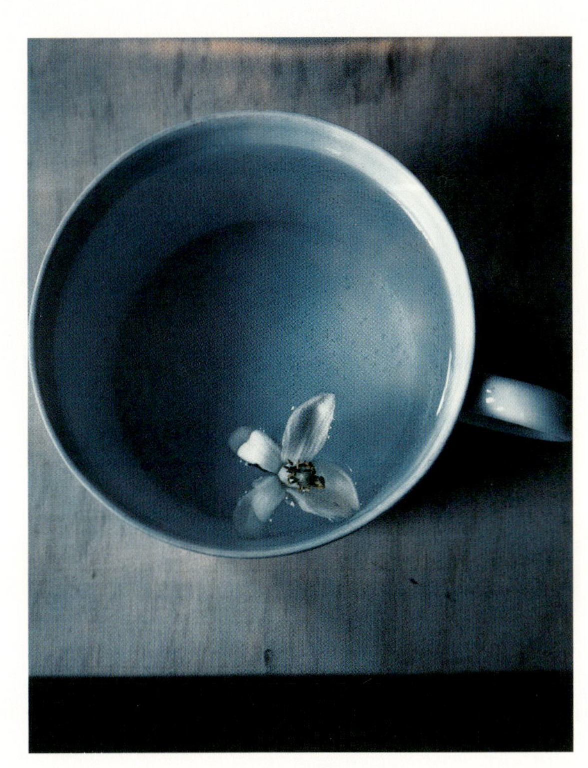

Plate 13. *Untitled*. 1970/73

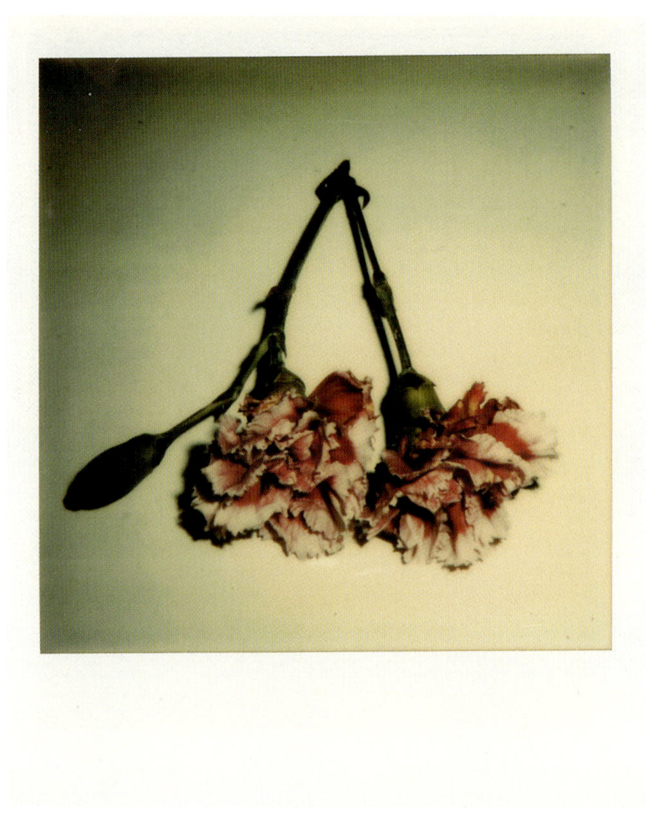

Plate 14. *Untitled*. 1975

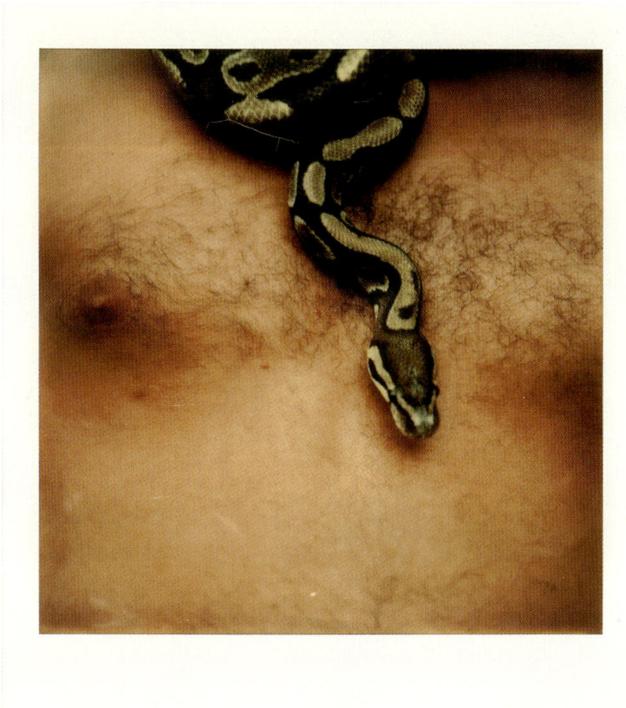

Plate 15. *Untitled*, 1975

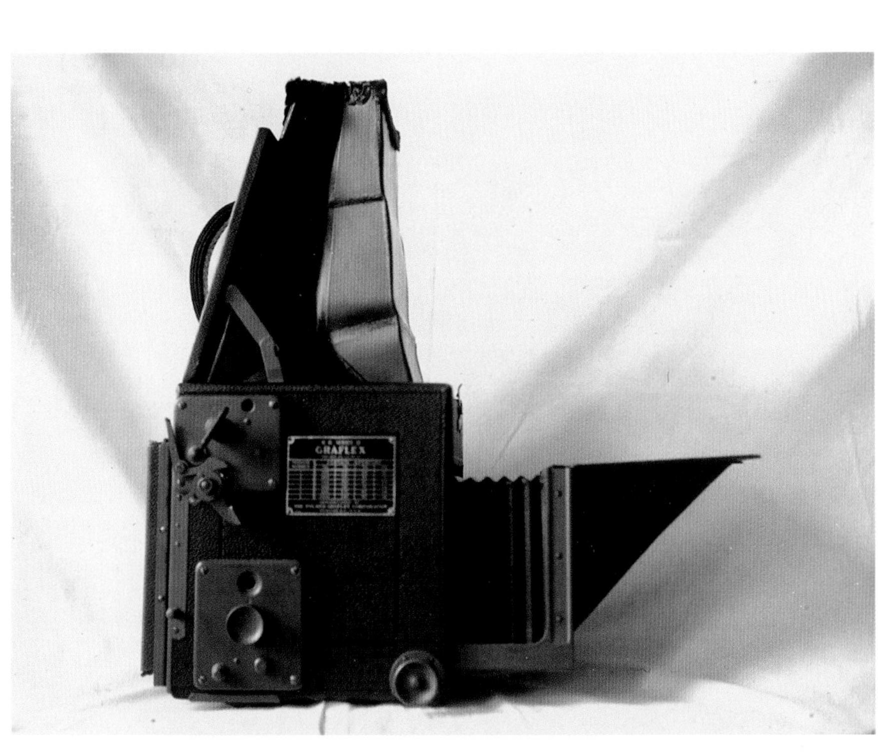
GRAFLEX

Polaroids
Mapplethorpe

Sylvia Wolf

PRESTEL
Munich · London · New York

Contents

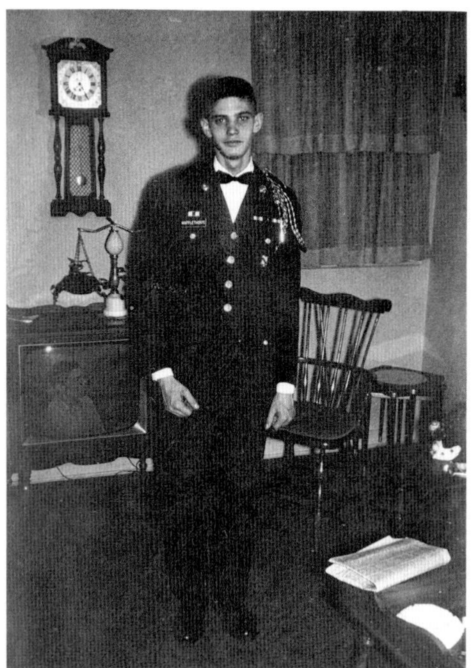

Fig. 1. Harry Mapplethorpe. *Robert Mapplethorpe in ROTC Uniform*. 1963. Gelatin silver print from color transparency, 7 x 5 in. (17.8 x 12.7 cm). Collection Edward Mapplethorpe

An Authentic Artlessness

Robert Mapplethorpe's Polaroids 1970–1975

In the summer of 1963, Robert Mapplethorpe was caught stealing a magazine of gay pornography from a newsstand in Times Square, New York. At age sixteen, working as a messenger in the months before entering art school, he had only just discovered that such publications existed and was legally too young to buy pornography, yet the longing to see proved too great for him to withstand. Gay pornography would make a lasting impression on him and would come to inform his artistic practice. In an interview in the late 1980s, he would recall,

I became obsessed with going into [magazine stands and storefronts] and seeing what was inside these magazines. They were all sealed, which made them even sexier somehow, because you couldn't get at them. . . . I got that feeling in my stomach, it's not a directly sexual one, it's more potent than that. I thought if I could somehow bring that element into art, if I could somehow retain that feeling, I would be doing something that was uniquely my own.[1]

For a young man who was only beginning to explore his sexual impulses, such raw and powerful emotions were both threatening and exciting—and the shame of being caught was likewise terrifying. (In fact, Mapplethorpe managed to break free of his captor and escape[2]). Perhaps out of fear, then, Mapplethorpe buried his feelings and in the year ahead renewed his efforts to conform to heterosexuality. But the desire to experience what is taboo, to get past veils of censorship and gain access to the forbidden, would return with visceral power, and in his second and third year in art school he would construct collages out of the very kinds of pictures found on Times Square newsstands. Later in his career, of course, his portraits, sexually explicit photographs, male nudes, and still lifes of flowers, all throbbing with homoerotic overtones, would make him famous.

The highly stylized, neoclassically inspired works that Mapplethorpe made between the late 1970s and his death, in 1989, did not emerge fully formed, however; nor did the homoerotic photographs that made him one of the most notorious photographers of the

1980s and a lightning rod for conservatives. His mature work was preceded by a largely unknown body of over 1,500 photographs, made with Polaroid cameras and film, during the six-year period 1970 to 1975. Unlike the carefully crafted and controlled images that Mapplethorpe would stage later in the studio, his Polaroids are marked by spontaneous invention. Some convey an unexpected tenderness and vulnerability; others have a toughness and immediacy that would give way in later years to a more-refined formalism. Compared to the work for which Mapplethorpe is best known, these are imperfect pictures that provide a glimpse of his early concern with light, composition, and design. An examination of this single aspect of his career, in the context of the period, the culture, and the artist's background, allows us a better understanding of the whole. Above all, though, Mapplethorpe's Polaroids give us access to his creative development at a time when he was shaping his identity as an artist and as a man.

In Formation

Before Mapplethorpe began experimenting with a Polaroid camera, he had shown no particular interest in taking pictures, despite the presence of photography in his history. His father, an engineer by profession, was an amateur photographer who kept a darkroom in the basement of the family home in Floral Park, Queens.[3] Robert's mother, in addition to maintaining the house, often assisted her husband in his hobby. Born on November 4, 1946, Mapplethorpe was the third of six children. Life in Queens was ordinary and unchanging: "I came from suburban America," he once remarked. "It was a very safe environment. And it was a good place to come from in that it was a good place to leave."[4] When it came time for college, Mapplethorpe longed to study out of state, but his father insisted that Robert attend his own alma mater, Pratt Institute, in the nearby borough of Brooklyn. Mapplethorpe enrolled there in September 1963 and declared a major in advertising design. Because he had graduated early from high school and was only sixteen when he entered Pratt, he spent his freshman year living at home.

Mapplethorpe's college years, from 1963 to 1969, coincided with a volatile time in American history. The civil rights movement, aimed at producing legislative change that would end discrimination against blacks, was becoming a powerful national force. In 1968 violent protests against the Vietnam War broke out across the country and Martin Luther King, Jr., and Robert F. Kennedy were assassinated. The women's movement was developing strength and visibility, as evidenced at the Miss America Pageant of 1968, where protesters threw bras, girdles, curlers, makeup, and high-heeled pumps into a garbage can, discarding them as "instruments of torture." On June 28, 1969, New York police officers raided the Stonewall Inn, a gay bar in

Greenwich Village, inadvertently sparking an assertive national gay-liberation movement.[5]

Against this backdrop of civic engagement and violence, a growing appetite for erotic experience emerged in both heterosexual and same-gender circles. In the decade to come, sex shops, x-rated movie houses, and adult bookstores would crop up not just in big cities but all over the country. New York's first gay cinema, the Park-Miller on 43rd Street, opened in the summer of 1969.[6] In 1971, Wakefield Poole's film *Boys in the Sand* would become the first gay pornographic film to receive crossover attention and widespread success. A year later, Gerard Demiano's *Deep Throat*, one of the first feature-length pornographic films, ran in theaters nationwide, achieving a cult status that signaled the potential of heterosexual pornography to move from an illicit form of entertainment to a popular one. By 1973, birth-control pills would be available at women's health centers across the country, and the Supreme Court decision in Roe v. Wade would legalize abortion.

During the growth of this sexual revolution, Mapplethorpe moved from conformism to rebellion. On entering college, he vowed to shed the homosexual desire that had nearly gotten him arrested that summer and to lead a "normal" life. In his freshman year he joined the ROTC and pledged the National Honor Society of Pershing Rifles, to which his father had belonged years before (fig. 1). The Pershing Rifles was a military-oriented drill company that prized leadership and discipline. Acceptance in this honorary fraternity involved weeks of training designed to break the spirit of the hopefuls. The trial period culminated in a night of brutal tests in which pledges were stripped of their clothes, blindfolded, and subjected to physical violence, sexual humiliation, and infantilizing cruelty.[7] Mapplethorpe endured the ordeal and was admitted into the fellowship. For months he projected an image of heterosexual masculinity, which included dating a Jackie Kennedy-like brunette, Nancy Nemeth, who was voted the queen of the 1965 ROTC Military Ball.

By the fall of that year, a growing number of students at Pratt were moving to the left, embracing the countercultural movement that would come to define the 1960s. Attracted by this lifestyle, Mapplethorpe began to distance himself from his military buddies and found kinship with the art students at Pratt. He switched majors from advertising design to graphic arts, which allowed him to study drawing and painting.[8] He also started to smoke marijuana, beginning a systematic use of drugs that would last the rest of his life. Mapplethorpe's works of these years reflect his appreciation for the Cubists, the Surrealists, and the artists Francis Bacon and Joseph Cornell. An untitled canvas from 1965, for instance, features a fragmented figure as a metaphor for multiple facets of the self, a motif that would reappear in his later collages and Polaroid photographs (fig. 2).

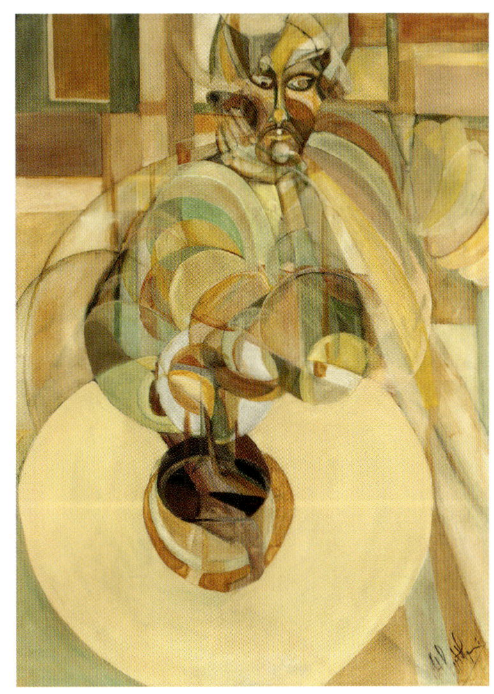

Fig. 2. Robert Mapplethorpe. *Untitled*. 1965. Acrylic on canvas, 30 x 22 in. (76.2 x 55.9 cm). Collection Edward Mapplethorpe

In the spring of 1967, Mapplethorpe met Patti Smith. Then a young poet, the future rock singer would become his soul mate. They lived together for the next five years, first as a couple, later as friends. Today, Smith remembers them as starving young artists who often had to decide between buying two sandwiches for dinner or sharing one to allow them to buy film or writing supplies.[9] They challenged one another, exchanged ideas, and fed off each other's energies and moods. Robert encouraged Patti to write and occasionally made artwork to accompany her poems. Patti read Rimbaud to Robert and contributed prized possessions to eclectic installations he made in their apartment.

Inspired and provoked by his Catholic upbringing, Mapplethorpe often made shrinelike works out of a broad range of materials, from men's underwear to prayer cards. Of his integration of the sacred and the profane, he once remarked that his most vivid memories of his childhood were of visits to Coney Island and to church.[10] The link between the two is not so distant: both incorporate visual stimulus, pageantry, and display. In Mapplethorpe's youth, the Catholic mass was held in Latin and included the burning of incense and the ringing of bells. "A church has a certain magic and mystery for a child," Mapplethorpe explained. "It still shows in how I arrange things. It's always little altars."[11]

In addition to the formal appeal of Catholic iconography, Mapplethorpe found fodder in stories and characters from the Bible. Extraordinary individuals who endured suffering and elicited devotion from the Virgin Mary to Andy Warhol, who had been shot in 1968—would be an ongoing fascination. (In 1987, after Warhol's death, Mapplethorpe would enshrine a portrait he had made of the artist, surrounded by a halo of light, in a cruciform frame.) For another of his early assemblages, *Tie Rack* (1969; fig. 3), Mapplethorpe enshrined a painting of the Madonna in black neckties. He marked the lintel of the frame with an X, as if it were a Station of the Cross, and outlined the Virgin's halo with a thin line of yellow pigment that pierces her neck. He also added sparkles to her white shift, over her chest and lungs, and painted a triangle over her eyes (the veiling or covering of eyes

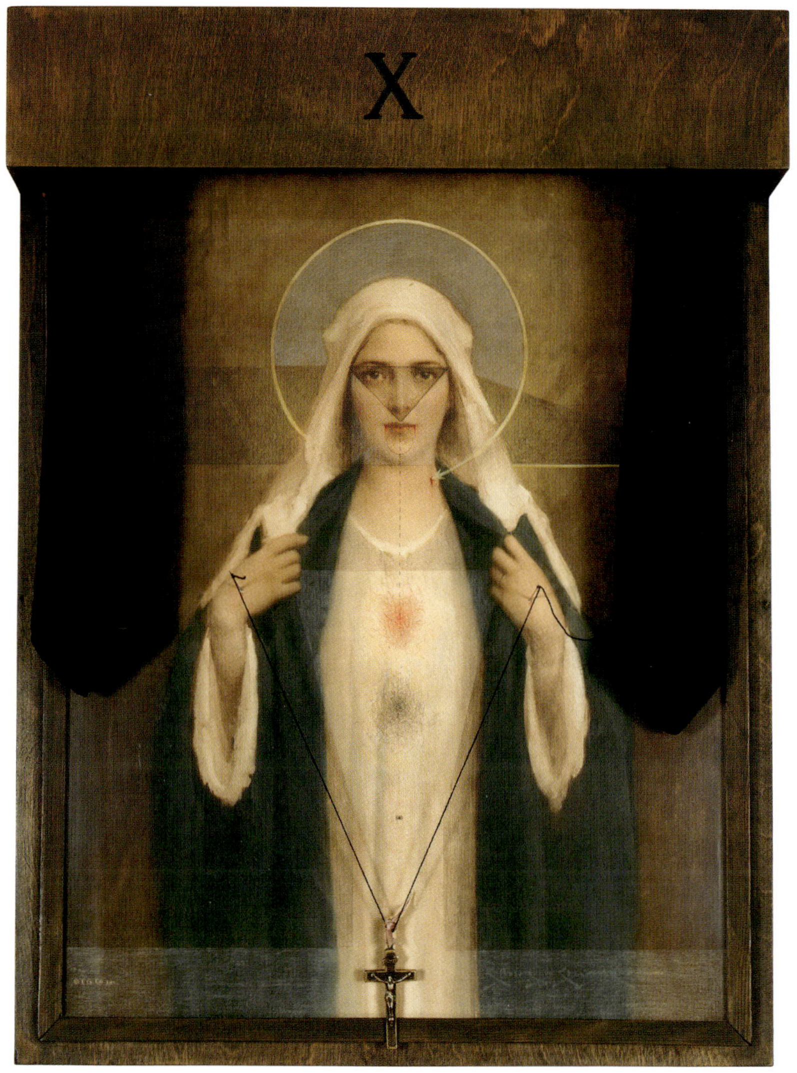

Fig. 3. Robert Mapplethorpe. *Tie Rack*. 1969. Mixed media, 24 x 18 x 4 1/2 in. (61 x 45.7 x 11.4 cm). Robert Mapplethorpe Foundation

would appear again and again in his work). It is common in portraits of the Virgin that she holds open her robe to reveal her heart. In Mapplethorpe's rendition, however, the gesture seems more like an erotic invitation, in part because of his alterations to the painting, which make it more a fetish object than a devotional image.

The sexualization of the spiritual has a long history in Catholic iconography, going back to the orgasmic swoon of Bernini's *Ecstasy of Saint Teresa* (1647–52) or the thinly veiled genitals of the damned and the saved in Michelangelo's *Last Judgment* (1535–41). Church doctrine is paradoxical in its ideas on the body, as the critic Eleanor

Heartney has written: its assertion that human beings are created in the image of God would suggest that human sexuality must be godly too, but instead the Church mandates that the demands of the flesh be harnessed or transcended rather than celebrated or indulged.[12] Mapplethorpe was not the only Catholic-raised artist to find contradictions in these teachings, nor was he the only one in our time to make art that is part reverent, part sacrilegious. (Among others are the filmmaker Martin Scorsese, the photographer Andres Serrano, the painter Chris Ofili, and the pop star Madonna). While Mapplethorpe may have been embittered by Catholicism's condemnation of homosexuality, he also found in it a resource for artmaking. He equally embraced the sacred and the profane, and even found a biblical alter ego in the fallen angel Lucifer.

Mapplethorpe's fascination with religious tradition and his burgeoning interest in homosexuality appear clearly in an album he made in 1970, a store-bought sketchbook that became a highly individual object of devotion. The album opens with a photograph of Mapplethorpe, nude, his genitals and nipples covered by red paper dots of the kind found in office-supply stores (fig. 4). The photograph is set above a small calendar for the year 1970. Turning the page reveals a collage that has windows, which open to reveal pictures, (fig. 5), just as Advent calendars mark each day of the four-week period of penitence and preparation before Christmas. Among these hidden images are store-bought angel stickers and hand-painted photo-booth snapshots of Patti Smith. Farther on, the album introduces homoerotic imagery with a magazine picture of a tumescent penis, framed with black tape and enclosed by four triangular panels that close over it in the peek-a-boo style of children's pop-up books (fig. 6). Mapplethorpe has painted the head of the penis red, placed a star above the photograph, and set the name "Davey" below. In addition to the questions that the collage invites (who is Davey? Is he red hot?), the star, the patriotic colors, and the typography recall the flags that were placed in windows during World War II when a loved one was lost in battle. Military motifs appear often in Mapplethorpe's early work, perhaps inspired by his ROTC experience.

With its range of subjects and materials, the album manifests a visceral discontinuity between the childlike and the erotic. The use of stars and stickers, for example, conjures up childhood arts-and-crafts projects, and the format of the Advent calendar reminds us of the impatience of youth. (What Catholic child has not had the impulse to open all of the windows in one of these calendars at once?) Inviting suspense and withholding gratification can be an agonizingly pleasurable experience, particularly in the realm of sex. By 1970, Mapplethorpe had begun to explore his sexual attraction to men, trying to determine whether he was gay, straight, or bisexual.

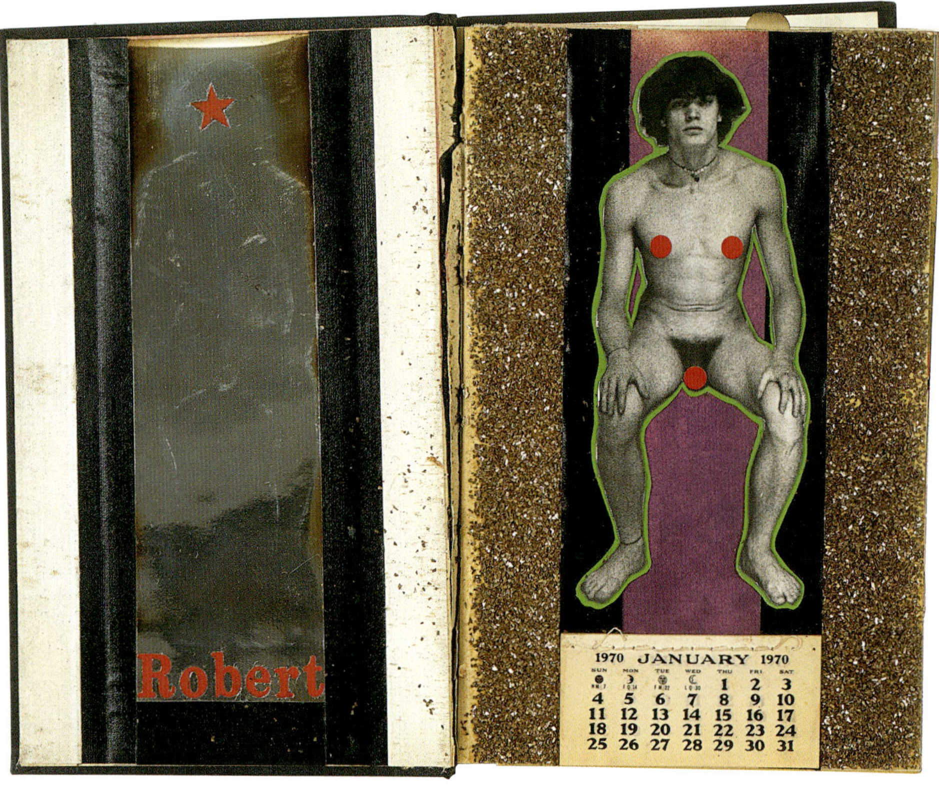

Fig. 4. Robert Mapplethorpe. *Untitled*. 1970. Mixed media, 8 1/2 x 5 1/4 x 1 in. (21.6 x 13.3 x 2.5 cm). Collection Philip Aarons and Shelley Fox Aarons

He had left Pratt and he and Smith were living at the Chelsea Hotel.[13] There Mapplethorpe met Sandy Daley, a filmmaker who lent him her Polaroid camera, accompanied him to leather bars, and introduced him to Max's Kansas City, the famous artists' restaurant and bar. Daley also showed him art books and encouraged him to submit his portfolio to galleries.

Mapplethorpe's works from the early 1970s reflect how quickly he embraced the gay fashion, lifestyle, and visual culture of the time. One collage, *Bull's Eye* (1970; fig.7), features a photograph clipped from a gay porn magazine of a male model standing with legs akimbo, wearing nothing but a black leather hat and riding boots—the clothes of a policeman or a biker. A translucent square of yellow paint veils his groin, sparkles pepper his chest, and two black bands perforated with holes frame the side edges, partly obscuring the figure while also invoking the halftone process of photomechanical reproduction. A black bar covers the model's eyes and face, a practice used in newspapers and early pornography either to protect the innocent or to conceal the identity of the sinner. Mapplethorpe has positioned a white dot with a red center

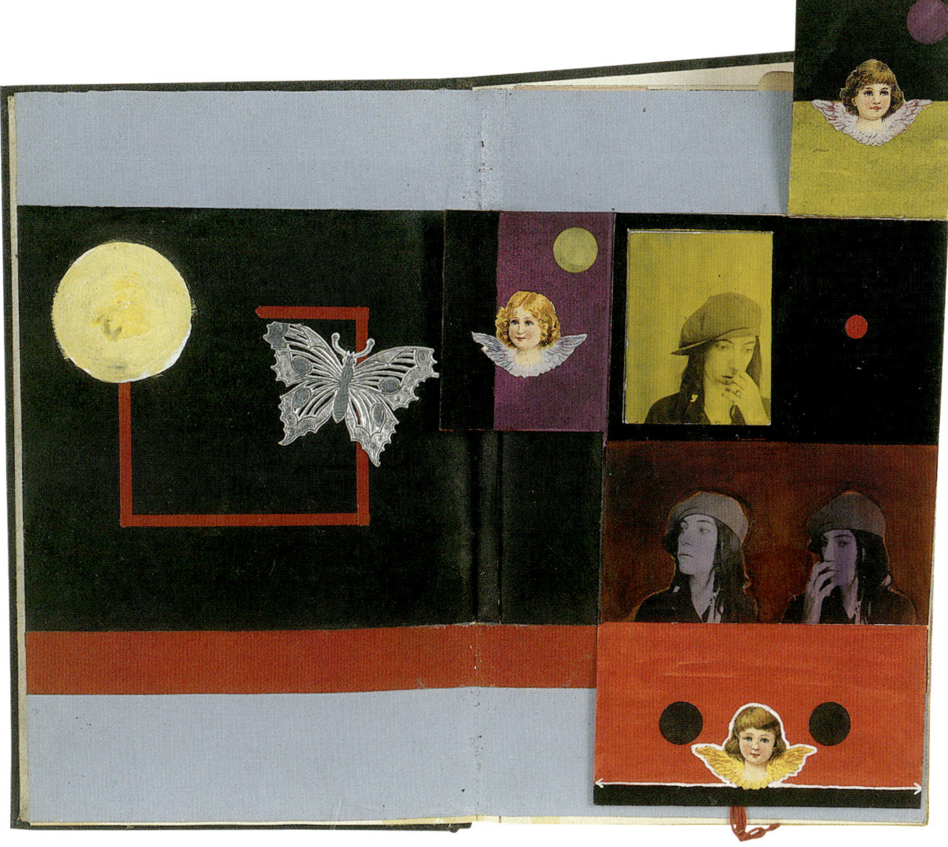

Fig. 5. Robert Mapplethorpe. *Untitled*. 1970. Mixed media, 8 1/2 x 5 1/4 x 1 in. (21.6 x 13.3 x 2.5 cm). Collection Philip Aarons and Shelley Fox Aarons

over the penis—the bull's-eye referred to in the title. The idea of the penis as both the locus of interest and a target involves both pleasure and pain; this castration aspect of the piece may reflect the artist's growing interest in sadomasochism.

Mapplethorpe once said that he first turned to Polaroids to make photographs for his homoerotic collages. He felt "it was more honest"—that rendering his personal experience was more authentic than using found images.[14] It was also more efficient and cheaper to take his own pictures than to buy porn magazines, which at the time were sold wrapped in cellophane and so could not be perused to see if they held material of interest. Also, if Mapplethorpe wanted a particular pose or sexual practice for a piece, he could enact it for the camera and get immediate results. Yet few of his collages make use of his Polaroid photographs. While he continued to utilize magazine images in his art well into the mid-1970s, he soon discovered the gratification of making Polaroid photographs to be appreciated in their own right.

Muses and Mentors

From the very beginning of his use of the Polaroid camera, Mapplethorpe

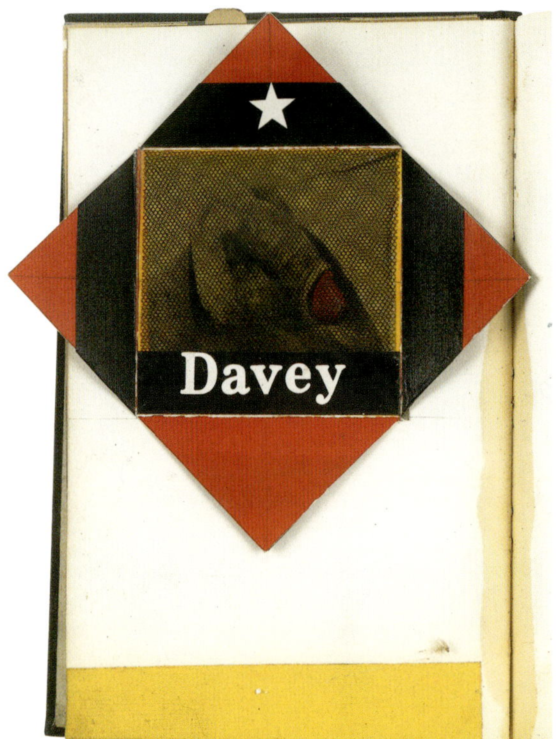

Fig. 6. Robert Mapplethorpe. *Untitled*. 1970. Mixed media, 8 1/2 x 5 1/4 x 1 in. (21.6 x 13.3 x 2.5 cm). Collection Philip Aarons and Shelley Fox Aarons

photographed Patti Smith. He took dozens of pictures of her during the first decade of their friendship, from their days as aspiring artists to their becoming well-known—Robert for photographs, Patti for rock 'n' roll (pls. 2–5, 30–41). Among the first of Mapplethorpe's portraits of Smith is a four-part piece shot in their Chelsea Hotel bathroom (pl. 2). Partly nude, her hair typically disheveled, she holds a towel to her chest. From photograph to photograph she looks to the left and to the right, then confronts the camera head-on. Mapplethorpe had yet to get the hang of the Polaroid process, which in those years required timing the development, separating the print from the negative at the right moment, then coating it with a fixing solution applied evenly with a roller. These four photographs are underdeveloped and poorly coated. Unwilling to discard them, however, Mapplethorpe applied splashes of color to their surfaces, much as he had covered parts of pictures with mesh or pigment in previous collages. He then sequenced them in spray-painted frames made from Polaroid film holders.

Some images of Patti are infused with the affection that comes with long friendship and intimacy. Others hint at Mapplethorpe's and Smith's ferocious attachment. Another piece contains four photographs of a pensive-looking Smith, wearing a man's white shirt buttoned to the top and hugging a white plaster wall; the center frame is a protective sleeve for Polaroid film, which warns "DON'T TOUCH HERE" (pl. 3). The words are the manufacturer's but the command may be read as spoken either by the photographer, possessively, or by the sitter, in defiance. Other photographs reference figures from film, art, and music. In one, Smith appears as an aloof bohemian with a cigarette, resembling the painter Lee Krasner or the Italian screen actress Anna Magnani. In another, her dark glasses, defiant posture, and bushy hair recall Bob Dylan album covers from the 1960s.[15]

In all Mapplethorpe's photographs of Smith, her charismatic presence and will engage the camera. Vanity, the desire to project beauty, or the need to exert control do not come into play here; instead we see Smith in various states of dress and

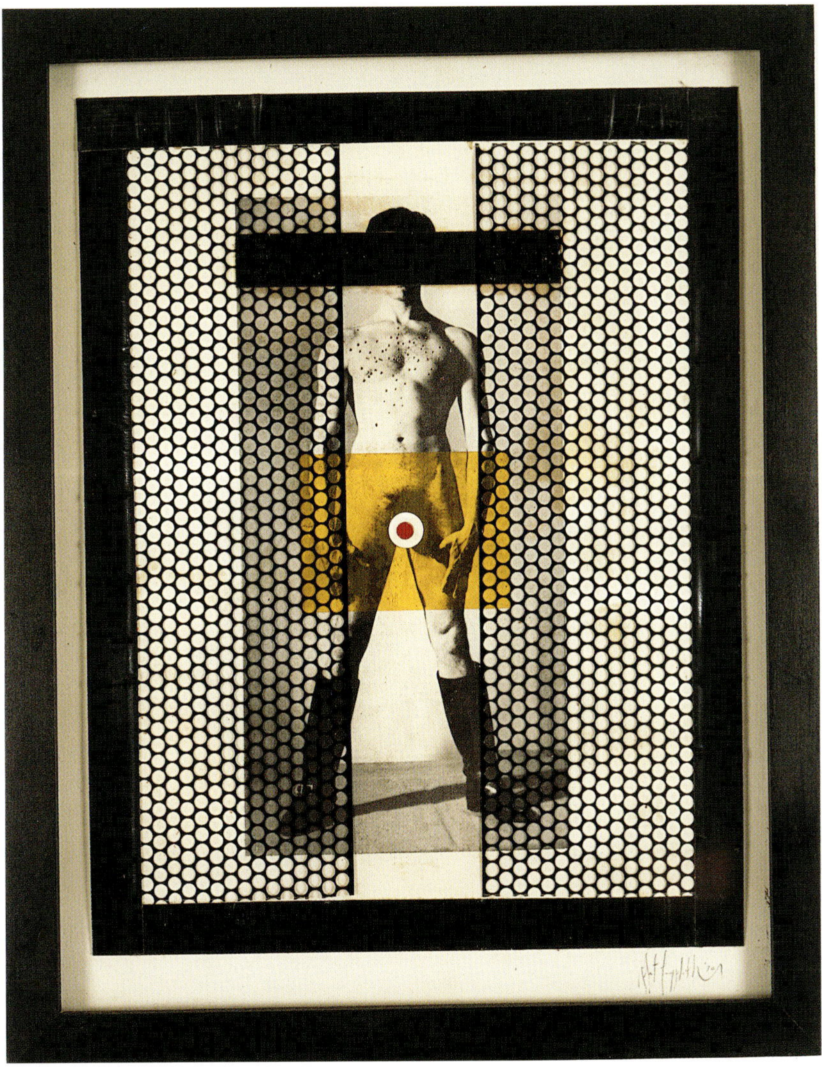

Fig. 7. Robert Mapplethorpe. *Bull's Eye.* 1970. Mixed media, 14 x 11 x 1 in. (35.6 x 27.9 x 2.5 cm). Private collection

mood, from vulnerable to tough, demure to defiant. More than any of Mapplethorpe's other portrait subjects, Smith was both a muse and a mirror for him. On the one hand, she offered inspiration, on the other she validated his endeavors with her participation. This may be why Mapplethorpe's photographs of her are intensely intimate, even when the two were no longer romantically involved. Smith was not a passive subject taking direction from Mapplethorpe (although he was known to be exacting when posing his models). Instead, the sessions were a collaboration. Indeed it was common for Smith to ask later, "How did we do?"[16]

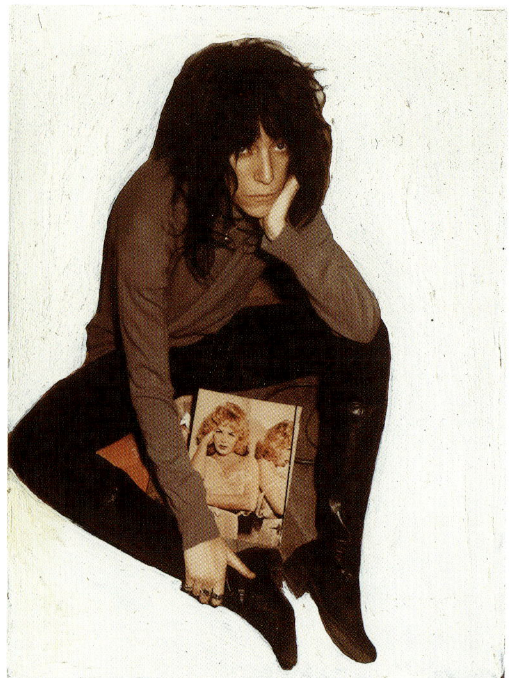

Fig. 8. Robert Mapplethorpe. *Untitled (Patti Smith)*. 1970/73. Internal dye diffusion transfer print (Polaroid) and pigment, 4 1/4 x 3 1/4 in. (10.8 x 8.3 cm). Private collection

Images of intimate partners are many in the history of photography, from Alfred Stieglitz's many portraits of Georgia O'Keeffe to Harry Callahan's dozens of photographs of his wife, Eleanor. Like these and other pictures of spouses and lovers, Mapplethorpe's images of Smith reflect the depth and complexity of their relationship and provide evidence of their shared sense of the importance of their work together. We, in turn, are third-party observers who get a privileged peek at the dynamic between two partners.

To make a different kind of portrait of Smith, Mapplethorpe used color Polaroid film to photograph her huddled on the floor, holding a glossy magazine (fig. 8). With her boyish attire, unruly hair, and apathetic slouch, Smith projects a counter-image to the glamour and sex appeal of the lingerie-clad blonde in the magazine picture. Mapplethorpe makes Smith float in a world of her own by applying white pigment to the print, eliminating the background. Mapplethorpe also experimented with a technique called emulsion-transfer in which a Polaroid print is soaked in hot water until the emulsion lifts from the paper support and can then be manipulated to create different shapes.[17] In one work made this way (fig. 9) Smith wears the straw hat that was part of her costume for the 1971 play *Cowboy Mouth*, which she cowrote with the playwright Sam Shepard.[18] Here Mapplethorpe stretched and distorted the image before applying it to a fresh sheet of paper, and highlighted the edges with paint. The reduced contrast and muted colors give the work a painterly quality. As such, these experiments may be viewed as linked to Mapplethorpe's early desire to be a painter. The impulse was short-lived, however: he produced less than a dozen emulsion transfers, focusing instead on making Polaroids.

Because relatively few of Mapplethorpe's Polaroid photographs are titled, signed, dated, or annotated in any way, it is often difficult to determine exactly when they were made. Time spans for their creation, however, can be estimated by determining when Mapplethorpe met a subject, by recollections of friends and sitters, by examining details of the pictures (the Chelsea Hotel bathroom, for example, implies a timeframe, as does the straw hat from *Cowboy Mouth*), and by considering the pictures' dimensions.

Fig. 9. Robert Mapplethorpe. *Untitled (Patti Smith)*. 1971/72. Synthetic emulsion on paper with ink, 13 1/2 x 10 3/4 in. (34.3 x 27.3 cm). Robert Mapplethorpe Foundation

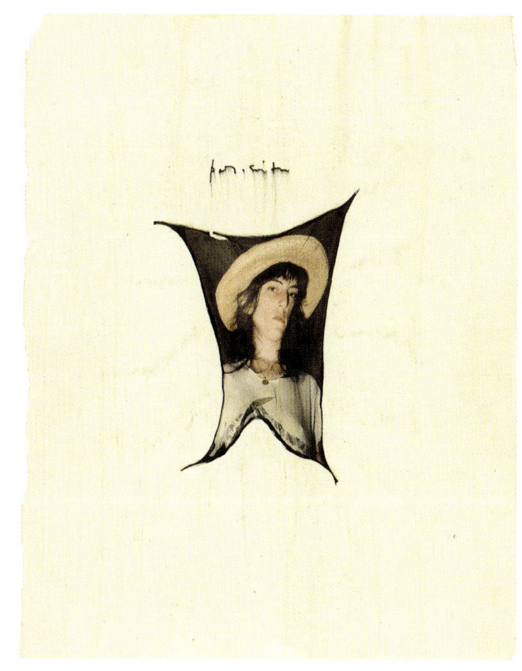

Prints measuring 3 1/4 by 4 1/4 inches are from the Polaroid Model 360 camera that Mapplethorpe used between 1970 and 1973. Prints measuring 4 1/8 by 5 1/8 inches were made between 1973 and 1975, with a Graflex camera outfitted with a Polaroid back. After 1975, Mapplethorpe stopped using Polaroid materials in any regular way.[19] The discussion of these works, therefore, is only loosely chronological. It is unclear, for example, exactly when Mapplethorpe first started working with a Polaroid. He borrowed Daley's camera sometime in early 1970. Later that same year, on Memorial Day, Mapplethorpe met David Croland, a young artist and model, born in New Jersey, with whom he began his first homosexual relationship. Croland recalls that Mapplethorpe began making Polaroids of him soon after they met.[20]

With the Polaroid camera, Mapplethorpe photographed Croland in erotically charged poses, including a color picture of him in leather briefs and jacket, fists clenched, legs spread, and looking off camera (fig. 10). The drama of the pose and Mapplethorpe's use of flash, which makes the leather shine and puts Croland in the spotlight, render the picture exhibitionistic and crude. Another photograph depicts Croland as submissive, lying on a tiled bathroom floor in a tuxedo vest, a bowtie, and no shirt. His arms are pressed rigidly against his side, as if bound, and his mouth is gagged—a reference to sadomasochism, perhaps, or to the silences surrounding homosexuality (fig. 11). Croland remembers that being photographed by Mapplethorpe was an erotic experience in itself—for Robert, taking pictures was a means of seduction and a catalyst for sex.[21] A camera that produces an instant photograph allows both photographer and model to respond to the image as part of their interaction. Indeed that was the primary appeal of the Polaroid process for Mapplethorpe: it was immediate.

Long before digital technology made instant viewing a standard part of picture-making, Polaroid cameras gave rapid results. Mapplethorpe said in 1988 that photography "was the perfect medium, or so it seemed, for the '70s and '80s, when everything was fast. If I were to make something that took two weeks to do, I'd lose my enthusiasm. It would become an act of labor and the love would be gone."[22] The Polaroid allowed Mapplethorpe to remain enthralled

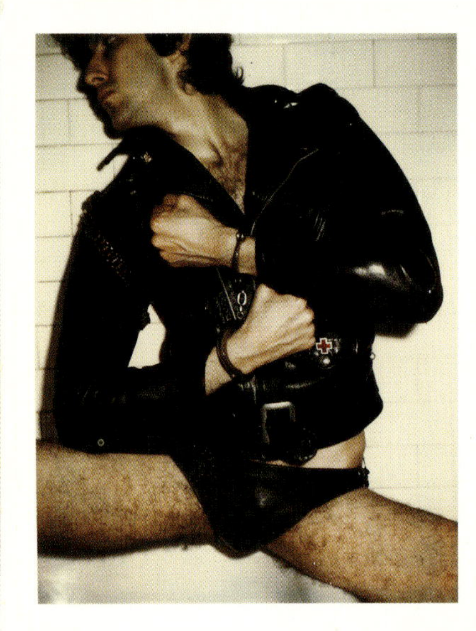

Fig. 10. Robert Mapplethorpe. *Untitled (David Croland).* 1972. Internal dye diffusion transfer print (Polaroid), 4 ¹/₄ x 3 ¹/₄ in. (10.8 x 8.3 cm). Robert Mapplethorpe Foundation

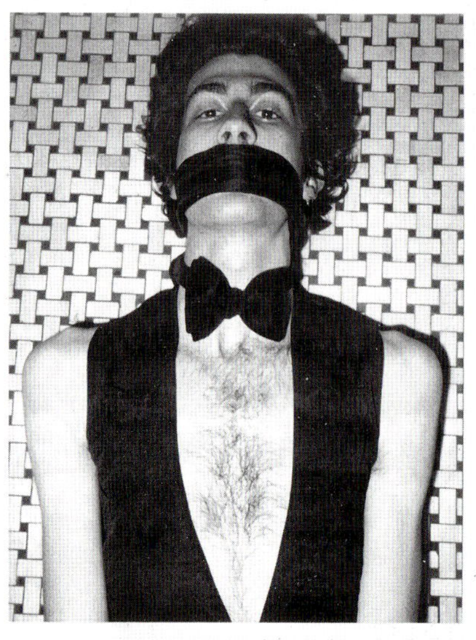

Fig. 11. Robert Mapplethorpe. *Untitled (David Croland).* 1972. Monochromatic dye diffusion transfer print (Polaroid), 4 ¹/₄ x 3 ¹/₄ in. (10.8 x 8.3 cm). Robert Mapplethorpe Foundation

with his subjects as he photographed the sexual energy between them. Arousal was heightened by working spontaneously. Moreover, seeing in the moment allowed for a free access to feeling and thinking. Making pictures was not a measured or heavily considered activity.

This visual responsiveness to the moment carried over into Mapplethorpe's picture-making outside of the bedroom or studio, and it is one of the distinguishing characteristics of this body of work. Of the hundreds of Polaroids Mapplethorpe took between 1970 and 1975, a significant percentage are of casual acquaintances, unremarkable subjects, and uninteresting stuff, but Mapplethorpe's use of natural light, the high silver content of black and white Polaroid prints, and the shallow depth of field of the particular camera he used give these images a broad tonal range and exquisite softness. In these small, intimate images we see Mapplethorpe looking at the world with curiosity and appreciation for the beauty of ordinary things. Photographs of a ceramic jug, for example (pl. 16), and of a shop-window display of children's shoes (pl. 26) reflect a childlike wonder and a pure delight in seeing. They also reveal his attraction to methods of presentation and to the sensuality of rounded forms, which would become defining characteristics of his mature work. Mapplethorpe made pictures of things around the house, from light fixtures to the contents of his refrigerator, which he arranged in triptychs in drugstore photo albums (fig. 12). He also found religious symbolism, displaced eroticism, and drama in the everyday. A telephone pole silhouetted against a cloudless sky, say, may

Fig. 12. Robert Mapplethorpe. *Untitled*. 1970/73. Three monochromatic dye diffusion transfer prints (Polaroids) in plastic sleeve, each 3 1/4 x 4 1/4 in. (8.3 x 10.8 cm). Robert Mapplethorpe Foundation

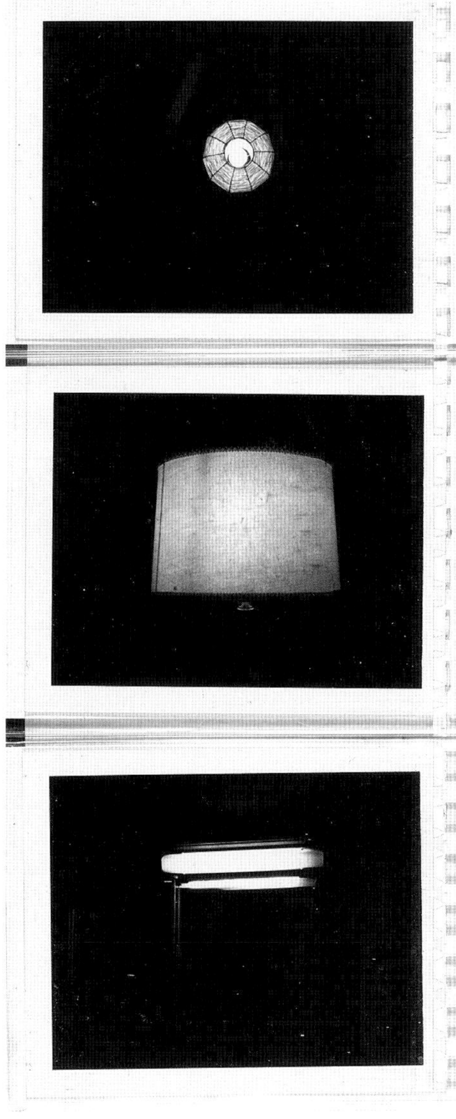

be read as a phallus or a crucifix (pl. 20), while city rooftops at night recall the deep shadows and dark mood of film noir (pl. 21). In their simplicity of composition, delicacy of tone, and diaristic quality, these are distinctly personal, almost tender pictures.

Other photographs show Mapplethorpe earnestly experimenting with camera angles, depth of field, light, and framing. One image depicts the Royal Artillery War Memorial at Hyde Park Corner, London.[23] Seen from below, the hulking cloaked figure looks more like an Arthurian knight than a soldier from World War I (pl. 19). Another picture made in London, through the lace-curtained window of an upper-floor flat, angles down on a storefront selling plumbing supplies, whose signage announcing "potties" would have appealed to Mapplethorpe's sense of humor (pl. 18). In a photograph of a rotary-dial telephone (pl. 17), Mapplethorpe throws the foreground out of focus by setting the camera at a low vantage point, and in a picture of a vase of roses (pl. 22), the camera is too close to the subject to register it in detail. The flowers' bloated overripeness and the chintzlike wallpaper barely discernible behind them lend the picture a Victorian melancholy. Unlike the flowers in Mapplethorpe's later photographs, shot in the studio and carefully arranged to suggest body parts or pure perfection (fig. 13), these are scraggly, scrawny stalks with blossoms that are well past their prime.

Many of the pictures mentioned above were made in London on a trip Mapplethorpe made at the invitation of his first significant benefactor, John McKendry, then curator of photographs and prints at New York's Metropolitan Museum of Art. Croland introduced Mapplethorpe to McKendry at a dinner party hosted by the

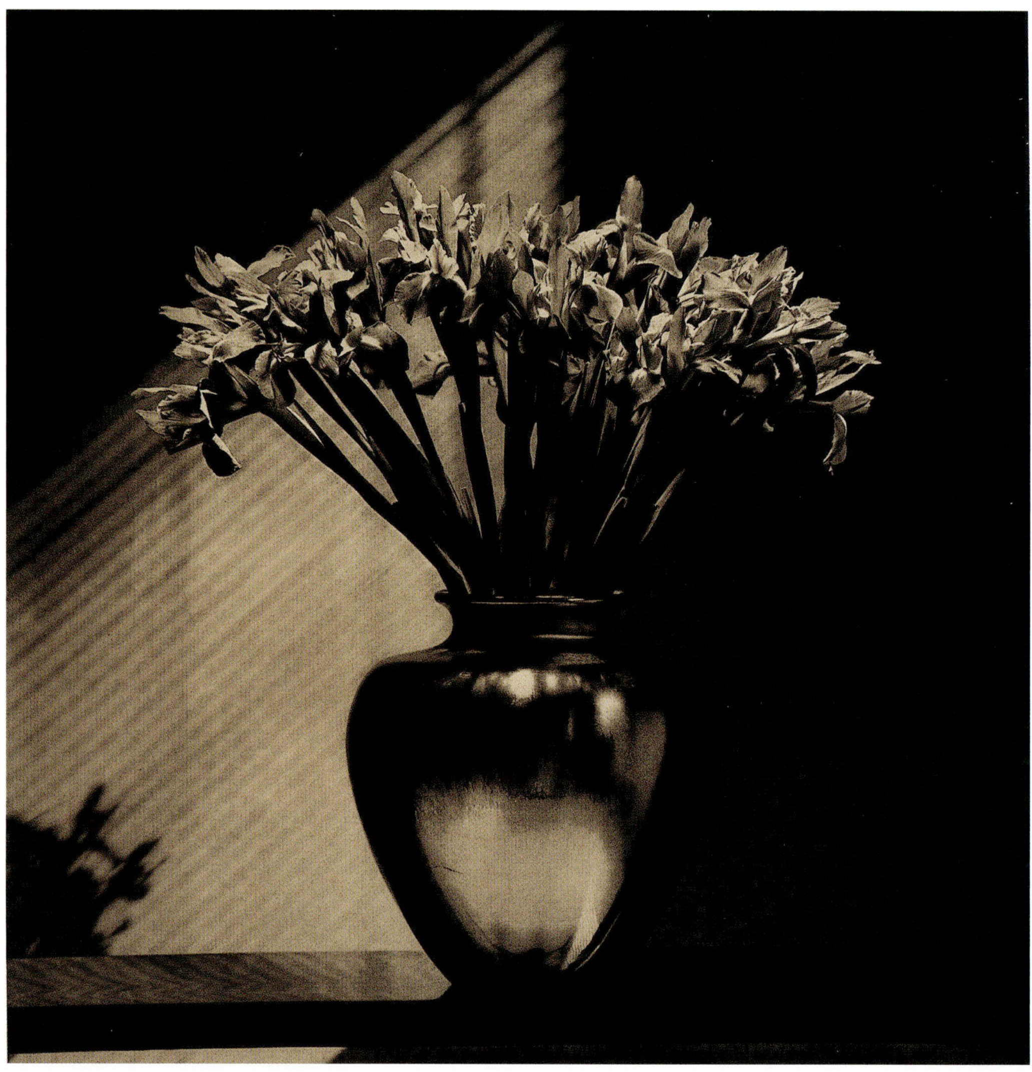

Fig. 13. Robert Mapplethorpe. *Irises.* 1986. Photogravure on silk mounted on paper, 46 x 39 1/4 in. (116.8 x 99.8 cm). Robert Mapplethorpe Foundation

curator and his wife, Maxime, a food editor at *Vogue* who had formerly been married to the French aristocrat Comte Alain de La Falaise. The McKendrys were known for their exotic soirées, which were attended by artists, musicians, and members of high society, including Warhol, Mick Jagger, and Diana Vreeland. This was the social circle that Mapplethorpe had been looking for. John McKendry was immediately charmed by Mapplethorpe, whose good looks and handmade necklaces laced with beads, feathers, and skulls appealed to his own Baroque sense of style. After a visit to Mapplethorpe's studio to view his homoerotic collages and ritualistic

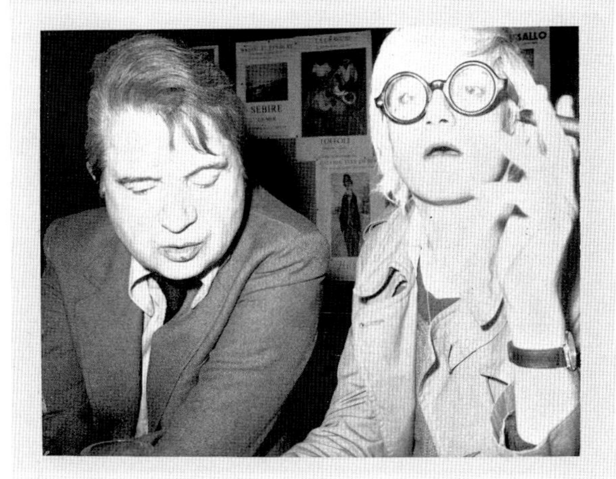

Fig. 14. Robert Mapplethorpe. *Untitled (Francis Bacon and David Hockney).* 1970/73. Monochromatic dye diffusion transfer print, 3 ¼ x 4 ¼ in. (8.3 x 10.8 cm). Private collection

assemblages, McKendry took the young artist under his wing.

First, McKendry invited Mapplethorpe to see photographs in the Met's collection, which, the artist later remarked, gave him an appreciation for fine print-quality.[24] Then, for Christmas 1971, McKendry bought Mapplethorpe his own Polaroid camera. In the spring, McKendry took Mapplethorpe to Boston to introduce him to executives at the Polaroid Corporation, which sponsored an Artist Support Program. Founded by scientist and inventor Edwin H. Land in 1937 to manufacture glare-resistant windows and glasses, the Polaroid Corporation became best known for the 1947 invention of a one-step process for producing a finished photograph.[25] In 1949, Land hired Ansel Adams as an artistic and technical consultant, beginning a decades-long collaboration with artists to test results in the field and improve Polaroid cameras and films.[26] The Artist Support Program provided photographers with free film and cameras—an initiative that continues to assist photographic artists today. With McKendry's support, the Polaroid Corporation invited Mapplethorpe to participate in the program, which gave him new freedom and facilitated his creativity. Still, Smith remembers that Mapplethorpe never squandered a sheet of film. Even when it was free, he took great care in selecting subject matter and composing pictures.[27]

Other photographers working with Polaroid in the early 1970s included Marie Cosindas, a consultant for Polaroid and one of the earliest photographers to use color Polaroid film.[28] Warhol began to experiment with instant photography in 1970, and in 1973 he began an aggressive program of portraits of celebrities and society snapshots using the Polaroid Sure Shot camera.[29] Mapplethorpe knew this work of Warhol's and shot some party pictures himself, including one of Francis Bacon and David Hockney (fig. 14), who would go on to make Polaroid collages of his own in the early 1980s. Apart from Warhol, the artist who has made the most use of instant photography over the years has been Lucas Samaras, who, in 1969, started an engagement with self-portraiture using Polaroid cameras that continues today (fig. 15).

Like Samaras, Mapplethorpe made self-portraits throughout his career. What may be his first photographic self-portrait is a nude composed of three Polaroids

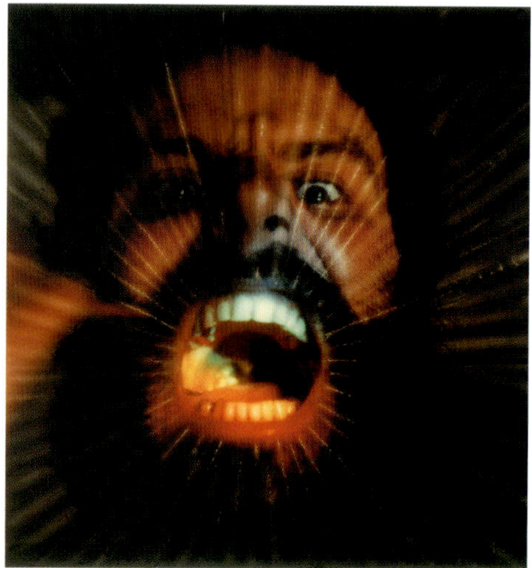

Fig. 15: Lucas Samaras. *Photo-Transformation.* 1973. Internal dye diffusion transfer print (manipulated Polaroid SX-70 photograph), 4 1/4 x 3 1/2 in. (10.8 x 8.9 cm). ©Lucas Samaras, Courtesy of the Polaroid Collections (79:651:02)

positioned behind the wire mesh of a brown-paper potato sack that was spray-painted purple (pl. 1). The figure stands against a white wall and is starkly lit. There is nothing particularly alluring or sexy about the depiction, which looks more like a full-body mug shot than a nude. Several devices here, however, would recur in Mapplethorpe's work: the veiling of a subject, for instance, which compels the viewer to look through to see in. Both breaking the body into fragments and making it up out of multiple images were also frequent exercises of Mapplethorpe's, as was hand-coloring his Polaroids or attaching found objects (figs. 16 and 17). He also staged erotic scenarios. In one image Mapplethorpe lies on a bed and holds a phone to his ear, as though it were a phallic device, or an erotic transmitter of a lover's voice; in another picture he clutches his crotch (pls. 42 and 43). More playful and inventive are Polaroids of his feet in the air with the ceiling as backdrop (pl. 49). Here, Mapplethorpe's experimentation with a radical point of view produces a dizzying inversion of conventional pictorial space. Images like these are private pictures. They may be seen as investigative, as though Mapplethorpe were trying on roles or postures to see how they might fit, feel, and look.

In photographic self-portraits, artists select a setting, position the camera, and decide when to trip the shutter (either remotely or with a pneumatic release, as Mapplethorpe did). Ultimately, however, they can never know what the camera sees at the moment of exposure, and images of unexpected candor or metaphoric potential may emerge. In one dreamlike sequence that borders on striptease, Mapplethorpe is beckoned by a robe hanging on the

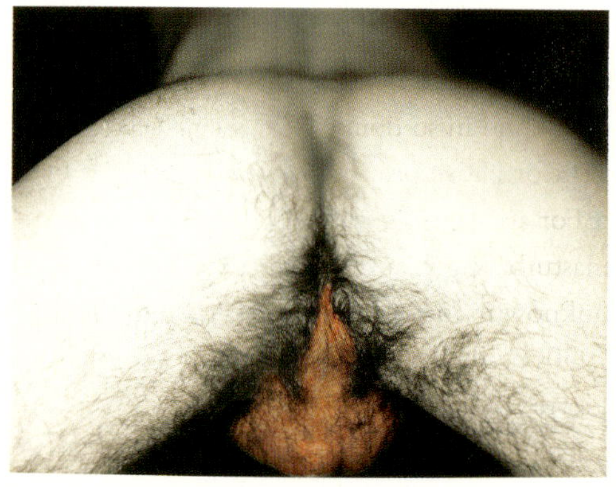

Fig. 16. Robert Mapplethorpe. *Untitled.* 1970/73. Hand-colored monochromatic dye diffusion transfer print (Polaroid), 3 3/4 x 4 1/4 in. (8.3 x 10.8 cm). Robert Mapplethorpe Foundation

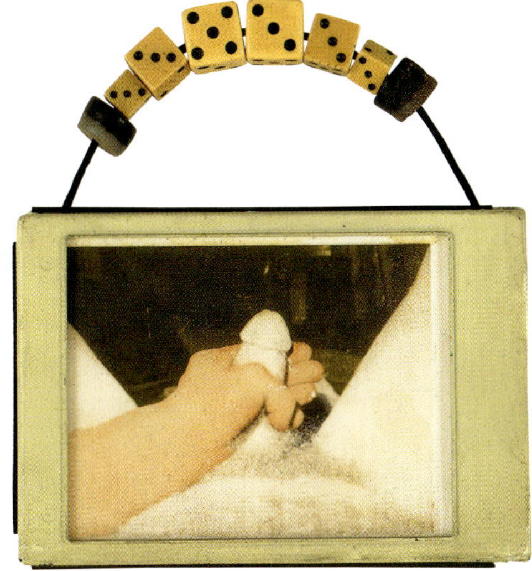

Fig. 17. Robert Mapplethorpe. *Untitled (self-portrait)*. 1970/73. Hand-colored monochromatic dye diffusion transfer print (Polaroid) in painted plastic mount with beads, string, and dice, 6 x 5 1/4 x 3 1/4 in. overall (15.2 x 13.3 x 8.3 cm). Collection David Croland

wall of his studio whose subtle movement makes it appear to shudder (pls. 50–55). As he reaches into the picture to grab the garment, we envision him as naked outside the frame, groping for cover. In sequential images, Mapplethorpe dons the robe, then discards it. Now stripped bare, he looks down and away, in a pose recalling classical sculpture. We are brought back to the carnal demands of the flesh in a final image in which Mapplethorpe joylessly strokes his partly erect penis. The sequence is at once seductive and suggestive of the occult, the robe acting as a garment imbued with powers that put its wearer in a trance. The artist sheds the robe—as a snake sheds its skin—and in so doing gains access to the transformative properties of sex.

For artists to portray themselves masturbating is rare in art history but not unknown. In several pictures made in the 1950s by the homoerotic photographer Pierre Molinier, for example, the masked artist looks crazed, his grimace a cross between pleasure and pain. Egon Schiele's pencil and watercolor *Semi-nude Self-portrait in Black Coat* of 1911 (fig. 18) depicts the artist with mournful eyes that express melancholy and shame. While these and Mapplethorpe's Polaroids are daring in their depiction of a sexual act, an unnatural self-consciousness prevails. The body may be exposed but little of the self is revealed. Instead, the works' transgressive nature provokes inquiry. Is it defiant to make a

Fig. 18. Egon Schiele. *Semi-Nude Self-Portrait in Black Coat*. 1911. Pencil, watercolor with protein-based binder on Strathmore Japanese vellum, 18 7/8 x 12 5/8 in. (47.9 x 32.1 cm). Albertina, Vienna

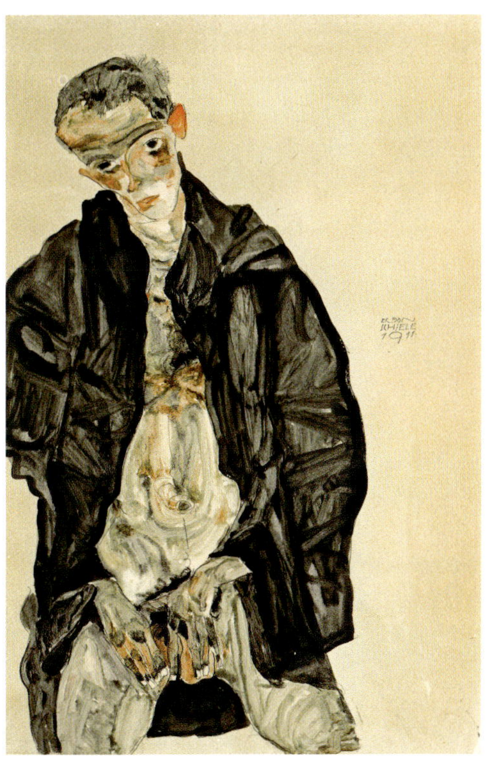

solitary practice public? Is it irreverent? Is it confessional? Asked whether he made sexually explicit pictures to shock, Mapplethorpe replied that his first priority was to satisfy his own curiosity: "It was about me wanting to see things... I was surprised that others found [such pictures] shocking. Once I had taken a photograph, it wasn't shocking to me anymore. I had been through the experience."[30] A self-portrait, in other words, both validated an experience and provided evidence of it.

Mapplethorpe was clearly not timid about exposing his body in self-portraits, but there were aspects of his psyche that he did not wish to show. In a 1987 interview he remarked, "I would never take a self-portrait when I was depressed, for example, I don't want to see that part of me."[31] This kind of avoidance of a darker side may seem unexpected from the artist who became notorious in the late 1970s for photographing himself with a whip inserted in his anus, but self-portraiture may be understood as a form less of self-disclosure than of play-acting—of concealing the self rather than revealing it. In 1976, addressing the works in which Max Ernst and Marcel Duchamp established fictional personas for themselves—"Dadamax" for Ernst, "Rrose Sélavy" for Duchamp—Kirk Varnedoe wrote of the seemingly contradictory aspects of modern self-portraiture:

Such surrogates... are confessions in code. Trick mirrors, they allow the artist to avoid direct reflection and thus, through his self-portrait as a symbolic equivalent, simultaneously to expand his persona and control access to his personality. This kind of image, motivated apparently by a desire both to define the self and obscure it, proposes impersonation as a fundamental modern means of self-expression.[32]

Varnedoe's observations may be applied as well to Mapplethorpe's self-portraits. The artist would go on in the 1980s to adopt personas representing social or sexual types—a biker or drag queen, for example—but there is a difference between impersonation and acting out personal fantasies (fig. 19). Exercising his erotic vision in his Polaroids, Mapplethorpe may have been asserting his sexual identity, but we see the self-exploration, not the self.

In the early summer of 1972, Mapplethorpe showed his Polaroids, assemblages, collages, and jewelry to Sam Wagstaff, who would become his lover, mentor, and greatest benefactor. Wagstaff had been a curator of contemporary art, first at the Wadsworth Atheneum in Hartford, Connecticut, then at the Detroit Institute of Art. At the age of fifty, after receiving a modest family inheritance that allowed him to quit his job, he moved to New York City.[33] A Brahmin, cultured gay man who had obscured his sexual orientation from public view, Wagstaff was captivated by Mapplethorpe's erotic imagery and brazen homosexuality. By then the twenty-five-year-old with intense green eyes, expressive

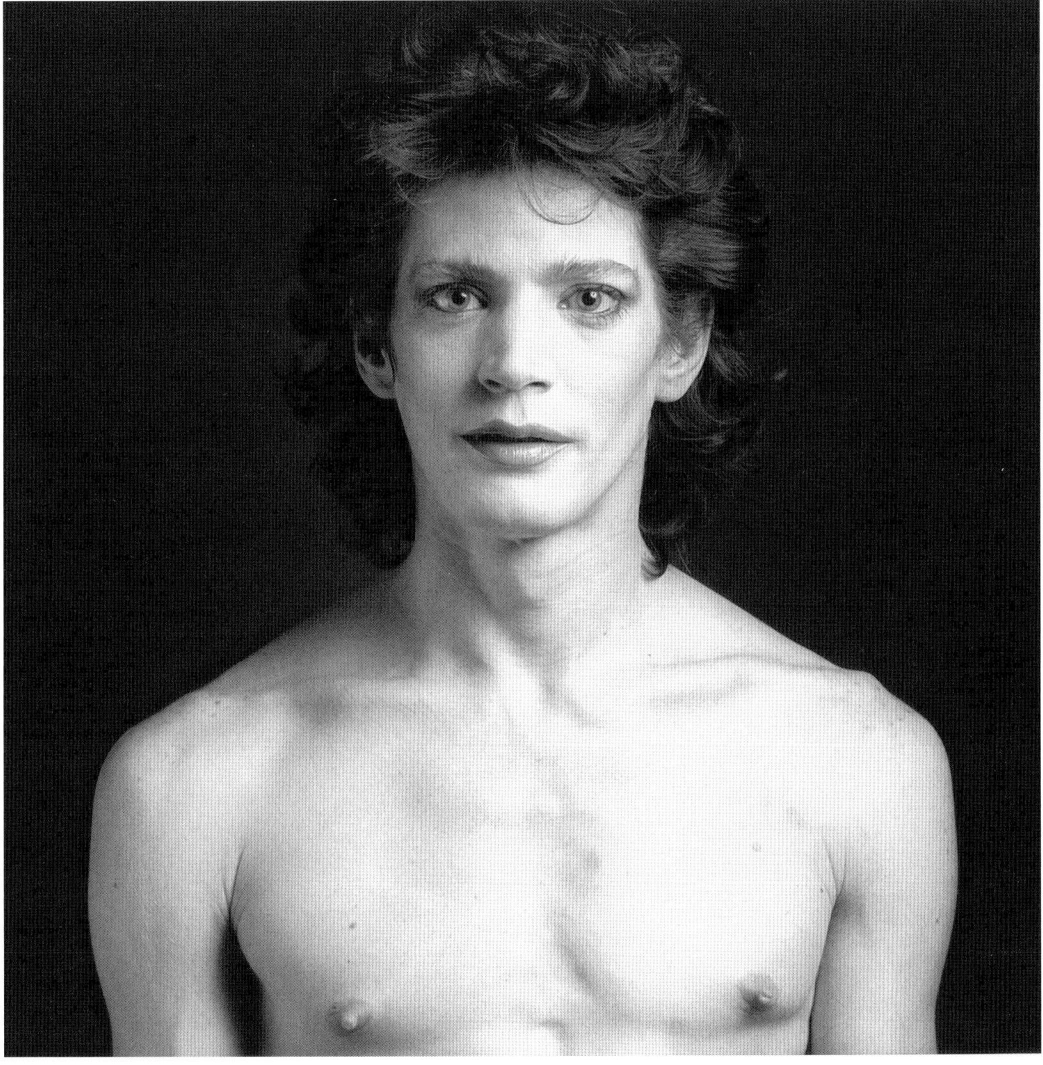

Fig. 19. Robert Mapplethorpe. *Self-Portrait*. 1980. Gelatin silver print, 16 x 20 in. (40.6 x 50.8 cm). Robert Mapplethorpe Foundation

hands, and leather attire was frankly and openly gay. Mapplethorpe provided youth, abandon, and the raw artistic talent that Wagstaff cherished. In turn, Wagstaff gave Mapplethorpe sophistication, access to high society, and financial stability.

Together the two made a handsome couple, attending cocktail parties and art openings, including one in 1973 at the Metropolitan Museum for the exhibition "The Painterly Photograph," organized by McKendry's assistant Weston Naef. At the sight of Edward Steichen's gum-bichromate-over-platinum print *The Flatiron* (1904, printed 1909), Wagstaff became enthralled with photography.

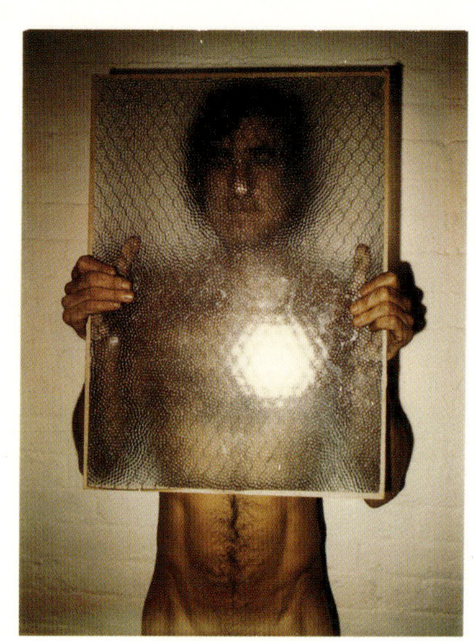

Fig. 20. Robert Mapplethorpe. *Untitled (Sam Wagstaff)*. 1973/75. Internal dye diffusion transfer print (Polaroid), 4 1/4 x 3 1/4 in. (10.8 x 8.3 cm). Robert Mapplethorpe Foundation

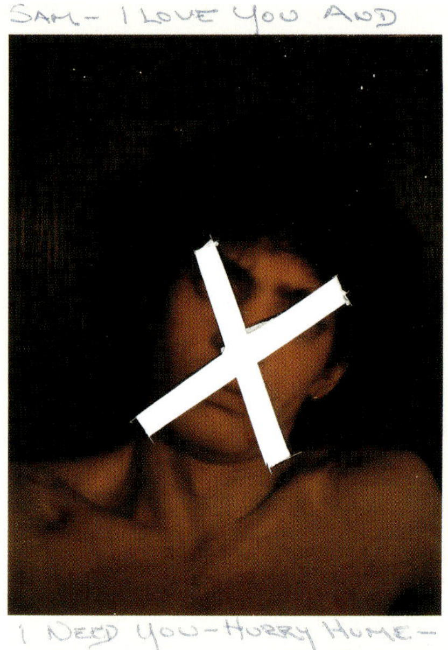

Fig. 21. Robert Mapplethorpe. *Untitled (self-portrait)*. 1974. Internal dye diffusion transfer print (Polaroid) with ink, 4 1/4 x 3 1/4 in. (10.8 x 8.3 cm). Robert Mapplethorpe Foundation

He had long been a passionate collector, amassing personal holdings of African tribal sculpture, American Indian artifacts, Greek coins, stamps, contemporary paintings and Minimalist art.[34] When he met Mapplethorpe, he was one of many in the art world who did not yet consider photography an art, but after his epiphany at the Met, he began voraciously buying photographs and went on to become a visionary connoisseur of the medium. Viewing, making, and collecting photographs would be one of the great pleasures that he and Mapplethorpe shared.[35]

As with all of his lovers and many of his friends, Mapplethorpe pressed Wagstaff into service before the camera. The resulting images run the gamut from beefcake pictures to cum shots to more staid portraiture that reflects the photographer's admiration for his lover and the depth of their connection (pls. 56–59). Color photographs of Wagstaff playfully peering through a meshed piece of frosted glass (another example of veiling a subject), and a love note from Robert when Sam was overseas, reveal the degree to which the two felt the photographs they made together were private (figs. 20 and 21). Unlike the pictures of Smith, which were intensely personal but rarely sexual, the photographs of Wagstaff evidence erotic longing and lust.

As example, Mapplethorpe constructed an album with images of Sam that are evocative and explicit. Some show Wagstaff on the toilet, or shaving in the tub (fig. 22)

Fig. 22. Robert Mapplethorpe. *Untitled (Sam Wagstaff)*. 1972/73. Three monochromatic dye diffusion transfer prints (Polaroids) mounted on paper with colored pencil, 9 1/2 x 6 1/8 in. (24.1 x 15.5 cm). Robert Mapplethorpe Foundation

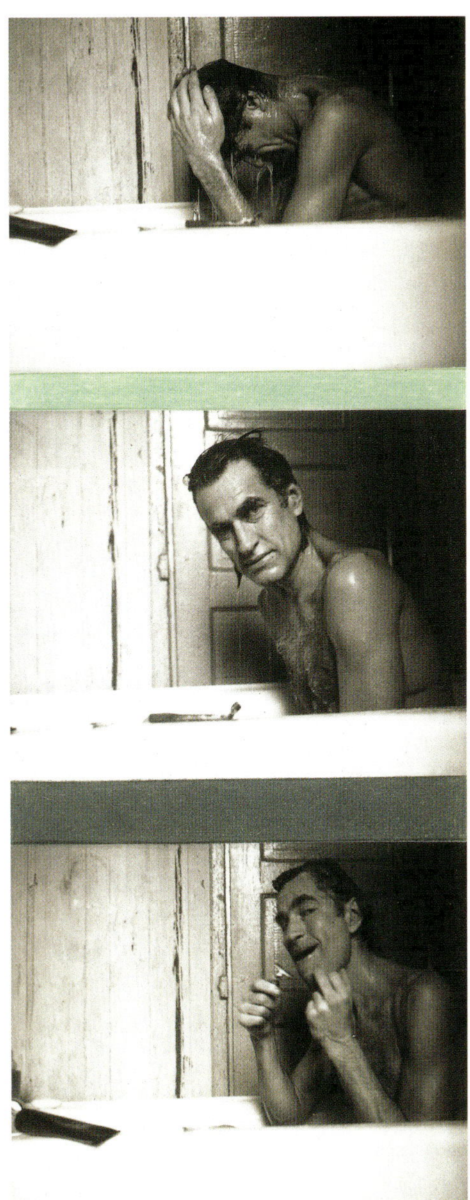

in a reversal of the common nineteenth- and twentieth-century art practice of representing women at their toilette.[36] Other photographs picture Wagstaff bending between his lover's legs, in one of the more suggestively sexual yet chaste scenarios of Mapplethorpe's photographic career (fig. 23). The pictures in this album are not particularly artful; Mapplethorpe seems to have paid more attention to the dynamic action between him and Wagstaff than to framing, lighting, and composition. Yet he carefully mounted the black and white Polaroids on the book's pages, and linked their frames by outlining or drawing shapes around them in colored pencil—a labor of ornament that adds to them a level of devotion, rendering each page a votive offering. The book is only partly filled, with a few loose items tucked in the back pages, and there is no title, date, or inscription to suggest that it was completed. Whether it was a work in progress or a visual diary is unclear. What is evident is that Mapplethorpe used the camera as a mediator of experience—as both companion to and verifier of the lovers' intimacy.

The Power of Suggestion

As well as outright depictions of nudity and sex, Mapplethorpe made many wryly humorous images that hint at coupling. In one photograph, twisted and crumpled bed linens suggest active love-making or tortured sleep (pl. 62), while in another, a hand tugging on a sheet against a striped mattress evokes the emotional push/pull of romance (pl. 68). A photograph taken in a shower of an arm reaching in for the nozzle indicates the presence of a lover beyond the curtain (pl. 63), as does an image of a hand positioning two pairs of boots to imply that their owners are locked in an embrace (pl. 66). (Mapplethorpe frequently used the device of reaching into the picture from outside it, drawing attention to the framing mechanism of photography and creating mystery by insinuating a presence just beyond our sight.) The anthropomorphizing of inanimate objects or animals is also often evident in Mapplethorpe's Polaroids, from two wicker chairs pictured side by side on a porch, like an old married couple sitting in the shade, to a pair of bats in a cage (pls. 64 and 65).

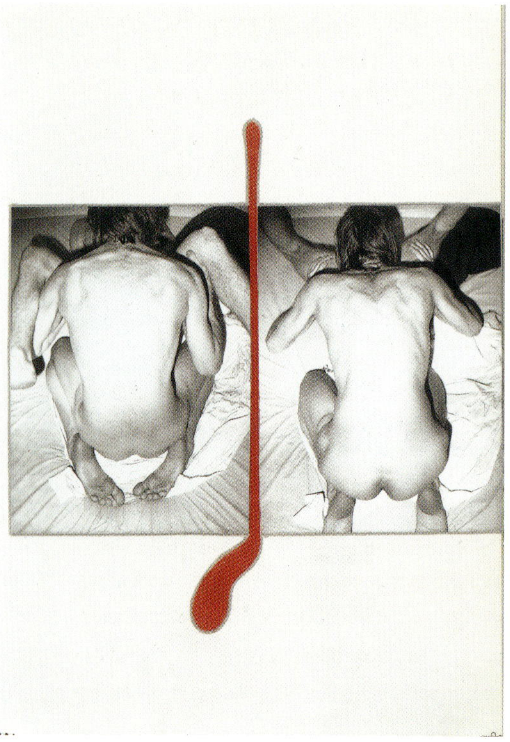

Some of these pictures were staged, but most were made spontaneously during visits to Fire Island, London, or the apartments and studios of fellow artists. While composed with care and attention to detail, they have the immediacy of snapshots taken when a photographer responds with delight to a situation, an idea, or the company of friends. More intimate pictures were made in the studio. In October 1972, when the lease expired on the 23rd Street apartment that Mapplethorpe then shared with Smith, Wagstaff bought him a loft on Bond Street, near his own home. (Smith moved to an apartment in Greenwich Village with her new partner, Allen Lanier, a member of the band Blue Öyster Cult.) Living alone, with ample space to set up a camera, Mapplethorpe was freer than before to entertain and photograph the men he met in leather bars in the West Village. He also made pictures of men and women, gay and straight, whose bodies and beauty he admired. These images fall into a number of stylistic categories, from wistful portrayals and classical nudes to amateur pornography.

Abundant photographs of handsome young men suggest varying degrees of engagement with the photographer. Jamie, with his long hair, deep-set eyes, pouting mouth, and sinewy posture, regards the camera with a sultry come-hither look (pl. 74), whereas Stewart strikes a more

Fig. 23. Robert Mapplethorpe. *Untitled (Sam Wagstaff)*. 1972/73. Two monochromatic dye diffusion transfer prints (Polaroids) mounted on paper with colored pencil, 9 1/2 x 6 1/8 in. (24.1 x 15.5 cm). Robert Mapplethorpe Foundation

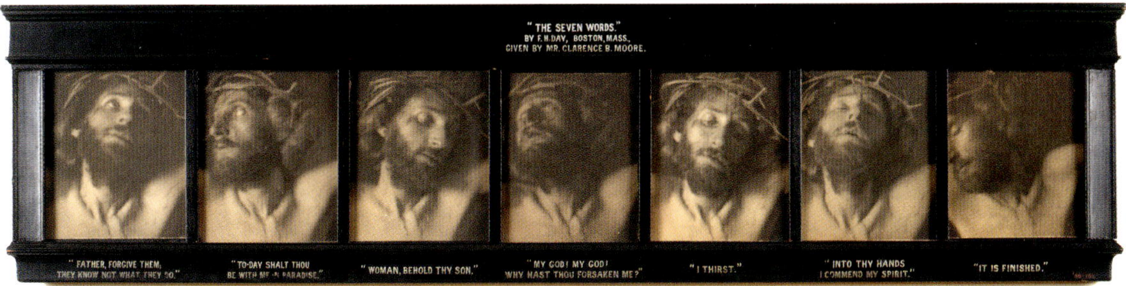

Fig. 24. F. Holland Day. *The Seven Words.* 1898. Seven platinum prints in frame, 8 1/2 x 34 1/2 in. (21.6 x 87.3 cm). Bruce Silverstein Gallery, New York. © F. Holland Day, courtesy Silverstein Photography

casual pose (pl. 84). Some sitters seem to be in various states of suspended consciousness or reverie. Nicholas, for instance, gazes to the side, his arm raised to reveal his armpit, in a gesture that signals openness and availability (pl. 79). By contrast, François looks at the camera with wide-eyed frankness but hugs his knees, perhaps out of modesty or self-protectiveness (pl. 83). Other pictures suggest religious iconography, as in Michael's Christ-like look of sadness (pl. 76) or Randy's chin perched on a flat surface, recalling the severed head of John the Baptist placed on a platter for Salome (pl. 80). Unlike the muscle-bound bodies, oiled to enhance their chiseled physiques, in later Mapplethorpe photographs, many of these figures have a soft, fleshy quality that makes them lifelike and approachable. Not all of Mapplethorpe's subjects were lovers or were gay. Still, he reveled in gazing at them and invites us to join him, his contemplation a form of erotic suggestion.

Several figurative works contain mirrors, glass, or windows. Croland's friend Eddie perches on a chair, first fully clothed, then nearly nude, behind an ornately framed glass fire screen, which reflects a window and, faintly, the photographer (pls. 98 and 99). Mapplethorpe's reflection reappears in a suite of pictures depicting the dancer Joshua Mores striking poses before a full-length mirror in the Bond Street studio. The fact that Mapplethorpe could have eliminated his image simply by repositioning the camera indicates that he intended these photographs as portraits of the artist and his model. At the same time, they act as metaphors for an inquiry into the psyche, the two figures symbolizing multiple facets of the self. Additional photographs of Mores made without the mirror, but repeating his image as angst-ridden double exposures, underscore this interpretation (pls. 116–21).

The theme of the mirror as a tool for self-representation, a symbol of vanity, and an aid to self-knowledge has appeared in the history of art since at least the fifteenth century.[37] It has also been used to comment on the act of looking. In Mapplethorpe's photograph of Boaz Mazor, assistant to fashion designer Oscar de la Renta, the subject's eye contact with the camera commands our attention and gives the picture a sexual charge (pl. 89). At the same time, the mirror to the right offers the voyeuristic experience of gazing at his physique. Our contemplation of the figure

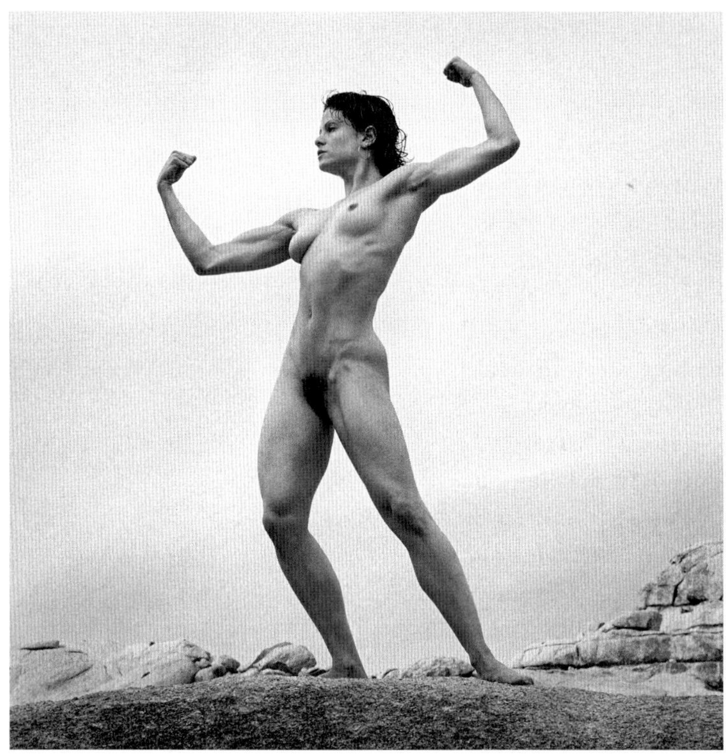

Fig. 25. Robert Mapplethorpe. *Lisa Lyon*. 1980. Gelatin silver print, 16 x 20 in. (40.6 x 50.8 cm). Robert Mapplethorpe Foundation

is triangulated as we are confronted with making a choice: to return his look or to admire his reflection. Mazor's steadfast stare makes us conscious of that choice, exposing our desire and shedding light on our prurient interests.

Historical precedent for Mapplethorpe's figurative work may be found in photographs by Minor White, Baron Wilhelm von Gloeden, and F. Holland Day (fig. 24), all of whom couched homoeroticism in formal, mythological, or religious symbolism. (Mapplethorpe and Wagstaff owned photographs by all of these photographers.)[38] Another favorite was Eadweard Muybridge. Like the nineteenth-century innovator's photographic studies of figures in motion, Mapplethorpe's Polaroids of men practicing yoga analyze the body as an anatomical structure or specimen performing remarkable feats of athleticism (pls. 100 and 101).[39] Neither erotic photographs of individuals nor metaphoric compositions, these sexy figure studies both celebrate and stimulate admiration for the fluidity and grace of the human form. So, too, does an image of a young man kneeling on a platform and bending forward, as though pouring down the platform's front (pl. 103).

Mapplethorpe occasionally made Polaroids of the female figure. Sometimes

Fig. 26. Cover of *Physique Pictorial,* vol.9, no.3. (winter 1955). Collection Ryan McGinley

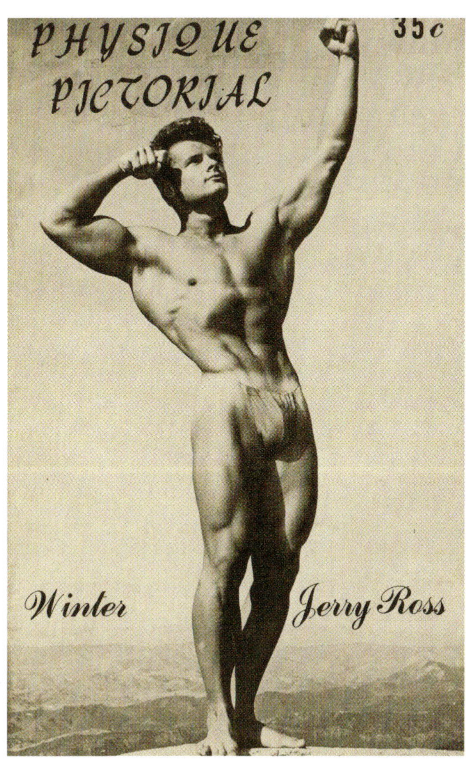

the bodies are fragmented, as in an image of a woman floating in a swimming pool, her legs bowed and her head truncated by the top of the frame (pl. 104). Images of broken or twisted doll parts by the Surrealist photographer Hans Bellmer come to mind. In two other photographs, an artist's model and one-time subject of Diane Arbus is sharply lit from the side, her head lost in shadow. With concave chest and bony hips, the figure appears androgynous, cadaverous (pls. 105 and 106).[40] Quite the contrary is an unromanticized close-up of the torso of a woman whose ample bosom and visible stretch marks speak of fertility and represent a real versus an exotic body (pl. 109).[41]

Among Mapplethorpe's more theatrical female figures are a transsexual thrusting out her chest (pl. 110) and a woman with flowing black hair, her head tipped back, her robe falling from her shoulders, who calls to mind the gypsy temptress of Bizet's opera *Carmen* (pl. 111). But perhaps the most exhilarating sequence of pictures of women was shot in Paris and shows a subject named Lucy (pl. 108). A saucy, shapely woman who is clearly enjoying posing for the photographer, Lucy is in full command of her power to hold his gaze and ours. In nearly a dozen photographs, Mapplethorpe captures the erotic energy she projects, enthralled by her responsiveness to the camera (pls. 112–14). When a male partner enters the picture—offering a tender embrace—he is the supporting actor to her starring role (pl. 115). Lucy's palpable, exuberant sexuality, and the pictures' spontaneity, are a far cry from photographs Mapplethorpe would make years later of the first women's world champion in bodybuilding, Lisa Lyon (fig. 25). His dozens of portrayals of Lyon—from athlete to choirgirl, from biker to bride—form a composite of types that render her as superhuman, hypersexualized, but unapproachable. Mapplethorpe once remarked that he was attracted to Lyon because she was an anomaly, a woman who was closer to the male physical ideal than any other he had seen. "Lisa Lyon reminded me of Michelangelo's subjects, because he did muscular women."[42]

A reverence for the male athletic build figures largely in Mapplethorpe's work, and in gay visual culture overall. Our modern-day appreciation for the athletic body dates back to the 1880s and '90s, when the changing nature of industrialization began to provide time and money for leisure activities among the concentrated populations of modern cities.[43] A growing participation in sports, as well as the revival of the Olympic Games in 1896, brought new audiences to physical competitions in which the male body was on display. Photographs of athletes were widely distributed in the 1890s as examples of the virtues of the ideal form.[44] With the invention of the halftone printing process around this time, which allowed for images to be reproduced in large numbers, publications associated with this new "physical culture" flourished in Germany, France, and beyond.[45]

Fitness magazines emerged in America in the 1930s, the decade that also presented the first Mr. America contest, in 1939. These "physique culture" magazines, as they were called, circulated among men in the service during World War II and flourished further in the 1950s, the focus on bodybuilding providing a smokescreen for monthlies that catered to men who enjoyed looking at photographs of other men. Operating under the claim of promoting art and health, publications like *Physique Pictorial*, which first appeared in 1953, offered photographs of bodybuilders striking athletic poses, wrestling with one another in G-strings, and mimicking characters from classical mythology (fig. 26).[46] The models often smile for the camera, defining themselves as wholesome specimens of muscular manliness.[47] In 1962, the U.S. Supreme Court ruled that male nudity in homoerotic magazines was no more obscene or objectionable than female nudity in publications for heterosexuals, allowing homoerotic monthlies to circulate freely to subscribers through the mail. These magazines continued to increase in popularity until more than one hundred English-language variations were distributed worldwide by the time of the Stonewall Rebellion of 1969.[48]

Mapplethorpe collected vintage muscle magazines from the 1950s and '60s and used images from some of these publications in his art (pls. 126 and 127). One aspect of the physique publications that would have appealed to Mapplethorpe's sensibility was the titillation that comes from viewing some but not all of a figure. As we have seen, he was fascinated with this manner of displaying the male body. The posing straps, as G-strings were called, left much to the imagination. Moreover, the subterfuge then necessary in publications directed at same-sex audiences may be thought of as informing Mapplethorpe's use of veils, mesh, chicken wire, and metal grillwork in his art.

While images of physically fit men adopting classical stances or imitating figures from folklore and legend may strike today's audiences as kitsch, that was part of their appeal for Mapplethorpe, who occasionally contrived to make similar photographs

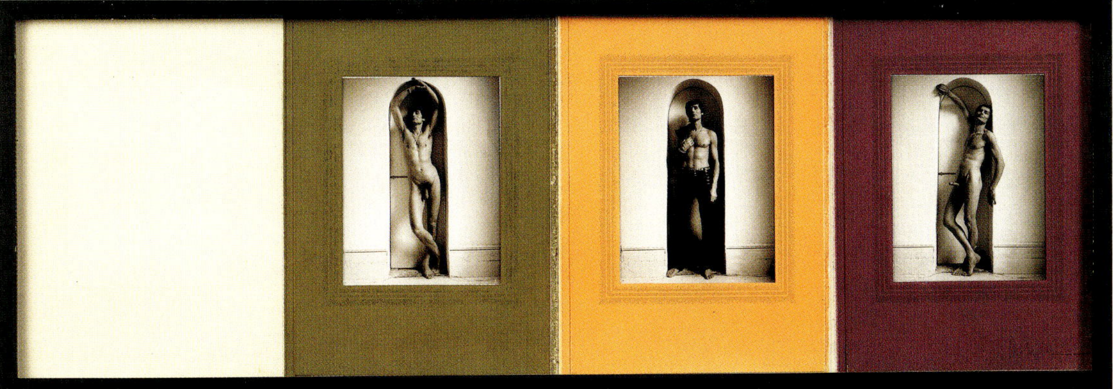

Fig. 27. Robert Mapplethorpe. *Manfred*. 1974. Three monochromatic dye diffusion transfer prints (Polaroids) with colored mats in wood frame, 8 x 18 x 1 in. (20.3 x 45.7 x 2.5 cm). Robert Mapplethorpe Foundation

himself. One sequence of pictures features Gyles Fontaine, a choreographer known for his work on the 1976 cult-horror film *Bloodsucking Freaks* (pls. 122 and 123).[49] Lean and muscular, and with a pendulous scrotum, he poses atop a pedestal next to a Corinthian column in what looks like a backstage storage area or prop warehouse. His emotive gestures suggest that he is portraying a character from mythology—a satyr, perhaps, or Pan. A more contemporary characterization appears in Mapplethorpe's Polaroids of the dancer and porn star Peter Berlin, who performs for the camera in an industrial elevator wearing the tight blue-jean cutoffs, leather boots, and military cap that were signifiers of gay culture (pl. 124).[50] Far from resembling classical nudes, these pictures were made to arouse.

The Naked and the Nude

Over the years, Mapplethorpe and his champions have made much of his visual inspiration in antiquity and neoclassical art, but his Polaroids invite a broader and more transgressive reading. A sequence showing a man identified as Manfred, for example, posing in a niche like a statue come alive, provides a glimpse into the range of possibilities Mapplethorpe considered in photographing the figure, from camp to classical, from erotic to heroic, from naked to nude. Single Polaroids of Manfred include front and rear views of him in various artistic poses including contrapposto, a common posture in Greco-Roman classical sculpture (pls. 128 and 129). Mapplethorpe chose three of these images for a framed piece, each projecting a distinctly different attitude (fig. 27). In one, a nude Manfred fills the niche, his arms raised, his legs casually crossed; in another he stands at attention in jeans; in the third he is undressed again, leaning casually on the side of the niche and sporting a proud erection. Mapplethorpe's choice of these less traditional stances for the final piece, as opposed to the more iconic poses, points to the tongue-in-cheek nature of his emulation of classicism. The framed piece also includes a device he would use throughout his career: an empty space left in the composition, to suggest absence,

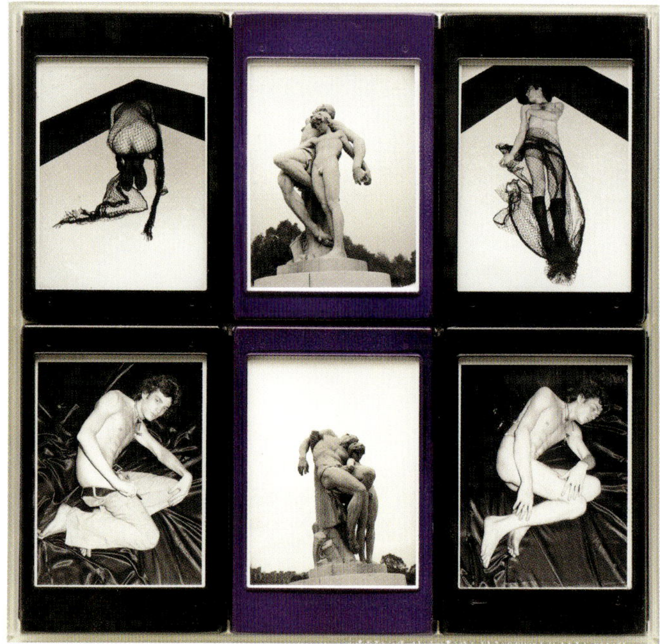

Fig. 28. Robert Mapplethorpe. *Untitled*. 1973. Six monochromatic dye diffusion transfer prints (Polaroids) in painted plastic mounts with Plexiglas frame, 10 ³/₄ x 11 ¹/₄ x 1 ¹/₂ in. (27.3 x 28.6 x 3.8 cm). Solomon R. Guggenheim Museum, Gift, Robert Mapplethorpe Foundation

create mystery, or perhaps provoke viewers to wonder what is held back, or what is yet to come.

During Mapplethorpe's first years of making pictures he took a number of photographs of public sculptures intended to broadcast noble, humanist ideals through the power of the body. His pictures, however, locate the erotic suggestion often present in such works. In one, a muscular male physique, leaning on a large sword, is shot from below and behind against a backdrop of silvery clouded skies (pl. 130). The vignetting at the edges of the frame, which abstracts the figure from its environment, gives it a heroic flavor, while the hitch of the hip suggests a confident swagger. Another such image of a sculpture features a young man supporting the limp limbs of an ailing elder (pl. 131). Shot from below against a neutral sky, the sculpture offers a mixed message: on the one hand the figures communicate pathos—this is a monument to sickness and succor, devotion and death—but on the other we see two nude male bodies, entwined in what could be a passionate embrace or surrender.

Mapplethorpe used images of this sculpture in a six-part composition that contrasts "high" and "low" representations of the male figure (fig. 28), recalling the well-known distinction between the naked and the nude made by art historian Kenneth Clark in his book *The Nude: A Study in*

Fig. 29. Robert Mapplethorpe. *The Slave*. 1974. Monochromatic dye diffusion transfer print (Polaroid), 5 1/8 x 4 1/8 in. (13 x 10.5 cm). Robert Mapplethorpe Foundation

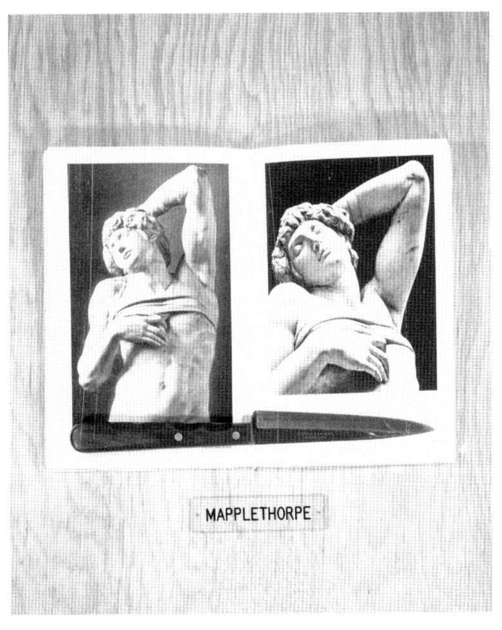

Ideal Form.[51] The naked, Clark proposed, is deprived of clothes—embarrassed and exposed—whereas the nude is confident and at ease. Nudity in classical art is often to be read as a state of grace, a noble link to godliness. In Mapplethorpe's composite, two Polaroids of the sculpture taken from different vantages occupy the center of the piece. They are framed in plastic film-holders spray-painted the rich purple of the vestments used in the Catholic mass during Lent. Flanking them are four photographs framed in black. The upper two are of Croland, seen from above and wrapped in fishnet fabric against a white floor; his veiled body, hidden eyes, and black knee-socks give the pictures a kinky element. The lower two photographs show Mapplethorpe, also seen from above but against a black satin backdrop, first pulling off a pair of jeans, then naked. Crouched in a fetal position and looking sheepishly at the camera and then away, Mapplethorpe appears afraid and ashamed, like Adam banished from the Garden of Eden. Despite his many unapologetic celebrations of physically beautiful men, and his provocative, sexually explicit self-portraits, in this piece he seems to struggle with inner demons.

Mapplethorpe nicknamed the sculpture featured in this piece "La Serpentine," perhaps in reference to the phrase *figura serpentinata,* or "figure in the form of a flame"—the term Michelangelo used to describe his marble sculpture *Dying Captive* (ca. 1513), also the subject of a Mapplethorpe work. To make *The Slave* (1974; fig. 29), Mapplethorpe took a Polaroid photograph of a tabletop collage he had made using a book open to reproductions of *Dying Captive.* The book is placed on a piece of plywood, suggesting the back of a picture frame. A kitchen knife lies across the bottom of the book, keeping the pages open but also intimating violence. A Plexiglas label printed with Mapplethorpe's surname rests below the book, as though the sculpture's authorship were reattributed: the photographer has inserted himself into the canon of classical art. Or perhaps Mapplethorpe identifies with Michelangelo's subject, a body intoxicated by sensation, the head thrown back in delicious, delirious martyrdom.

Pleasure and pain are associated in many ways in art history. One of the most

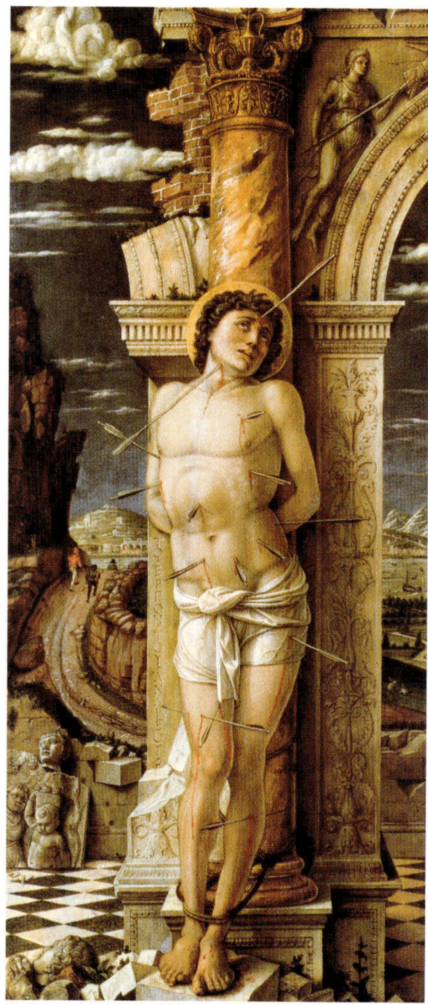

Fig. 30. Andrea Mantegna. *St. Sebastian*. ca.1459. Oil on wood, 26 3/4 x 11 3/4 in. (68 x 30 cm). Kunsthistorisches Museum, Vienna

notorious subjects of religious painting, from Mantegna to El Greco and beyond, is Saint Sebastian, the martyr tied up and shot with arrows for refusing to denounce Christianity (fig. 30). Many images of Sebastian share a languid display of the male body, scantily clad, with arms and feet bound to a post. Sometimes his physique is robust and mature, sometimes he is a frail youth; but he almost always gazes to heaven in ecstatic rapture, his faith transcending earthly matters of the flesh. Such images are favored icons in gay visual history. It is worth noting that if, in Catholicism, the word "passion" refers to the suffering of a martyr or of Jesus on the cross, in other contexts it more often describes ardent affection. Saint Sebastian, then, can be seen as symbolic of both religious devotion and erotic display.

Mapplethorpe's photographs of men in bondage are more ambiguous in treating the pleasure of pain. In one picture a masked figure, his mouth open, his arms bound and raised, appears enraptured. Soft light from the side illuminates the contours of his slight physique (pl. 132). In another, a gaunt man with slumped shoulders and concave chest pinched with nipple clamps gazes at the camera with a look of strained resignation; in the next photograph we see a four-pound weight tethered to his genitals (pls. 134 and 135). Although these pictures suggest extreme situations and behaviors, there is no evidence of resistance on the men's part, no tension on the ropes, no indication of physical pain. Rather than document the gritty realism of sadomasochistic sex, Mapplethorpe presents elegant postures and carefully orchestrated poses. More convincing is an early self-portrait of the artist reclining, wearing a harness and nipple rings (pl. 138). With one hand he cradles his trussed penis; with the other he depresses the cable-release bulb to take the picture. Although he looks directly at the camera, his face is masked, so we cannot read his expression. Here, the classically portrayed

Fig. 31. Robert Mapplethorpe. *Untitled*. 1973. Six internal dye diffusion transfer prints (Polaroids) in painted plastic mounts with Plexiglas frame, 11 x 11 x 1 ½ in. (27.9 x 27.9 x 3.8 cm). Private collection

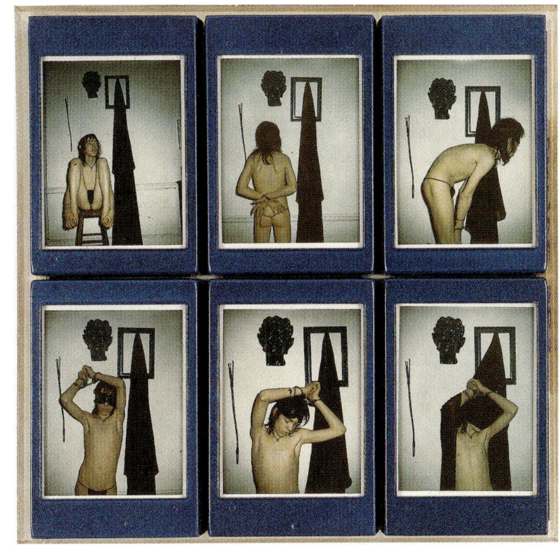

figure has given way to the exotic trappings of sexual deviance. The nude is now naked—at least in terms of the display of sadomasochistic desire.

As we have seen, the masking of a subject's identity appears repeatedly in Mapplethorpe's art in different ways, but as an accouterment of sadomasochistic sex the mask has a particular value related to fear and shame. At the same time, the participant's loss of sight heightens his other senses, loosens his inhibitions, and demands that he give up a degree of control—attractive experiences for Mapplethorpe, who saw making love and taking pictures as a form of losing himself: "When I have sex with someone I forget who I am. For a minute I even forget I'm human. It's the same thing when I'm behind the camera. I forget I exist."[52] For Mapplethorpe, immersion in sex and in photography brought liberation, both of and from the self. He used the camera to breach the boundaries of consciousness and let loose the psyche.[53] Moreover, both looking at and being seen were triggers for arousal. This does not mean that the Catholic attitudes toward good and evil that were ingrained in Mapplethorpe in his childhood were set free. On the contrary, part of the appeal of engaging in illicit activity was the thrill of being bad.

In an effort to inject his work with the energy of forbidden sex—to invoke "that feeling in my stomach" that so moved him ten years before—Mapplethorpe applied the conventions of porn to his art, with greater and lesser degrees of success. One six-part piece depicts a young man in a G-string against a backdrop that includes a devil's head, a whip, an empty frame, and a swath of black mesh (fig. 31). The amateurish posing, the flat lighting from flash, and the camera's distance from the subject are reminiscent of the home use of Polaroids for private sex pictures. Made primarily to elicit arousal, such photographs were often hastily taken and poorly composed. But in homemade pornography the subject may engage the lover with a seductive look, or smile mischievously at the familiar partner behind the camera. In Mapplethorpe's piece the sitter is either masked, draped, or looks away. Although Mapplethorpe does bring the camera progressively closer, a psychic distance between photographer and subject remains.

Quite contrary is a framed work featuring close-up pictures of anonymous body parts. *Made in Canada* (1973; fig. 32, pls.

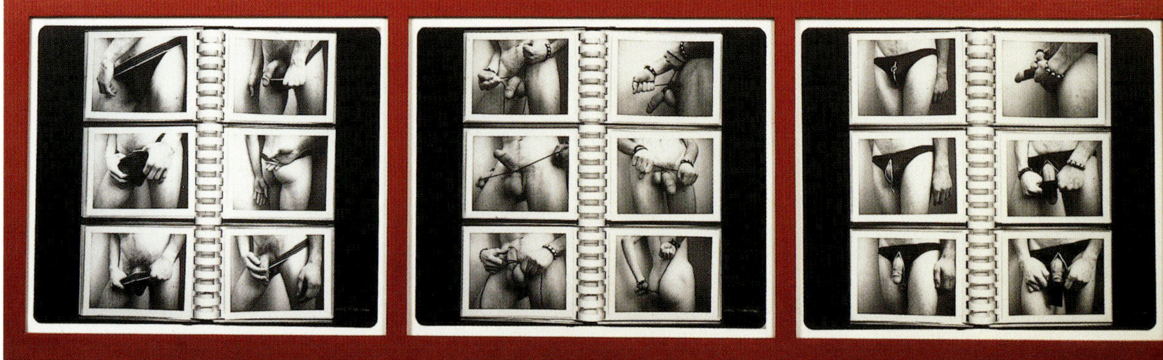

Fig. 32. Robert Mapplethorpe. *Made in Canada.* 1973. Three gelatin silver prints in painted wood frame, 22 x 72 x 1 ½ in. (55.9 x 182.9 x 3.9 cm). Robert Mapplethorpe Foundation

140–43) contains eighteen images of a man's hips, front and rear view, with garments and gear designed to heighten suspense, prolong arousal, and enhance pleasure and performance. The original sitting was shot with black and white Polaroid film and the photographs were placed in a photo album (the title of the piece refers to the manufacturer's imprint, visible on the album's lower-right corner). Mapplethorpe then photographed spreads from the album, enlarged the pictures that resulted, and placed them in sequence to offer a progression of images. In other words, Mapplethorpe has framed these images three times: first in the original Polaroids, then by rephotographing the spreads, then by setting those new photographs together in a red wooden frame. The images themselves resemble product shots, providing the maximum of information about the subject's anatomy and accompanying equipment. Here the penis is alternately fetish and trophy, and picture-making is a form of possession. Works like this are less about coupling or intimacy than about objectifying the body, breaking down all sense of it as a unified whole or as attached to an individual identity, and, in so doing, abstracting the idea of sex.

At the other end of the spectrum are over a dozen pictures of two men cavorting on a mattress in a corner of Mapplethorpe's studio. In *Untitled (Charles and Jim)* (1974; pls. 146–49), a single bed in a room that appears otherwise unfurnished evokes the pared-down atmosphere of the gay bathhouses of New York in the 1970s and '80s, where men met for anonymous sex. There is nothing particularly romantic or aesthetically pleasing about this stark white space, to which fluorescent lighting lends a clinical air. The camera starts at a distance, as though looking through a keyhole, and moves forward for scenes of passionate kissing and fellatio, then retreats to render postcoital languor. The most authentic part of the sequence is the kissing, largely because the close-up perspective and blurriness from motion imply intimacy. Even here, though, the action is directed to the camera, with a self-consciousness that touches on exhibitionism. This is not a sentimental portrait of romance,

Fig. 33. Robert Mapplethorpe. *Charles and Jim*. 1974. Three gelatin silver prints in wood frame, 48 x 16 x 1 in. (121.9 x 40.6 x 2.5 cm). Solomon R. Guggenheim Museum, Gift, Robert Mapplethorpe Foundation

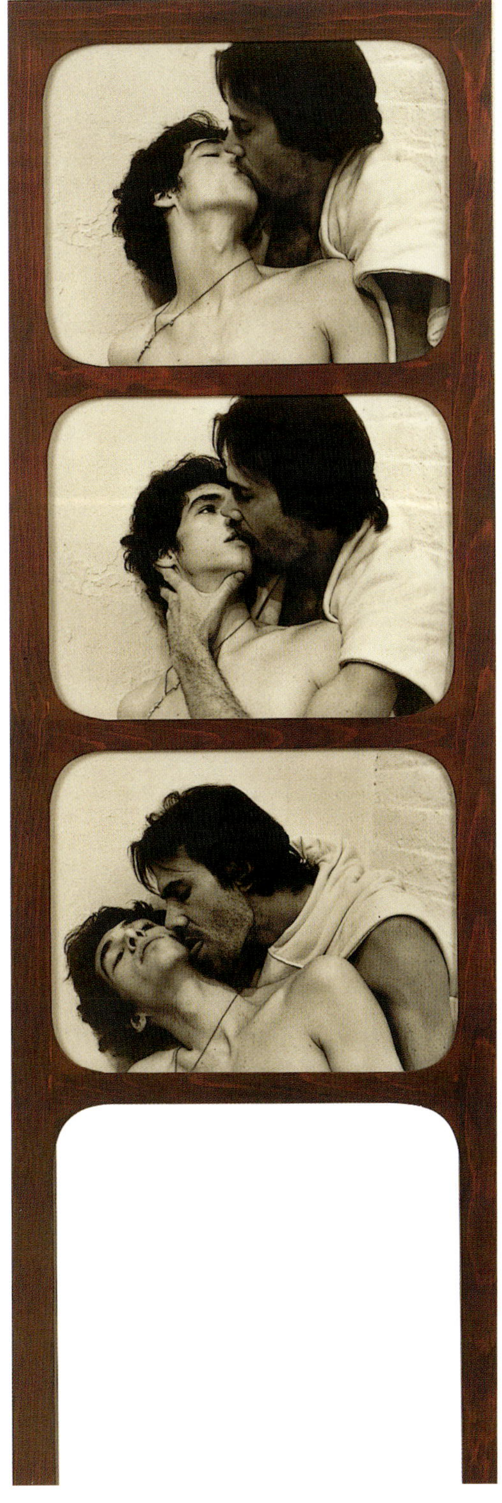

courtship, and lovemaking, nor does it describe the bump and grind, the groping and urgency, of real sex. Mapplethorpe later edited and narrowed down the pictures of Charles and Jim to two framed works. One is a memento mori of sorts, a single image of two figures spent after climax. The other resembles a filmstrip, with a vertical progression of three photographs of the couple kissing (fig. 33). The brown wood frame extends beyond the bottom photograph and is open-ended, as if to suggest that the kissing goes on.

Mapplethorpe photographed Charles and Jim a decade after Warhol made *Kiss* (1963/64; fig. 34), a series of thirteen three-minute silent films of kissing couples in various combinations (heterosexual, homosexual, interracial). Each of these black-and-white films was shot in a single take, and close up, so that the lovers' faces fill the frame. A range of approaches to kissing is depicted, from tender to aggressive, from thirsty to detached. The films were shown at an art house before the main feature, to audiences who probably had never before seen kisses like these onscreen: at the time, Hollywood movies limited kisses to a few seconds, highlighting their romantic meaning over the physical sensation of mouth-to-mouth contact. Mapplethorpe was in art school when Warhol's *Kiss* was first shown, and whether he saw them then is uncertain, but he is likely to have known about them when he photographed Charles and Jim. In the early 1960s, *Kiss* broke

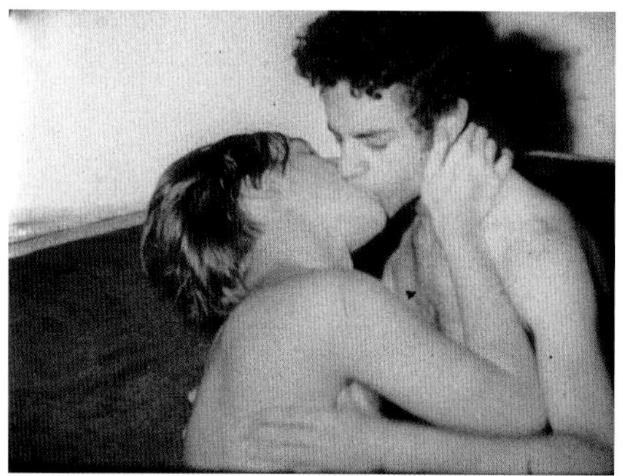

Fig. 34: Andy Warhol. *Kiss*. 1963. Film still. © 2007 The Andy Warhol Museum, Pittsburgh, a museum of Carnegie Institute. All rights reserved. Film still courtesy of The Andy Warhol Museum.

taboos with its defiant display of erotic action. A decade after its release, it was still transgressive to photograph two men kissing.

Mapplethorpe returned to the subject again in 1979 with *Larry and Bobby Kissing* (fig. 35). Far more stylized, this photograph depicts the lovers against a studio backdrop. Quartz lighting enhances the details of their clothing and the texture of their skin and hair. Unlike the action in *Untitled (Charles and Jim)*, this single kiss is frozen by a rapid exposure. There is no foreplay or afterglow, no look of wonder, as there is in the earlier work. In roughly six years, Mapplethorpe had significantly refined his aesthetic, and the style he would become known for was in full bloom. Much as before, his artistic development during that period was facilitated by the good will of patrons and benefactors, many of who were introduced to Mapplethorpe's work in 1973, the year his career as a photographer was publicly launched.

Poses, Products, and Presentation

Mapplethorpe opened his first solo show on January 6, 1973, at Light Gallery, 1018 Madison Avenue, New York. Later that year he participated in a show of Polaroids at Gotham Book Mart with Warhol and Factory figure Brigid Polk. For the Light Gallery invitation, he took a self-portrait in a mirror, holding his Polaroid camera before his bare crotch (pl. 182). Three hundred gelatin silver prints were made from the negative and embossed with Mapplethorpe's name. A label was affixed to the back of each photograph with information about the show's place and time. Either a red or a white paper dot was applied to the front to conceal the penis (pl. 183)—yet another example of veiling the forbidden, and a tongue-in-cheek dig at earlier laws forbidding the circulation of nudity through the mail. The invitation was then slipped inside the protective paper that came with Polaroid film, on which was printed "DON'T TOUCH HERE," and was posted in a cream-colored Tiffany envelope. Harold Jones, then director of the gallery, remembers the opening as crowded with uptown collectors, downtown hustlers, artists, musicians, and celebrities.[55] The "scene" that Jones recalls was an early indicator of Mapplethorpe's appeal across socioeconomic lines. It also signaled a growing audience for photography.

In the 1970s, New York had far fewer venues for photography exhibitions than it does today. In the commercial realm, the Lee Witkin Gallery and the SoHo Photo Gallery were devoted to photography. Pace Gallery exhibited photographs by some

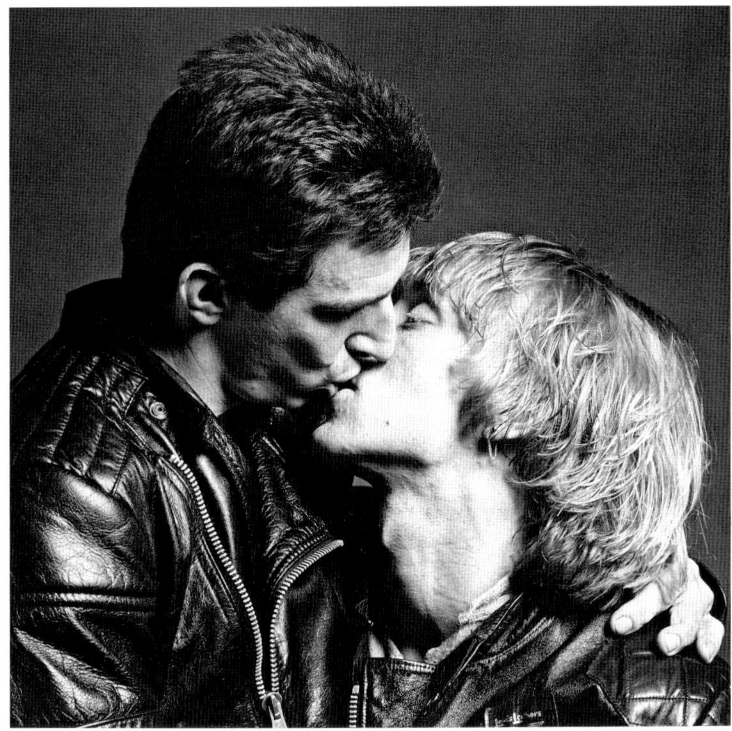

Fig. 35. Robert Mapplethorpe. *Larry and Bobby Kissing.* 1979. Gelatin silver print, 16 x 20 in. (40.6 x 50.8 cm). Robert Mapplethorpe Foundation

of its artists who also worked in other mediums: Samaras, for example, showed 405 Polaroid self-portraits there in 1971.[56]

Among public spaces, The Museum of Modern Art was the primary magnet for those interested in the medium. Starting in 1964, it began to show photographs in galleries designated to feature a historical survey from its permanent collection.[57] The Metropolitan occasionally presented photography exhibitions, as did the Whitney Museum of American Art.

Among the artists showing male nudes in New York at the time was the New Orleans photographer George Dureau, who made portraits of friends and neighbors with physical anomalies and exquisite physiques (fig. 36). Mapplethorpe collected at least three dozen of Dureau's pictures, which he most likely came to know through the Robert Samuel Gallery, the primary site featuring work by gay and lesbian artists.[58] Arthur Tress exhibited homoerotic fantasies at the SoHo Photo Gallery in 1973, and Duane Michals showed photographic narrative sequences at The Museum of Modern Art in 1970 and at Light Gallery in 1974 and 1975.[59] New York photographer Peter Hujar was also making portraits and nudes in his studio on 23rd Street, which he would exhibit at the Marcuse Pfeiffer Gallery in 1979.[60]

Philippe Garner, then photography specialist at Sotheby's in London, met

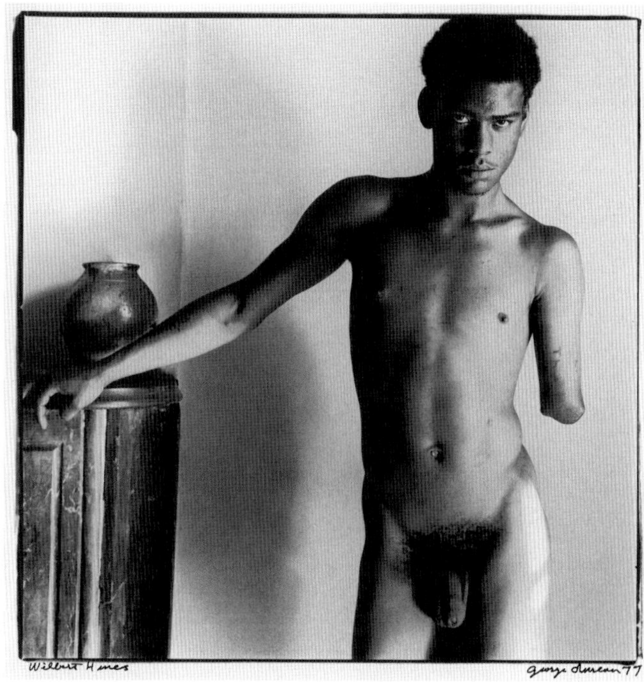

Fig. 36. George Dureau. *Wilbert Hines*. 1977. Gelatin silver print, 10 x 10 in. (25.4 x 25.4 cm).
© 2007 George Dureau

Mapplethorpe and saw an album of his Polaroids in 1974. He remembers Mapplethorpe as an intensely contained individual, a man of few words who nonetheless commanded attention with his exotic personal style. The work was shown without preamble or explanation. It comprised tough sex pictures, which, although this was becoming a period of extended license in publishing, were unlike any photographs Garner had seen. The mainstream French magazine *Photo* was beginning to feature increasingly challenging sexual imagery, but Mapplethorpe's works seemed to Garner more raw, more direct, and more personal: "I'm not sure I would have called them works of art at that time, and it is perhaps to their credit that they were not self-consciously aestheticized. Mapplethorpe clearly took them very seriously. They were tough and immensely powerful, had a total integrity, and were evidently an essential part of his personality."[61]

Photographs that exposed fringe behavior or depicted those on the social margins were not new. Historical precedents include the portraits of prostitutes that E. J. Bellocq made in New Orleans's legalized red light district at the turn of the nineteenth century and Brassaï's photographs in French brothels in the 1930s. More contemporary were Diane Arbus, whose photographs of circus performers, drag queens, midgets, and giants were exhibited in The Museum of Modern Art's 1967 exhibition "New Documents"

Fig. 37. Robert Mapplethorpe. *Untitled (Ruth Kligman)*. 1972/73. Three internal dye diffusion transfer prints (Polaroids) in plastic sleeve, each 3 1/4 x 4 1/4 in. (8.3 x 10.8 cm). Robert Mapplethorpe Foundation

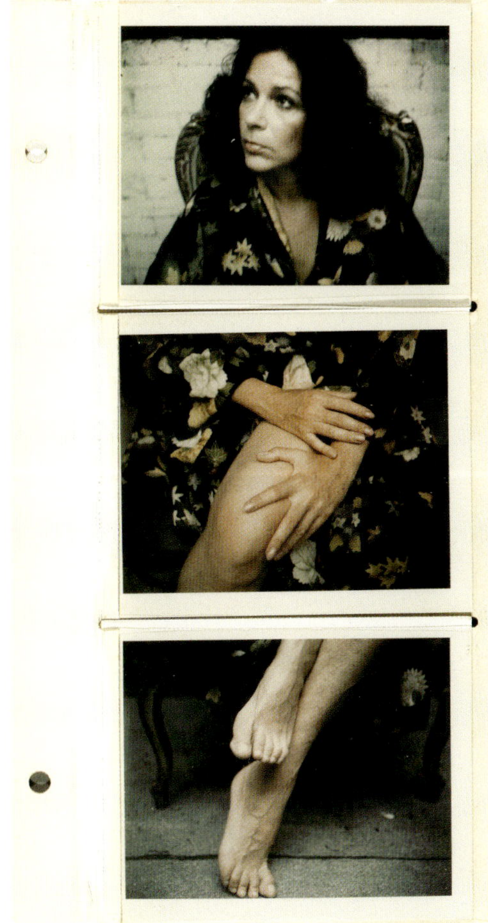

and published in a posthumous retrospective monograph of her work in 1972, and Larry Clark, whose images of teenage drug addicts from his hometown in Oklahoma were published in the book *Tulsa* (1971).[62] Like Arbus and Clark, Mapplethorpe did not act merely as a documentarian—he participated in and was committed to the world he depicted. At the same time, he occupied a parallel universe: when not photographing a conquest or acquaintance, he increasingly made portraits of the cultural elite whom he met through his benefactors.

Starting in the mid 1970s, portraiture would become a central focus of Mapplethorpe's career and his means of earning a living. The connections he made through McKendry and Wagstaff gave him entrée into high society, where he found numerous patrons. His expanding career as a photographer further enlarged his pool of portrait subjects to include artists, actors, musicians, and designers. Mapplethorpe photographed Nicky Weymouth, a socialite and member of Warhol's circle, as an ethereal figure, seemingly floating underwater, her hair flowing effortlessly behind (pl. 162). Her husband, Nigel Weymouth, by contrast, cradles an armload of tulips and looks slightly stunned, like a frightened beauty queen (pl. 163). The Warhol superstar Candy Darling talks on the telephone or lounges like a mermaid in a metallic, form-fitting evening gown (pls. 6 and 7). Darling is acutely aware of the camera in all of the pictures; alternately flirtatious and seductive, she is always on. Photographs of the British curator Clarissa Dalrymple, on the other hand (pl. 157), and of Smith's friend the photographer Judy Linn (pl. 152) are calm, solemn, and penetrating.

When a subject and a photographer come together and agree to make a portrait, a complex dynamic is set in motion. Vanity comes into play, as does the model's comfort or discomfort at being scrutinized by the camera. Cultural influences may affect body posture and expression, as does the relationship between the photographer and the sitter: do they know each other, and if so, is there trust or intimacy between them? In the most compelling portraits there is often a collision of wills, an exposure of vulnerability, a seduction or surrender. The public face that a subject would like the world to see is tempered by something deeper. Multiple layers of experience are brought to the surface and the inside is turned out for us to see. Mapplethorpe's portrait of the British singer and songwriter Marianne Faithfull—sitting in a plush armchair, wearing a ruffled blouse, and holding a cup of tea—is a particularly lovely example of photography's capacity both to register a subject's physical characteristics and to hint at the complexity within (pl. 159). In her soft eyes and gentle hint of a smile are a refinement and sweetness that run contrary to her history with drug addiction and her volatile partnership with Rolling Stone singer Jagger in the 1960s.

Like the portrait of Faithfull, several more of Mapplethorpe's images show a touch of Victorian wistfulness. The soft focus and flowing hair in a photograph of the painter Helen Marden, for example, recall

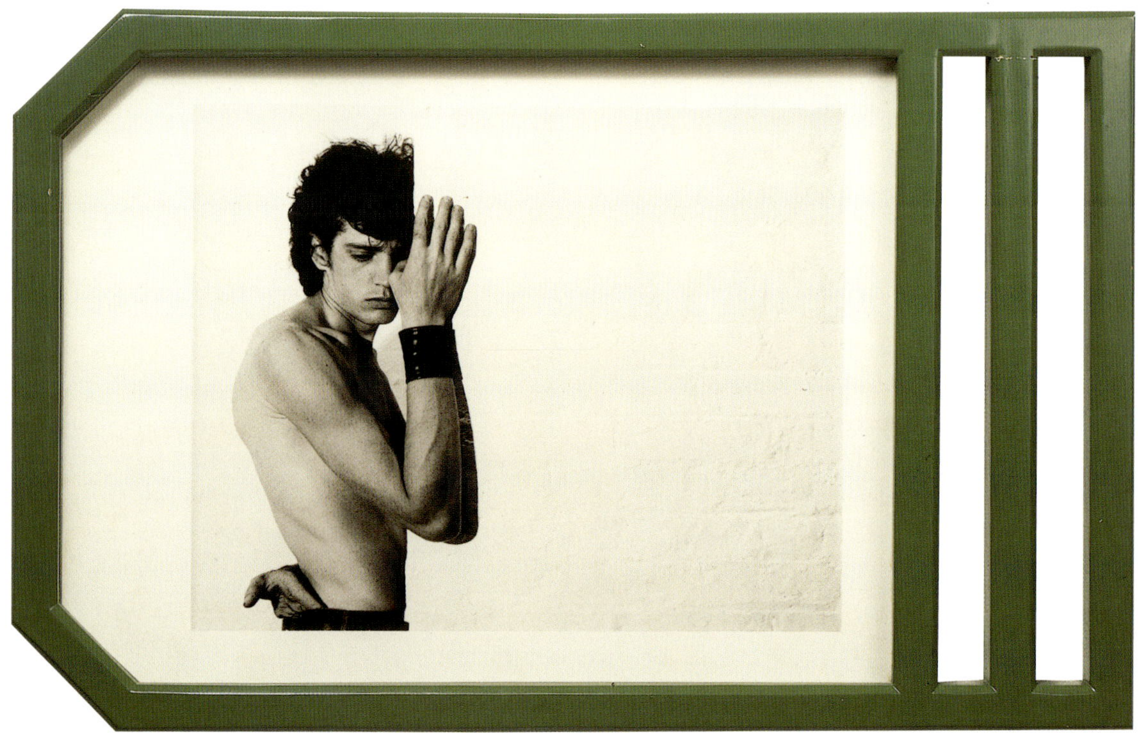

Fig. 38. Robert Mapplethorpe. *Untitled (self-portrait).* 1974. Gelatin silver print in painted wood frame, 14 1/2 x 23 1/2 x 1 in. (36.8 x 59.7 x 2.5 cm). Solomon R. Guggenheim Museum, Gift, Robert Mapplethorpe Foundation

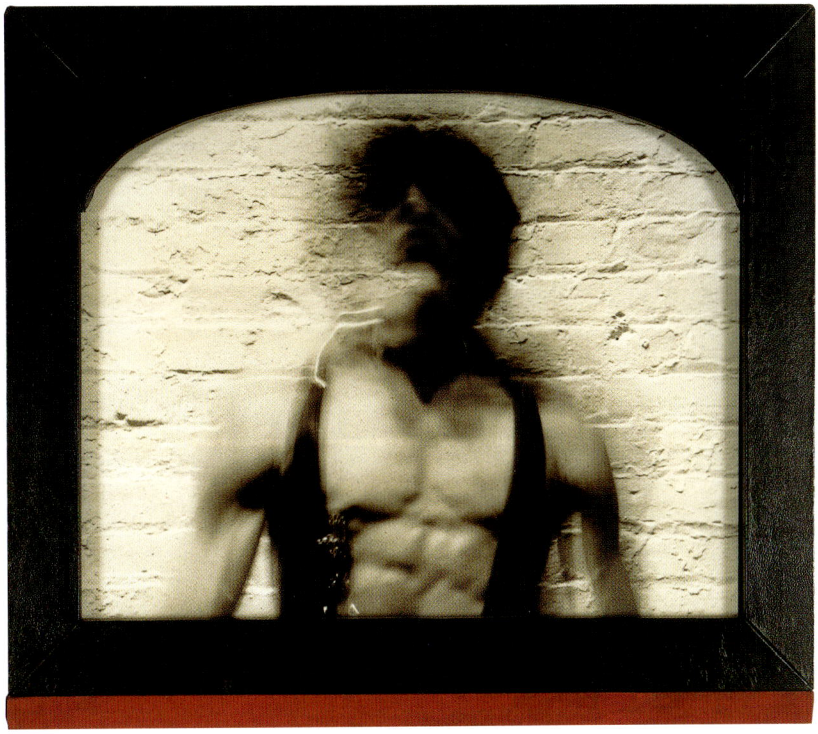

Fig. 39. Robert Mapplethorpe. *Untitled (self-portrait)*. 1973. Gelatin silver print in leather and felt frame, 14 x 16 x 1 in. (35.6 x 40.6 x 2.5 cm). Solomon R.Guggenheim Museum, Gift, Robert Mapplethorpe Foundation

the work of the nineteenth-century British photographer Julia Margaret Cameron (pl. 156). Cameron is one of the photographers whom Mapplethorpe and Wagstaff collected in depth. They also owned pictures by the mid-nineteenth-century French caricaturist and portrait photographer Gaspar Félix Tournachon Nadar. Some of Mapplethorpe's studio photographs of men in dapper dress—of the fashion designer Ozzie Clark, for example, or the British antique dealer Christopher Gibbs—recall Nadar's portraits of men of position and power, or of luminaries of the arts and letters (pls. 158 and 160). Mapplethorpe occasionally photographed members of the art community in domestic décor, as he did with the Metropolitan Museum of Art's contemporary art curator Henry Geldzahler (pl. 155) and with Ruth Kligman, the artist and former lover of Jackson Pollock (fig. 37). But more often than not he invited subjects to his studio, where he could control the conditions of the session. The Polaroid portraits that Mapplethorpe made from 1973 to 1975 show him moving toward the refined style of his later images in their stark formalism, their mastery of light, and in the aura of personality projected by his subjects (pls. 166 and 167).

Apart from portraiture, Mapplethorpe experimented in the studio with pictures in the style of commercial advertising,

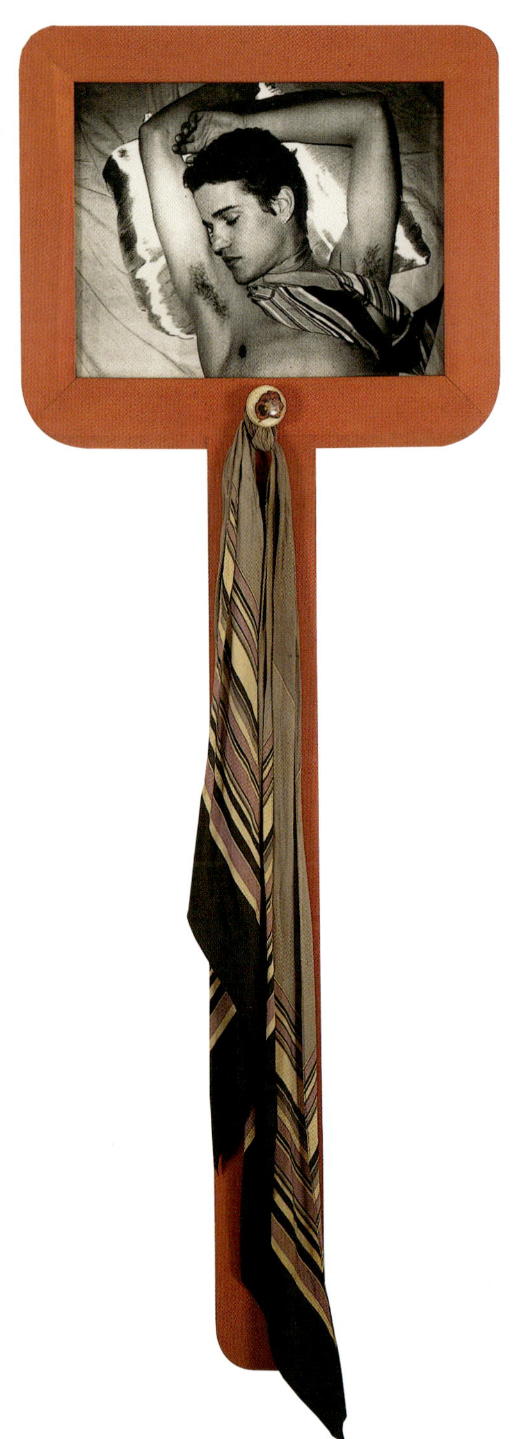

Fig. 40. Robert Mapplethorpe. *Jay Johnson Kiss.* 1973. Gelatin silver print in wood frame, metal knob, and silk scarf, 47 x 17 1/2 x 1 in. (119.4 x 44.5 x 2.5 cm). Private collection

including an oblique view of a pack of Kool cigarettes (his brand) and a frontal depiction of a bottle of Dom Perignon champagne that he shot for a New Year's card he sent to friends (pls. 172 and 175).[63] In these photographs, objects are isolated from their functions and appreciated for their form. A bird's-eye view of a cup of black coffee against a checkered kitchen cloth is a classic tabletop image (pl. 173), whereas a vacuum cleaner hose flanked by a broom with a wedge cut out of it, and the resulting pile of shavings, call to mind late-night television advertisements demonstrating new home products (pl. 170). Where Mapplethorpe's early constructions had a quality of baroque excess, we see here the beginnings of the cooler, bolder, more graphic style that would characterize his later works.

Many of these photographs were taken with the Graflex, which Mapplethorpe acquired toward the end of 1973 and outfitted with a Polaroid back (frontispiece, p. 16). Around the time he picked up this camera, he began to enlarge the Polaroid negatives he had made—both the Graflex and his earlier Polaroid, the Model 360, took positive/negative film[64]—and to embellish their presentation with wooden frames designed and constructed to his specifications by carpenter Robert Fosdick. Among these framed objects are several self-portraits, including an image of the artist hugging the brick wall in his studio with one hand slipped seductively into the back of his pants (fig. 38). The shape of

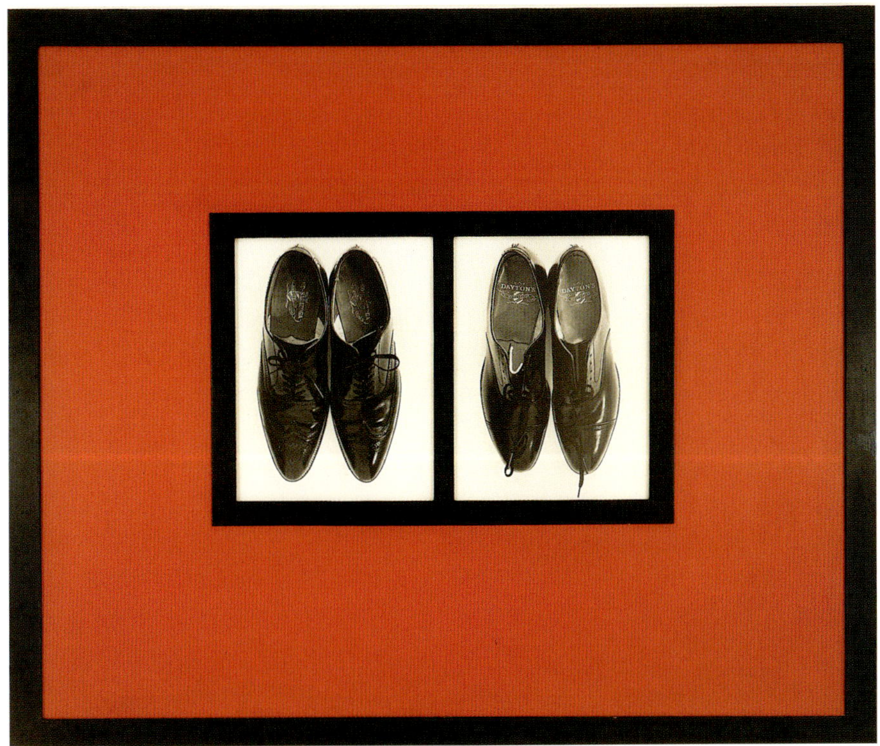

Fig. 41. Robert Mapplethorpe. *Black Shoes*. 1974. Two gelatin silver prints in wood frame, 37 x 42 1/2 x 1 in. (94 x 113 x 2.5 cm). Museum of Fine Arts, Houston, Gift, Michael A. Caddell and Cynthia Chapman

the green frame on the piece mimics the shape of the Polaroid Type 52 film he often used. In another piece, Mapplethorpe is dressed in leather vest and nipple clips, a frightening howl recorded by the blur of a long exposure (fig. 39). The photograph is framed in black leather and red felt with a vignette across the top, as in an altar or a niche. Unlike his early Polaroids, which reflect an innocence about seeing and being seen, these are self-conscious, provocative pictures that are neither neutral nor discreet.

Less aggressive are framed works made with irony and a wry sense of humor. A portrait of Jay Johnson wearing a silk scarf, with the scarf itself hanging from a knob on the frame (fig. 40), reads as a devotional object—the scarf a relic left over from the affair. In *Black Shoes* (1974; fig. 41), two pairs of patent-leather men's dress shoes are photographed against a white background and scaled to fill the frame. The shoes conjure up images of stature, wealth, and glamour, yet Smith remembers that they found one of these pairs on the street; the other pair belonged to Mapplethorpe.[65] Both of these works address the difference between objects in the real world and their photographic representations—a topic that would move to center stage in the 1970s as photography gained attention in the realm of art and academia.

When Mapplethorpe made these works, the field of photographic art was entering a period of extraordinary development. Accompanying a growing appreciation for the medium as a fine art was an increase in critical discourse in art journals and the press. In the early 1970s the cultural critic and historian A. D. Coleman began to write regularly on photography for the *New York Times,* while in the *New York Review of Books* Susan Sontag was publishing the essays that would become the contents of her seminal book *On Photography* (1977).[66] The first photography auction to take place in the United States was held at Sotheby's, New York, in 1975. In art schools and universities the number of academic programs in photography was growing, with ensuing developments in the study of the medium's history and of its social and political implications. Walter Benjamin's 1939 essay "The Work of Art in the Age of Mechanical Reproduction," translated into English in 1968, was widely read and debated; Benjamin identified photography and film as mediums of duplication and dissemination, undermining the "aura" and sense of uniqueness of works of art and precipitating a new form of cultural experience in which "creativity and genius, eternal value and mystery were brushed aside as outmoded concepts."[67]

In the context of these developments, Mapplethorpe's decoratively framed photographs of common subjects may be seen as both high art and a form of typology—a deadpan consideration of the subjects' stark forms. It is paradoxical that as he used the Polaroid negative to make photographic duplicates, he then framed them as unique objects, subverting the medium's link to replication. But then Mapplethorpe had always dressed up photographs and would continue to do so throughout his career. It gave them authority, he felt, and placed them more squarely in the realm of art. Shortly after making the enlarged framed Polaroids, Mapplethorpe entered a new chapter in his career—the one he would become known for—and embarked upon the quest for perfection that would engage him for the rest of his life. Once again, a piece of technical equipment and the largess of an admirer were the catalysts of change.

Moving Forward, Looking Back

In 1975, Wagstaff made Mapplethorpe the gift of a Hasselblad 2 1/4-inch camera, a model often used by studio photographers to make portraits and advertising images. Among the many benefits of the Hasselblad was its use of roll film, which allowed for continuous exposure. The momentum of a shoot was not interrupted by developing each sheet of film, as with the Polaroid. The Hasselblad's superior lens also offered better resolution and clarity, and the finely tuned machinery yielded greater shutter control. There was no immediate gratification, as with a Polaroid camera, but by the time Mapplethorpe started to use the Hasselblad he was ready for the heightened precision, detail, and image quality it provided. He

Fig. 42. Robert Mapplethorpe. *Untitled*. 1975. Chromogenic color print, 9 x 9 in. (22.9 x 22.9 cm). Robert Mapplethorpe Foundation

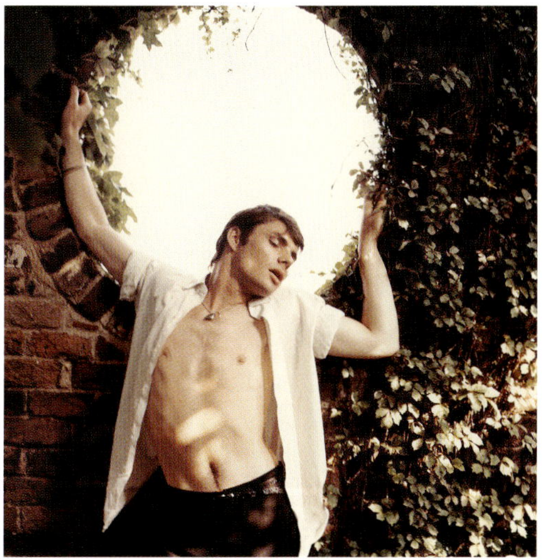

was also making money on his photography and could afford to hire a darkroom assistant to process his film and enlarge his negatives. (Mapplethorpe is not known ever to have made his own prints during his career).[68]

The Hasselblad, a square-format camera, offered an altogether different experience from composing for a rectangle. In fact, it provided a new way of looking: the human eye does not see in a square. Mapplethorpe had toyed with the square frame before, making quirky color pictures with a Polaroid SX70 camera (pls. 14 and 15), but only a few of these remain in the Robert Mapplethorpe Foundation archive; the artist appears not to have embraced the square format until he acquired the Hasselblad. Early rolls of 2 1/4-inch film show Mapplethorpe developing themes and motifs that would emerge more fully later, including juxtaposing the figure against a geometric form (fig. 42). Perhaps influenced by magazine photographer and celebrity portraitist Francesco Scavullo, Mapplethorpe sought high-profile subjects and posed them against neutral backdrops. Rock singer Deborah Harry, architect Philip Johnson, bodybuilder Arnold Schwarzenegger, and composer Philip Glass with avant-garde theater director Robert Wilson project distinct personas and personal styles. Photographs like these drew the attention of curators, collectors, and gallerists, including the New York dealer Holly Solomon, who commanded an elite clientele. She offered Mapplethorpe a show at her SoHo gallery in early 1977. He had also agreed to an exhibition at the performance space The Kitchen. With the two shows opening simultaneously on February 4, Mapplethorpe straddled downtown and uptown audiences, appealing to the rough and the refined.

Neither installation photographs nor checklists are available to confirm what was shown in either of these exhibitions, but reviews make no mention of Polaroid works.[69] By this time Mapplethorpe seems to have thoroughly embraced the 2 1/4-inch format and the Hasselblad camera, which he would use for the remainder of his career. In later years he would employ one of his early Polaroids (pl. 181) to make the announcement for the show "Seven Artists' View of the Male Image," which opened at the Robert Samuel Gallery on March 11, 1978, and in 1984 he would produce four color pictures of Ken Moody with the Polaroid Corporation's twenty-by-twenty-four-inch camera (fig. 43).[70] He would also use instant photography to test

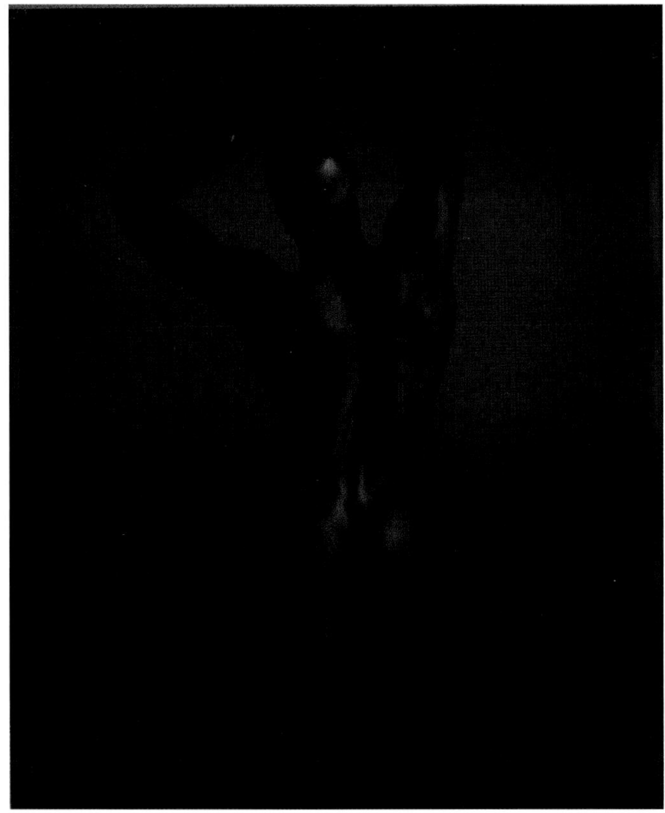

Fig. 43. Robert Mapplethorpe. *Ken Moody*. 1984. Internal dye diffusion transfer print (Polaroid), 24 x 20 in. (61 x 50.8 cm). Robert Mapplethorpe Foundation

lighting, exposure, and composition for studio portraits and still lifes, but here the Polaroid cameras were at the service of the Hasselblad: they were measuring tools, not instruments of the imagination.

This was not so when Mapplethorpe began. His photographs from the start of his career show little interest in achieving perfection or rendering exquisite beauty, as would those from later in his life. Instead, Polaroid materials provided the vehicle for his inquiry into the impulses and energies that drove his desire to be an artist. While many contributed to this quest—including lovers, mentors, and friends—his true companion was the Polaroid camera, an alter ego of sorts. In addition to giving him immediate feedback that helped him to refine his skills, instant photography provided a mode of entry into his creative ambition, his sexual desires, and the art world at large.

What, though, do we make of the fact that Mapplethorpe's Polaroids received only limited exposure during his lifetime? Are we to consider them incidental or immature? His organization of some pictures in triptychs, and of others in handmade or highly crafted frames, certainly suggests serious intent. He also showed portfolios of his Polaroids to gallery directors in the United States and abroad, and a postcard he sent to Croland from France on October 27, 1971, states "The only thing that might keep me here being a book of Polaroids on the people of Paris"—an indication that there was the possibility of a publication.[71]

Mapplethorpe's own remarks about the instant gratification of the Polaroid suggest that it is unlikely he would have gotten from point A (his early collages and assemblages) to point C (the photographs that are the markers of his career) without the intermediate, limit-testing phase of picture-making with Polaroid materials. What may have kept many of Mapplethorpe's Polaroids in boxes and notebooks in his studio, and in the Robert Mapplethorpe Foundation archive after his death, is the zeal with which he embraced more sophisticated equipment and the notoriety he achieved for these later photographs. Historians, critics, and artists themselves often attend to the most recent work at the expense of previous innovation. Reflecting on earlier production may occur only after an artist's death. Mapplethorpe said that his vision was already fully formed when he started taking photographs, and there is, indeed, a consistency of subject matter throughout his career, from self-portraits and flowers to sex pictures and nudes. Yet the Polaroids reveal an evolution in his thinking and seeing. What comes through in the early work is a spontaneity, charm, and toughness—an authentic artlessness that makes his Polaroids disarming and unique.

With the instant camera and film, Mapplethorpe defined his sexual identity and artistic persona, developed the basic style and subject matter of his work, and established the personal relationships that would become the foundation of his artistic success. But above all, Mapplethorpe learned how to see photographically with the Polaroid camera. In a picture from his early years as a photographer, he captures himself in a rare moment of candor, with uncombed hair and piercing eyes looking intently in the direction of the camera but not at the lens itself (pl. 48). It is a deceptive, seemingly naïve photograph, as the artist gropes for the shutter. Yet it is emblematic of this body of work for its display of the intensity with which Mapplethorpe sought access to inner worlds through photography. His was not merely a need to get past the veil of normalcy, it was also a quest for understanding. The Polaroid provided instant gratification, but more important it ignited a lifelong passion for using the camera to penetrate appearances and get at the complexity within.

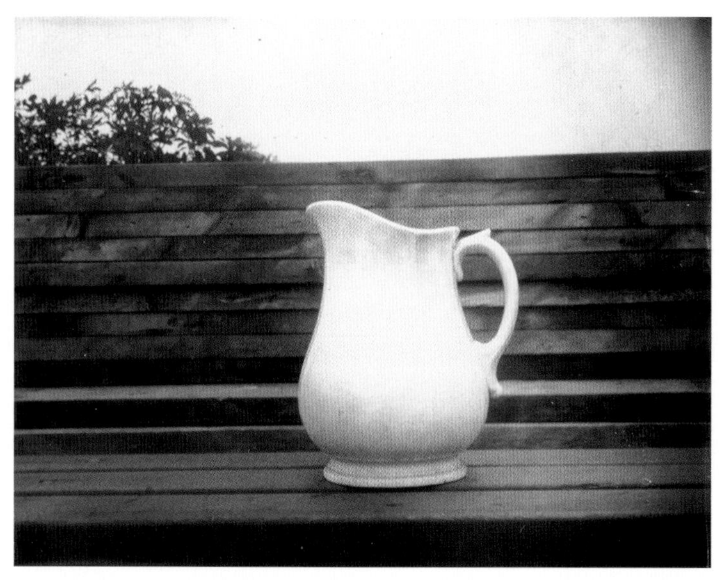

Plate 16. *Untitled*. 1970/73

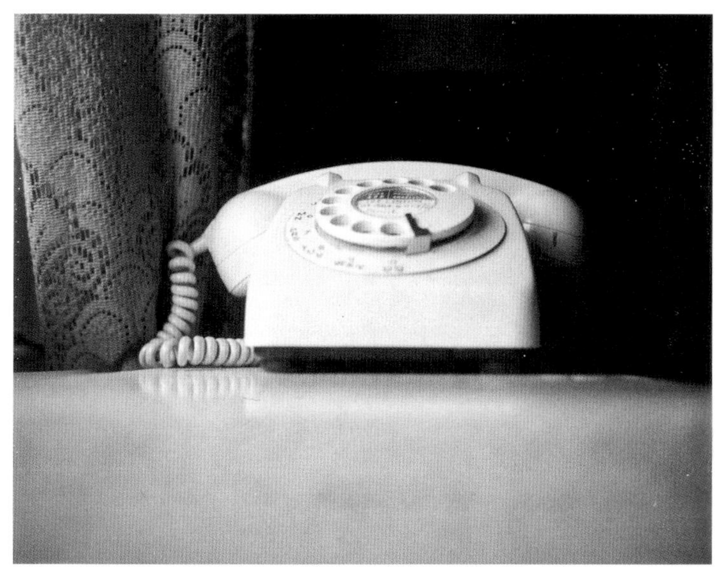

Plate 17. *Untitled*. 1971/73

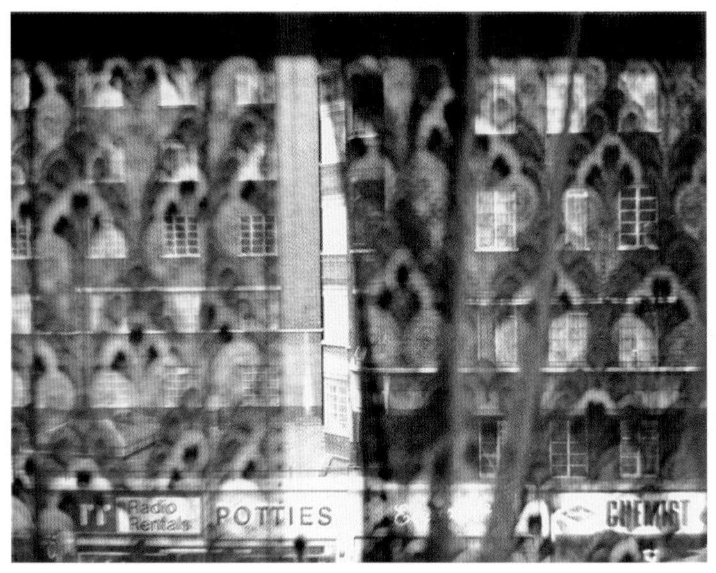

Plate 18. *Untitled*. 1971/73

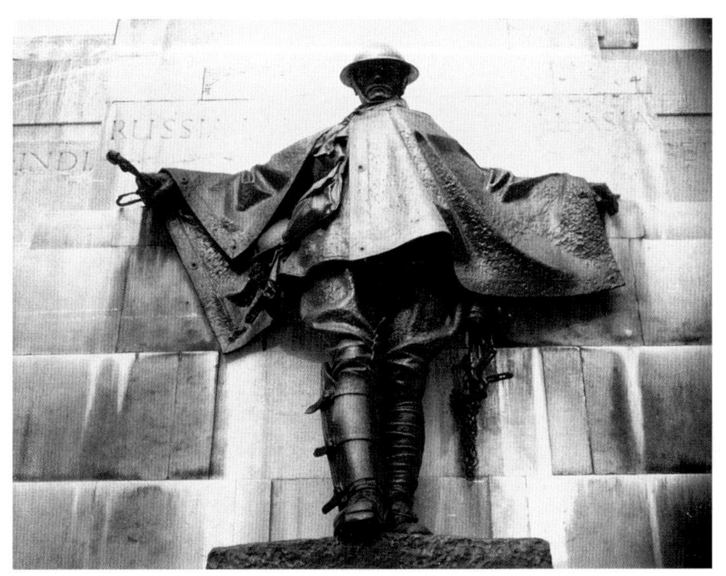

Plate 19. *Untitled*. 1971/73

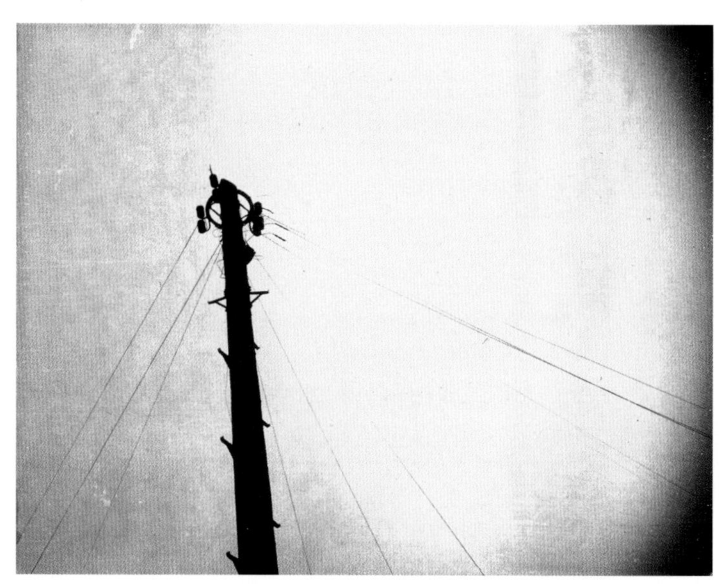

Plate 20. *Untitled*. 1970/73

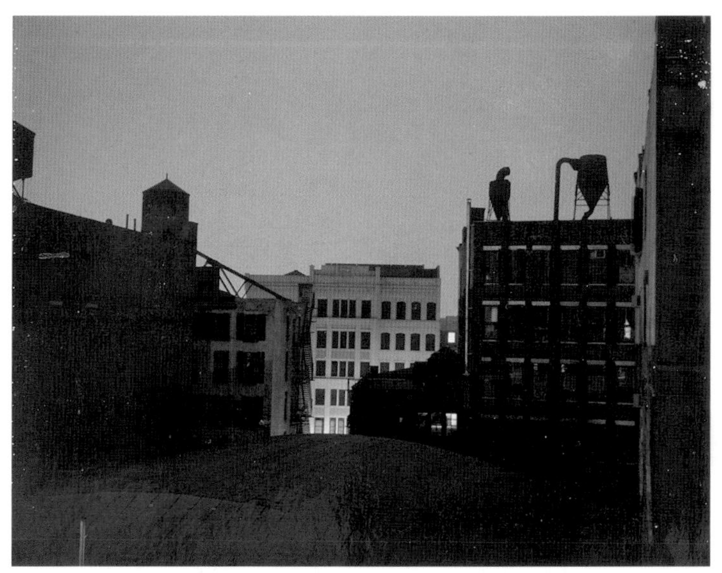

Plate 21. *Untitled*. 1970/73

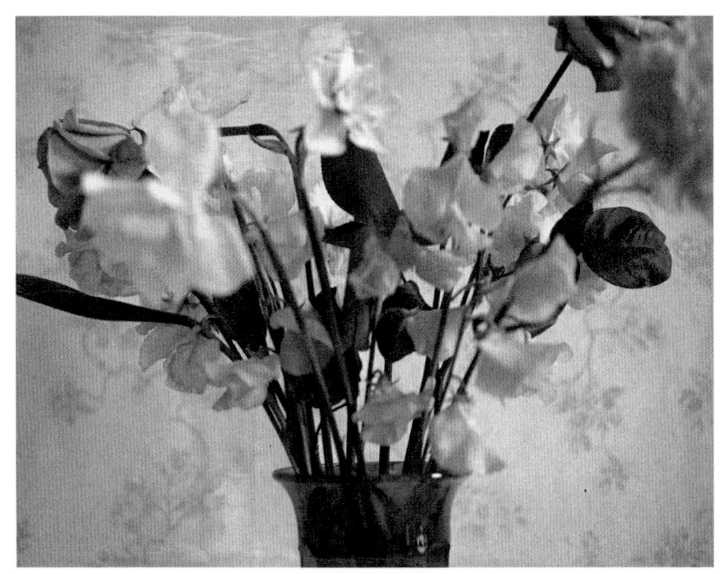

Plate 22. *Untitled (Catherine Tennant's House, London)*. 1973

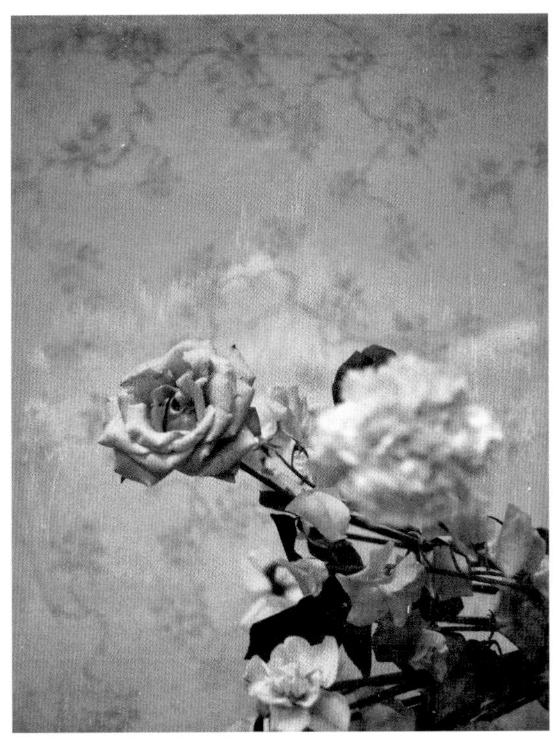

Plate 23. *Untitled (Catherine Tennant's House, London)*. 1973

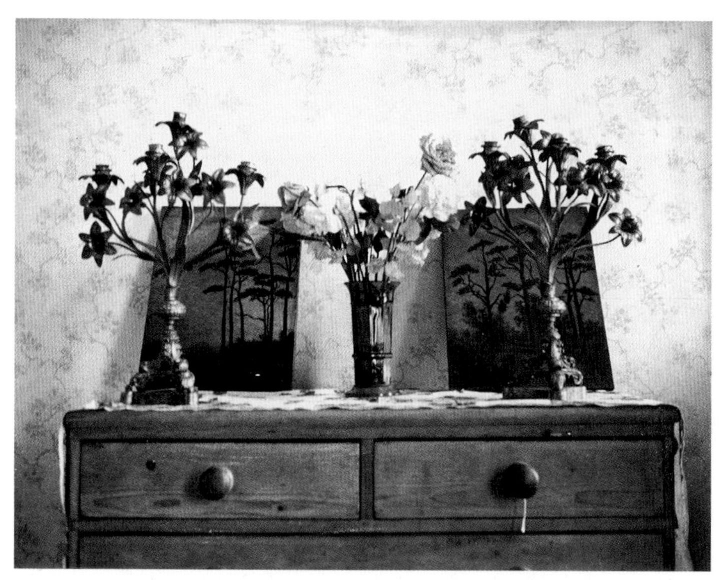

Plate 24. *Untitled. (Catherine Tennant's House, London).* 1973

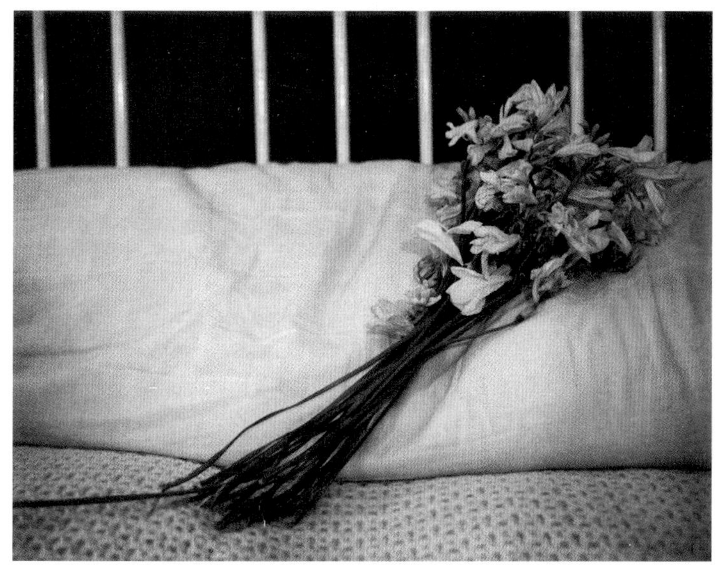

Plate 25. *Untitled*. 1973

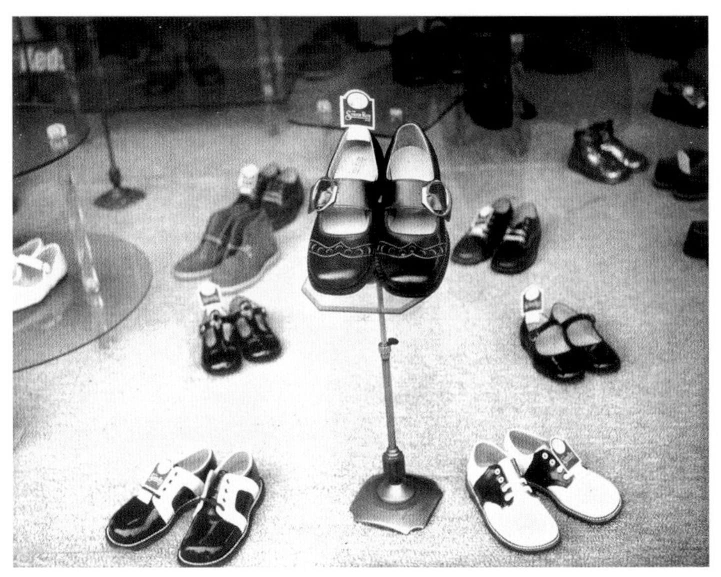

Plate 26. *Untitled*. 1970/73

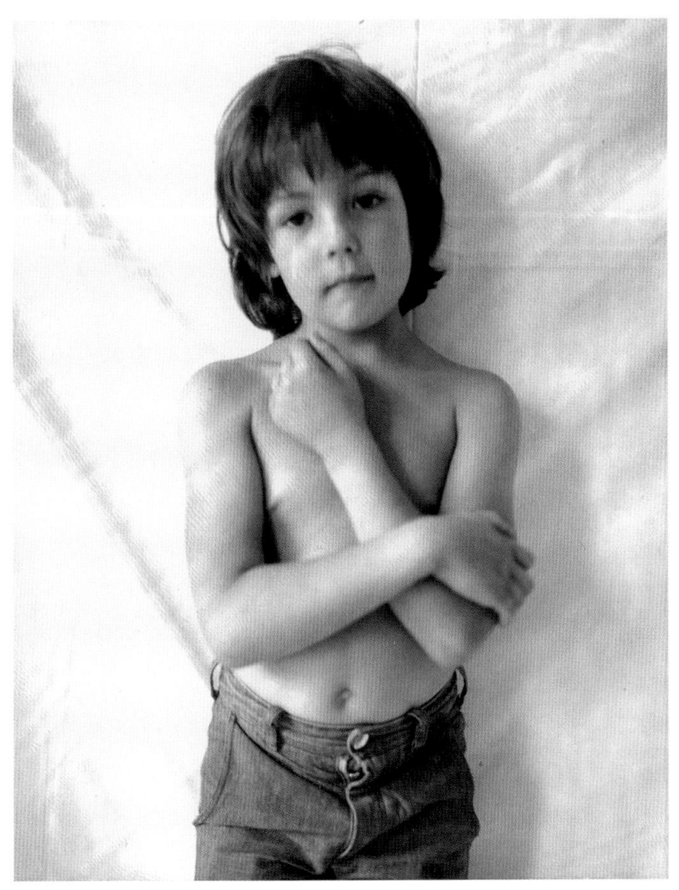

Plate 27. *Untitled*. 1973/75

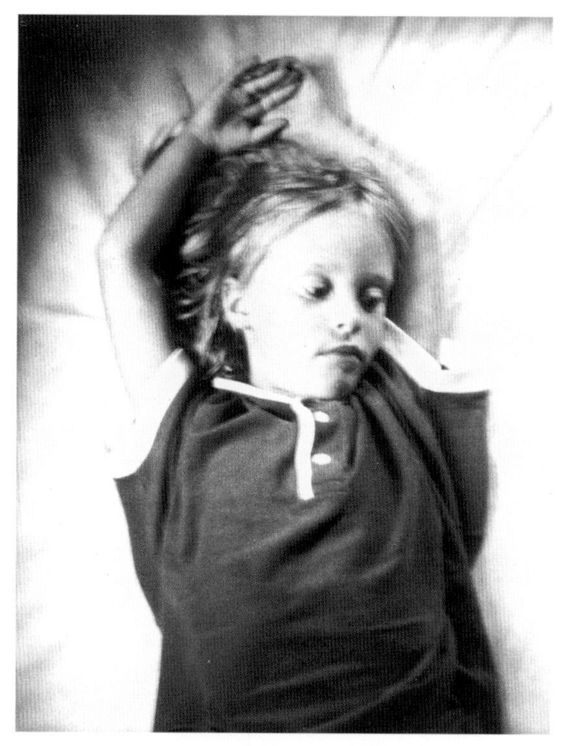

Plate 28. *Untitled*. 1970/73

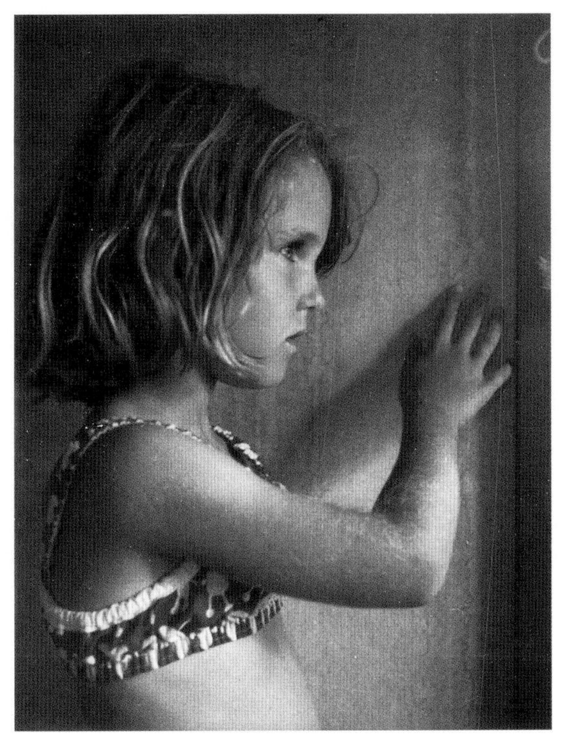

Plate 29. *Untitled*. 1970/73

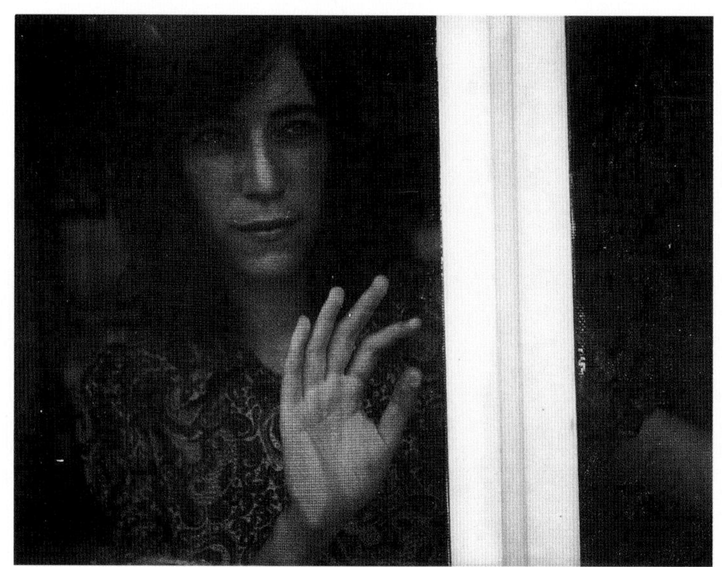

Plate 30. *Untitled (Patti Smith)*. 1973

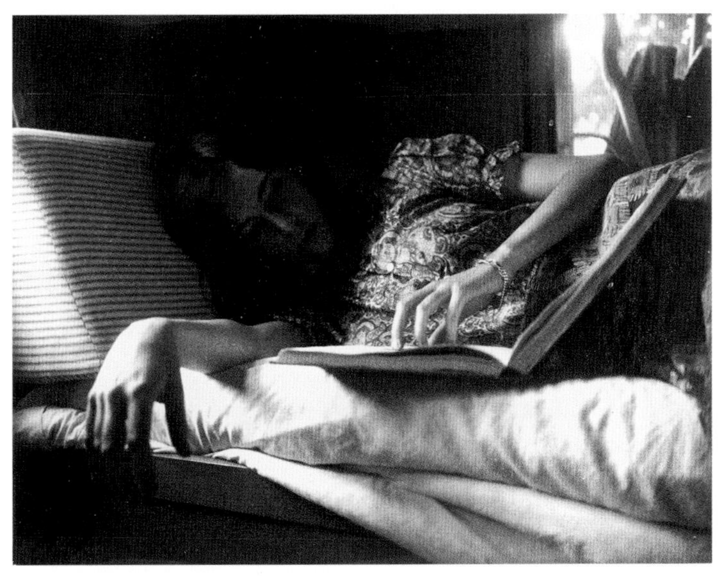

Plate 31. *Untitled (Patti Smith)*, 1973

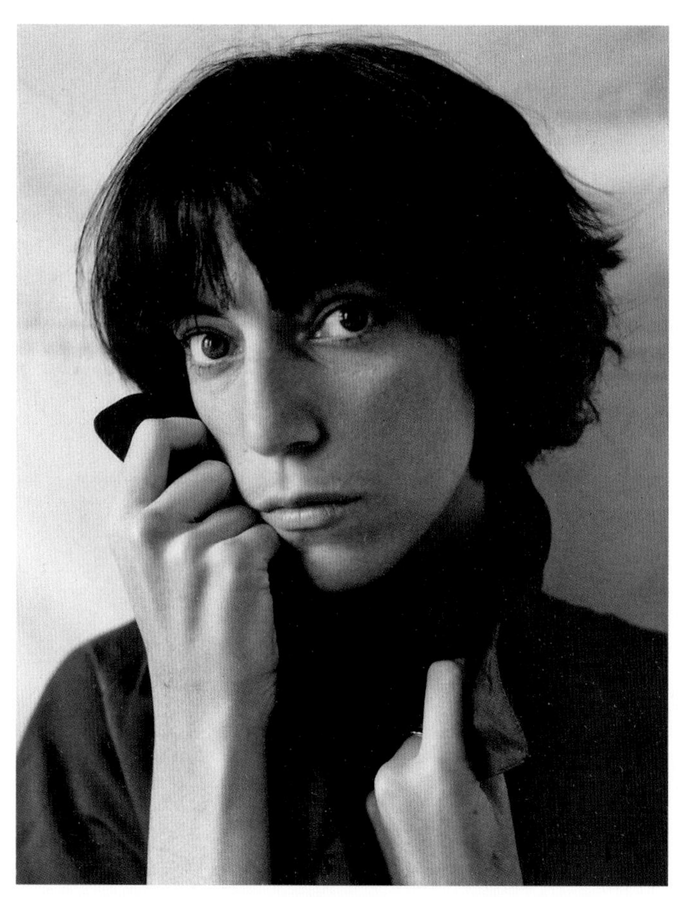

Plate 32. *Untitled (Patti Smith)*. 1973/75

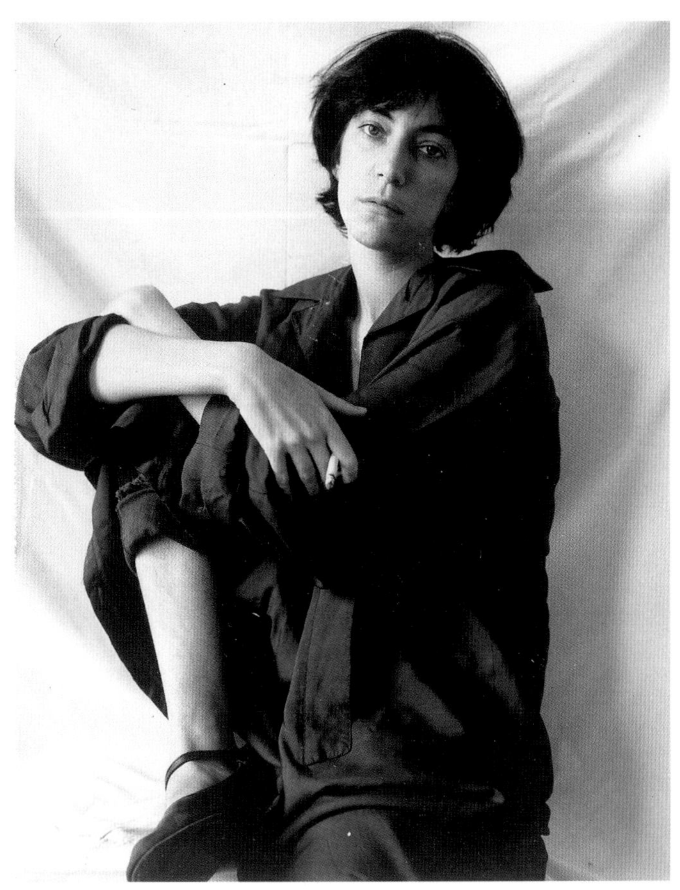

Plate 33. *Untitled (Patti Smith)*. 1973/75

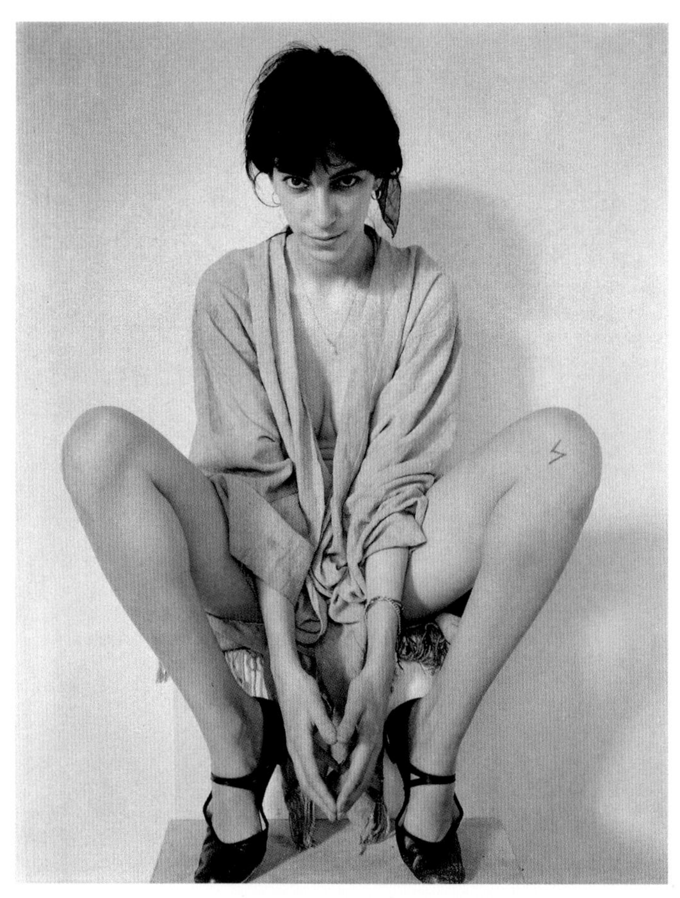

Plate 34. *Untitled (Patti Smith)*. 1973/75

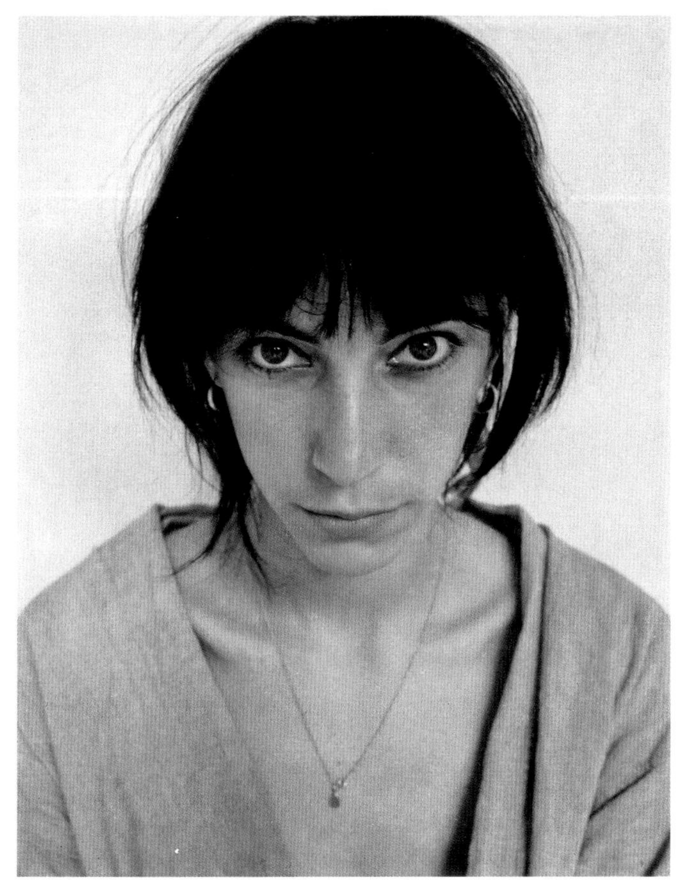

Plate 35. *Untitled (Patti Smith)*. 1973/75

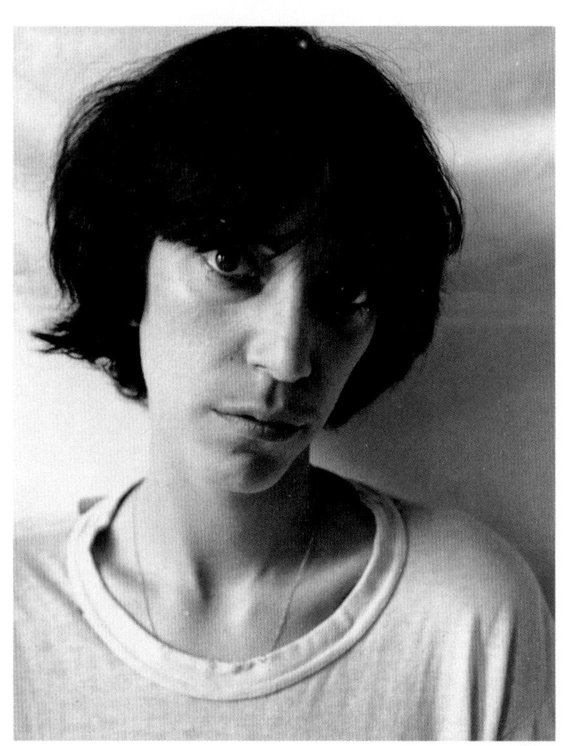

Plate 36. *Untitled (Patti Smith)*. 1970/73

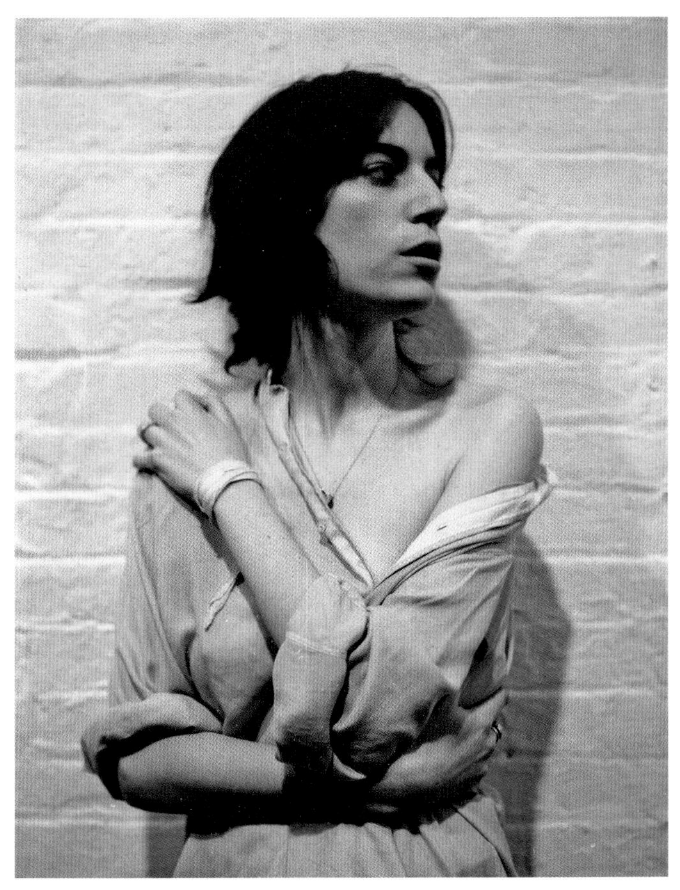

Plate 37. *Untitled (Patti Smith)*. 1973/75

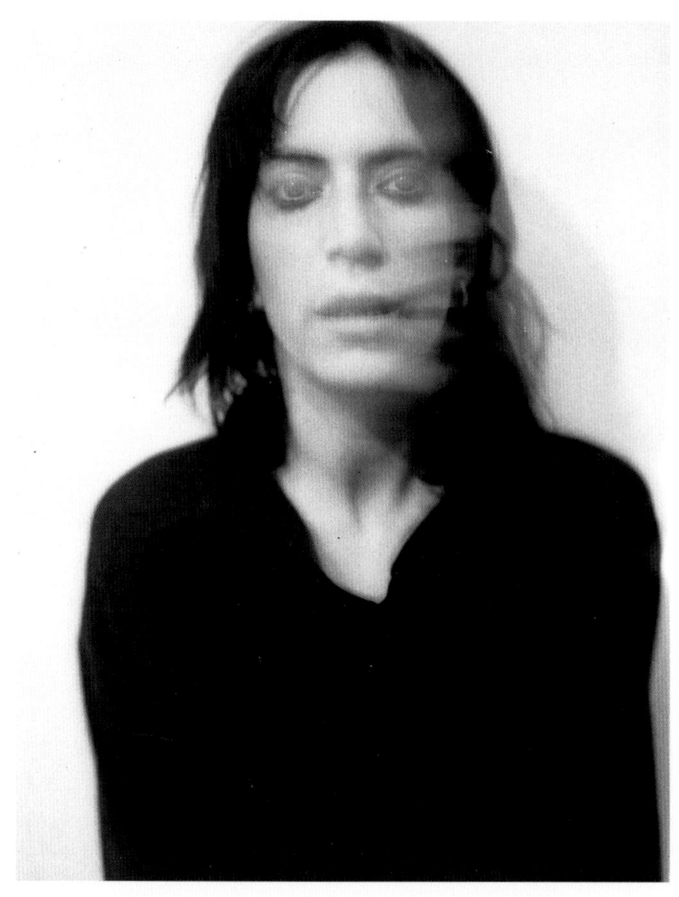

Plate 38. *Untitled (Patti Smith)*. 1973/75

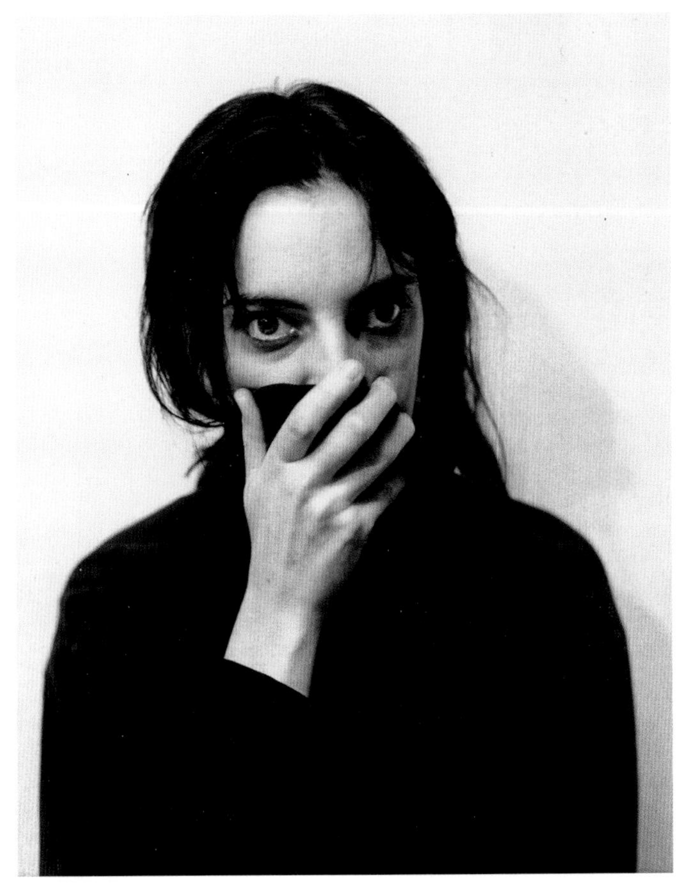

Plate 39. *Untitled (Patti Smith)*. 1973/75

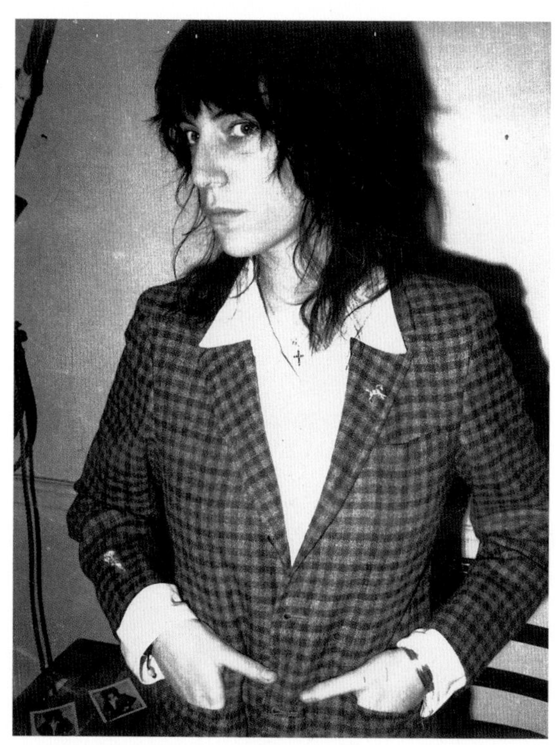

Plate 40. *Untitled (Patti Smith)*. 1970/73

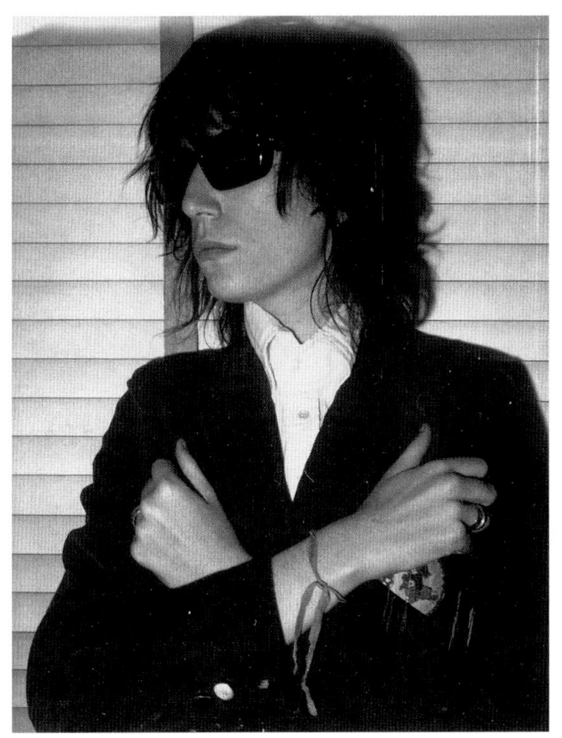

Plate 41. *Untitled (Patti Smith)*. 1970/73

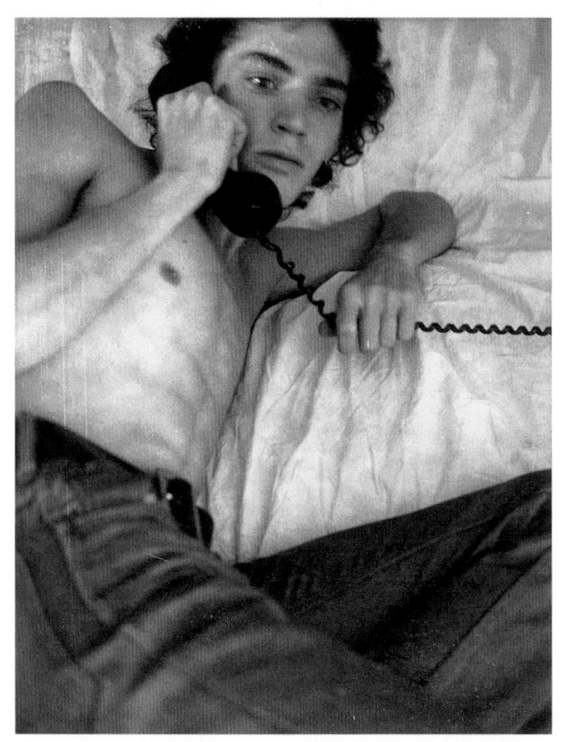

Plate 42. *Untitled (self-portrait)*. 1970/73

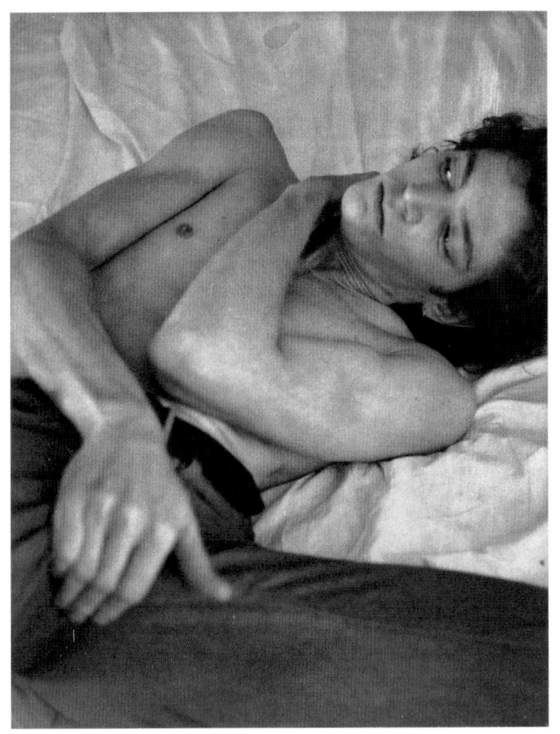

Plate 43. *Untitled (self-portrait)*. 1970/73

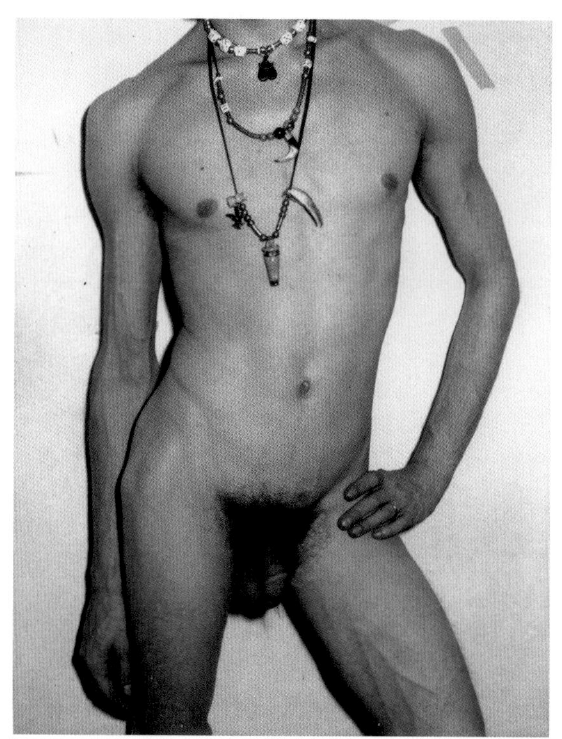

Plate 44. *Untitled (self-portrait)*. 1970/73

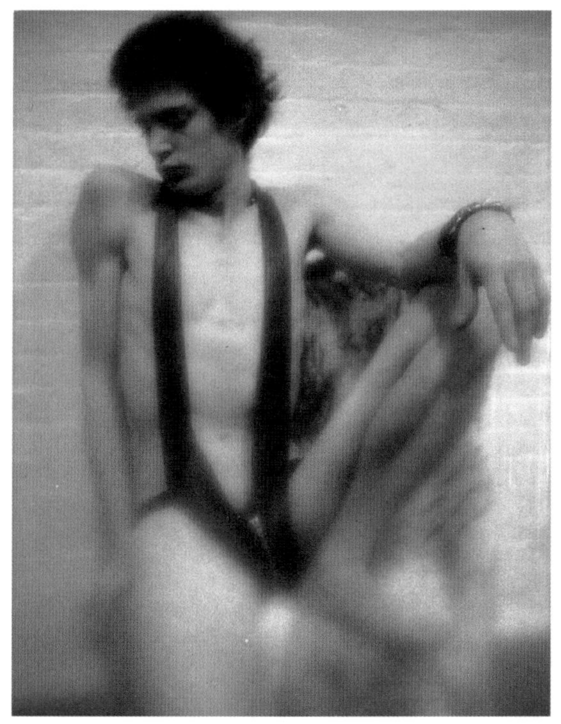

Plate 45. *Untitled (self-portrait)*. 1972/73

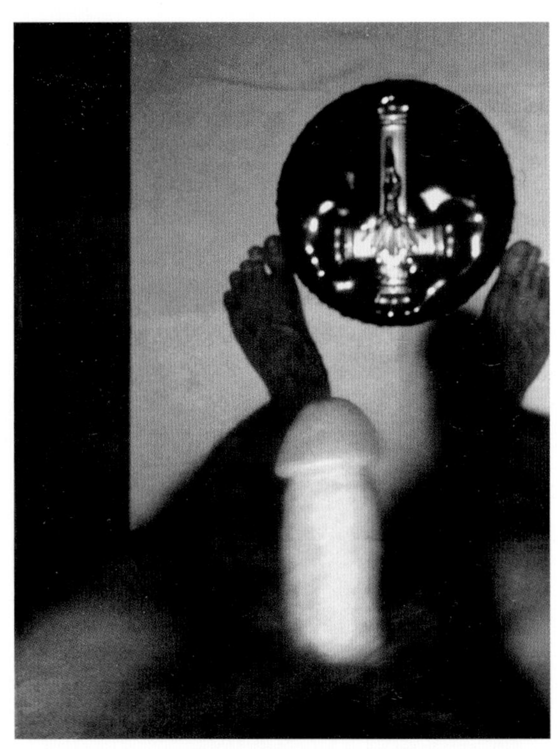

Plate 46. *Untitled*. 1971/72

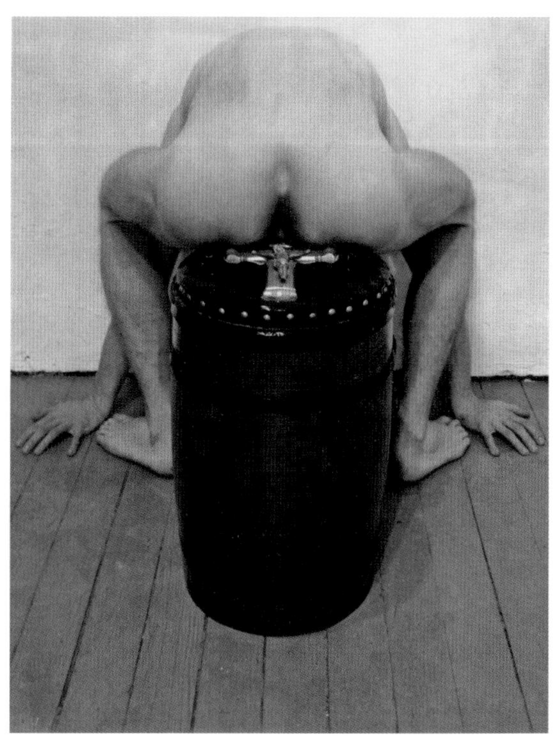

Plate 47. *Untitled*. 1970/73

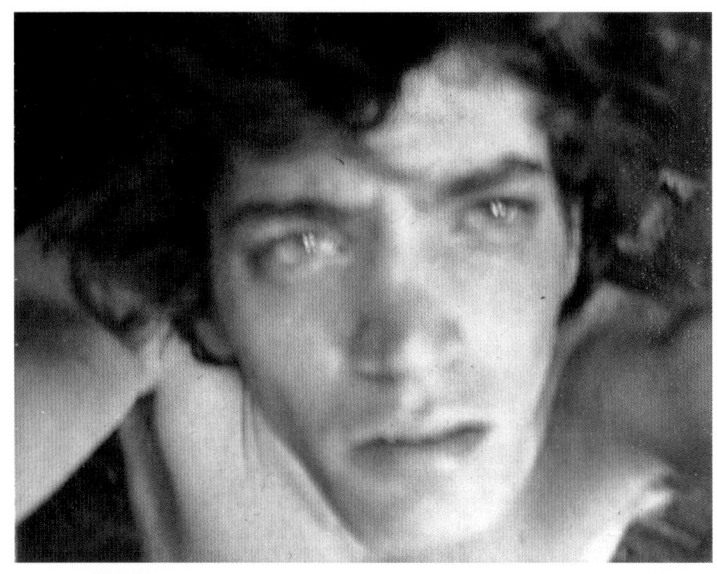

Plate 48. *Untitled (self-portrait)*. 1972

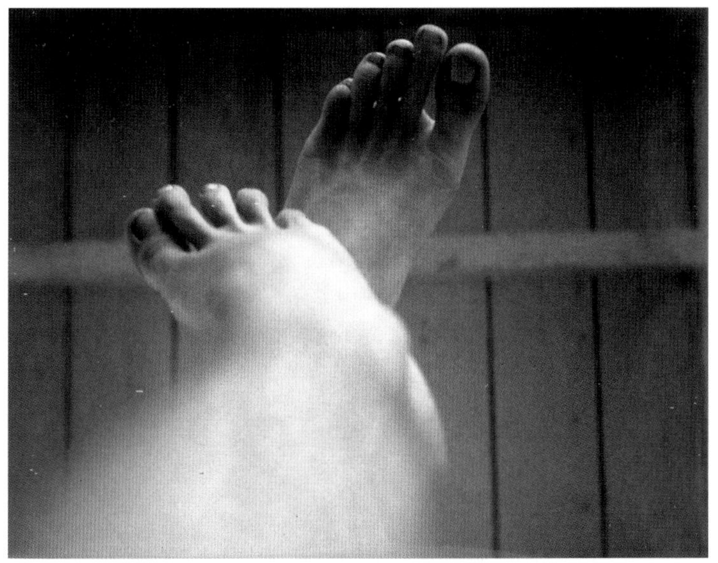

Plate 49. *Untitled (self-portrait)*. 1970/73

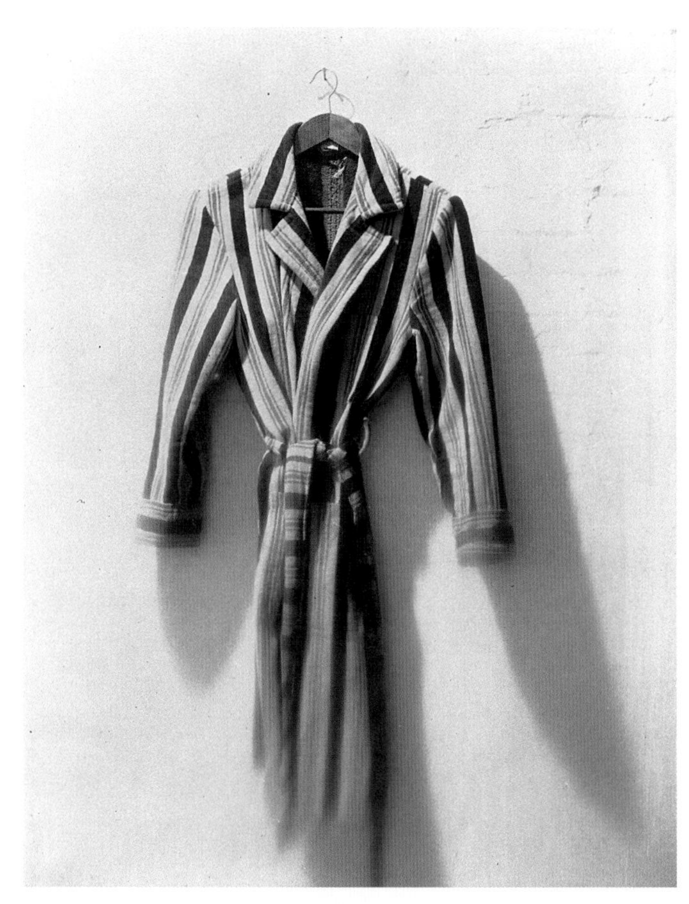

Plate 50. *Untitled*. 1973

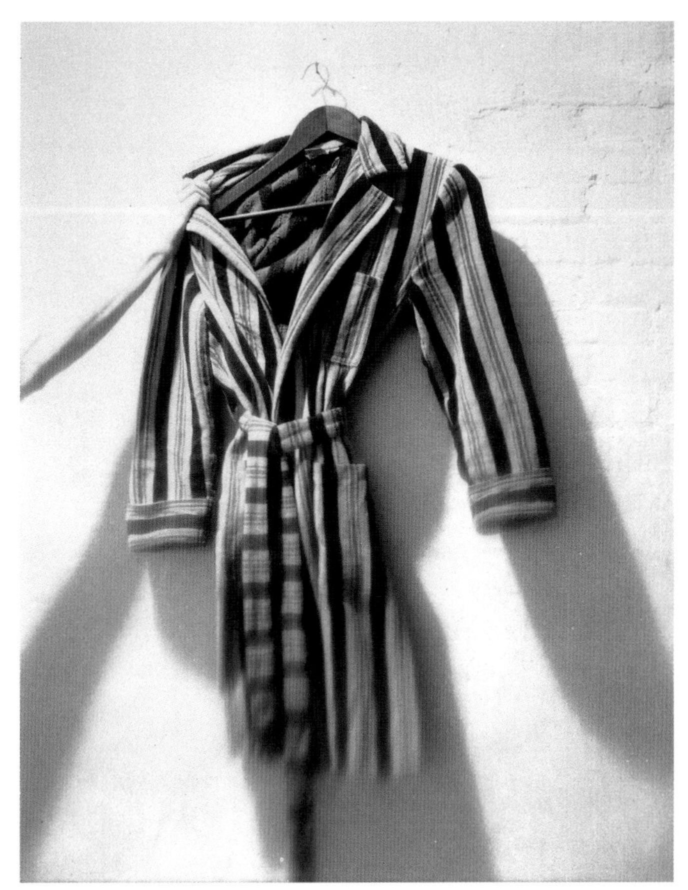

Plate 51. *Untitled*. 1973

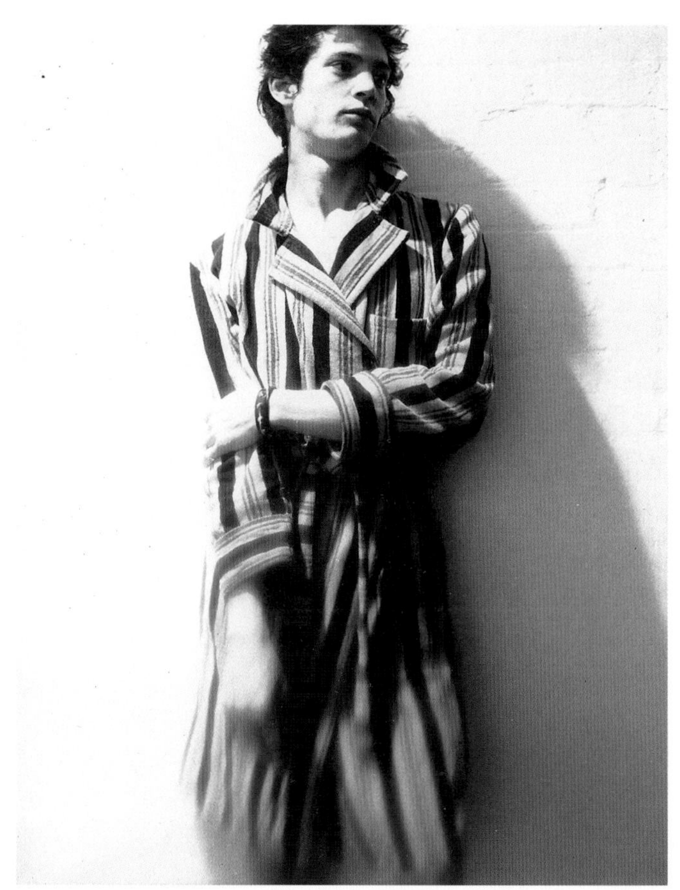

Plate 52. *Untitled (self-portrait)*. 1973

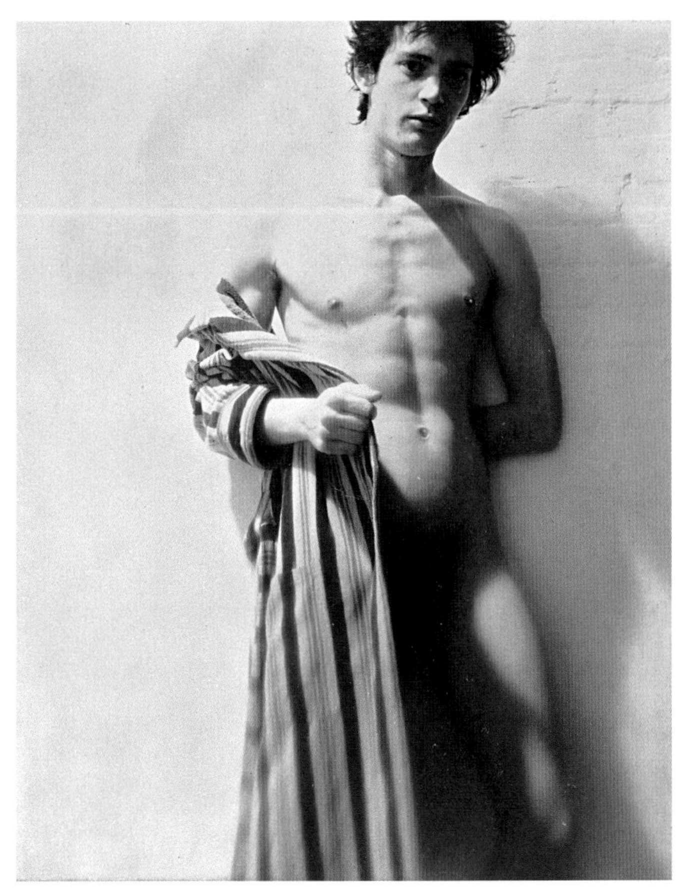

Plate 53. *Untitled (self-portrait)*. 1973

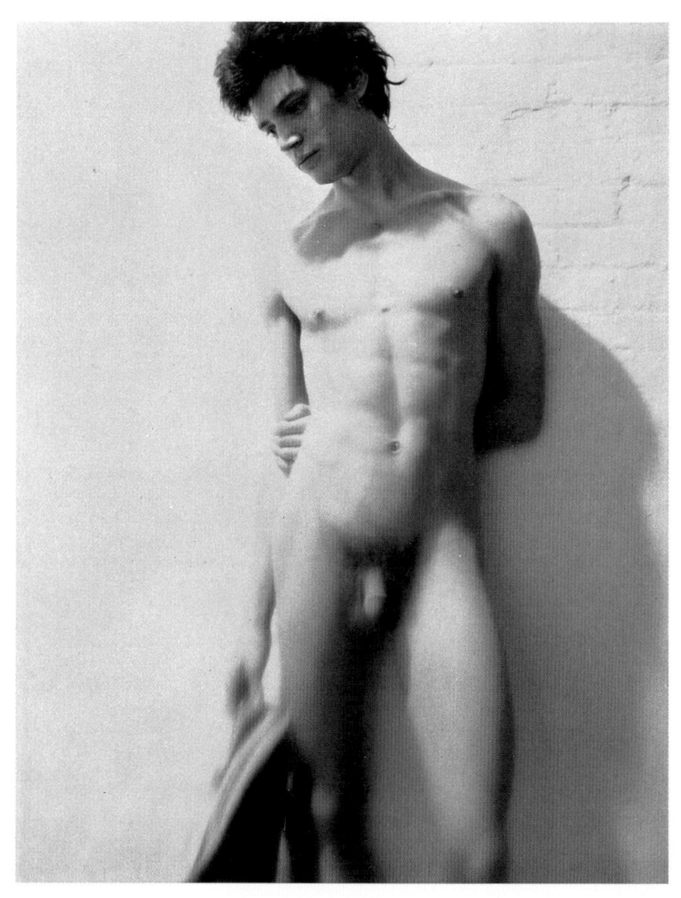

Plate 54. *Untitled (self-portrait)*. 1973

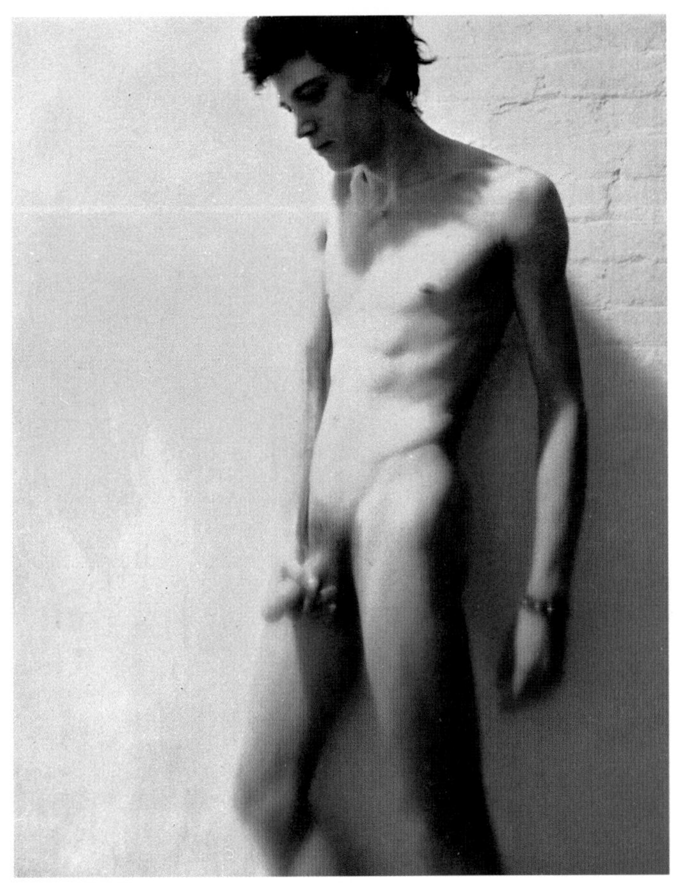

Plate 55. *Untitled (self-portrait)*. 1973

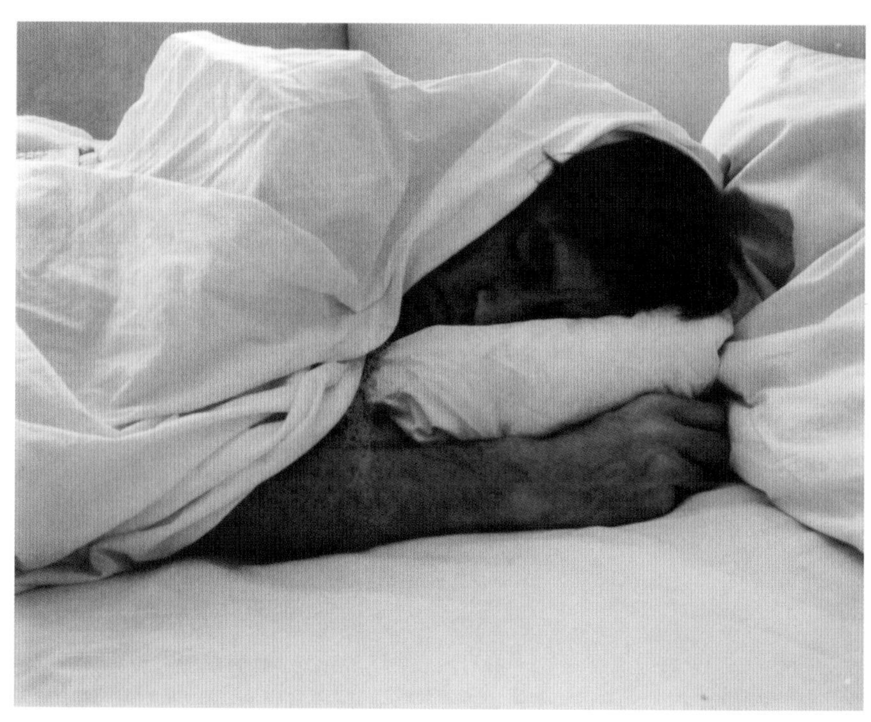

Plate 56. *Untitled (Sam Wagstaff)*. 1973/75

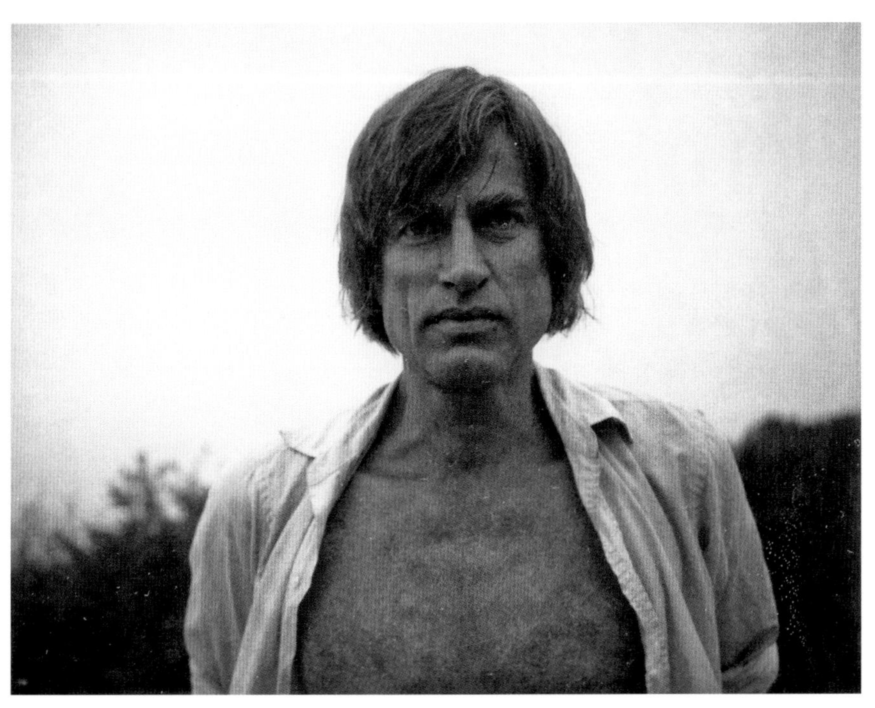

Plate 57. *Untitled (Sam Wagstaff)*. 1973

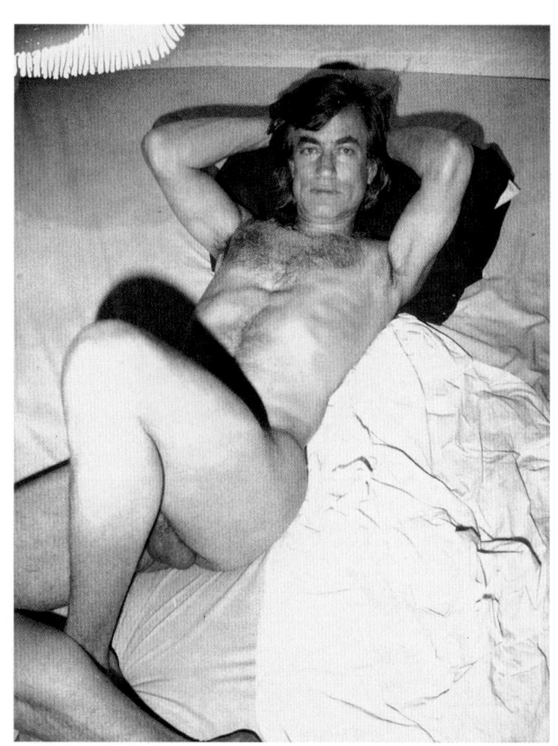

Plate 58. *Untitled (Sam Wagstaff)*. 1972/73

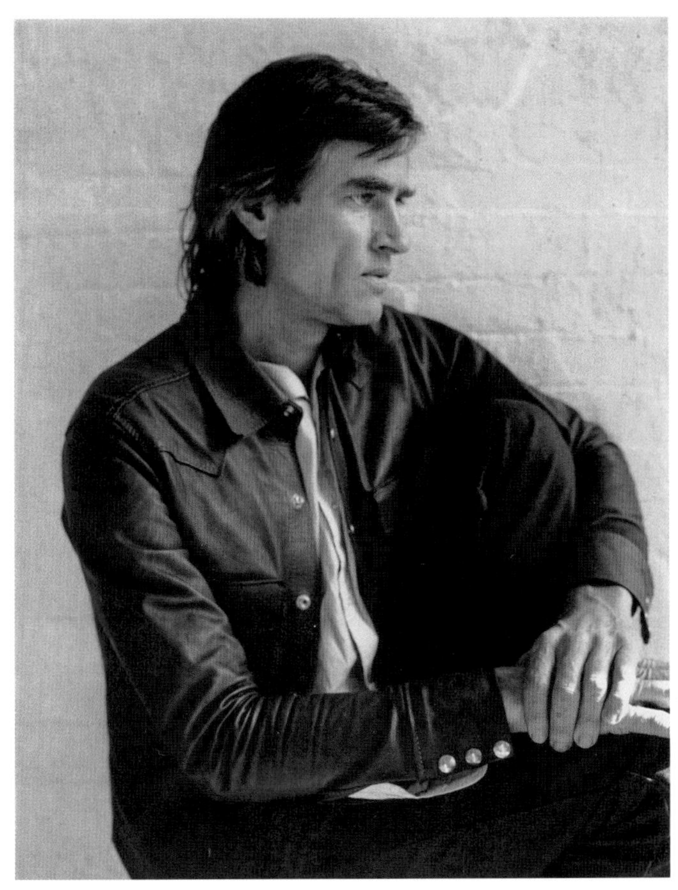

Plate 59. *Untitled (Sam Wagstaff)*. 1973/75

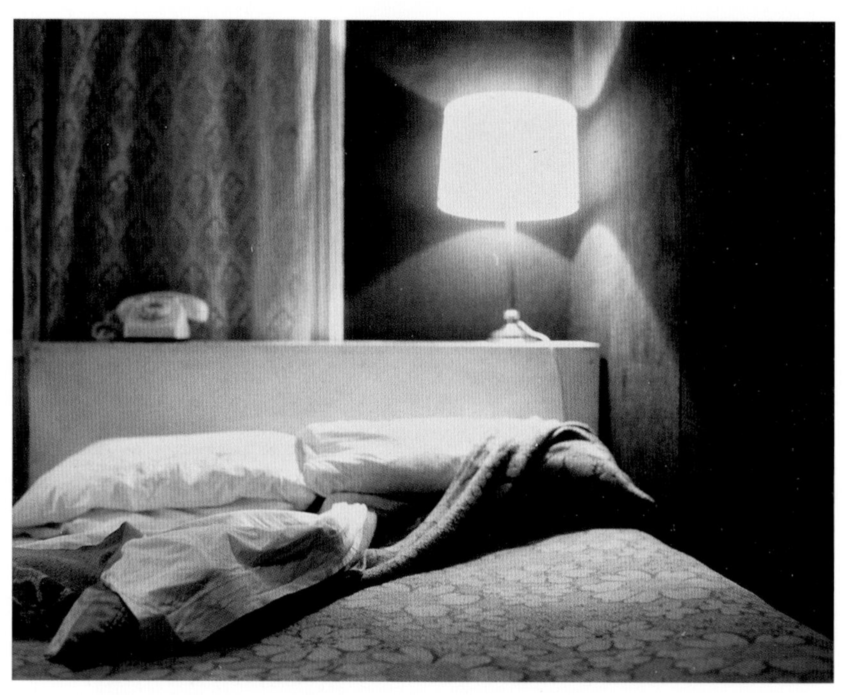

Plate 60. *Untitled*. 1973/75

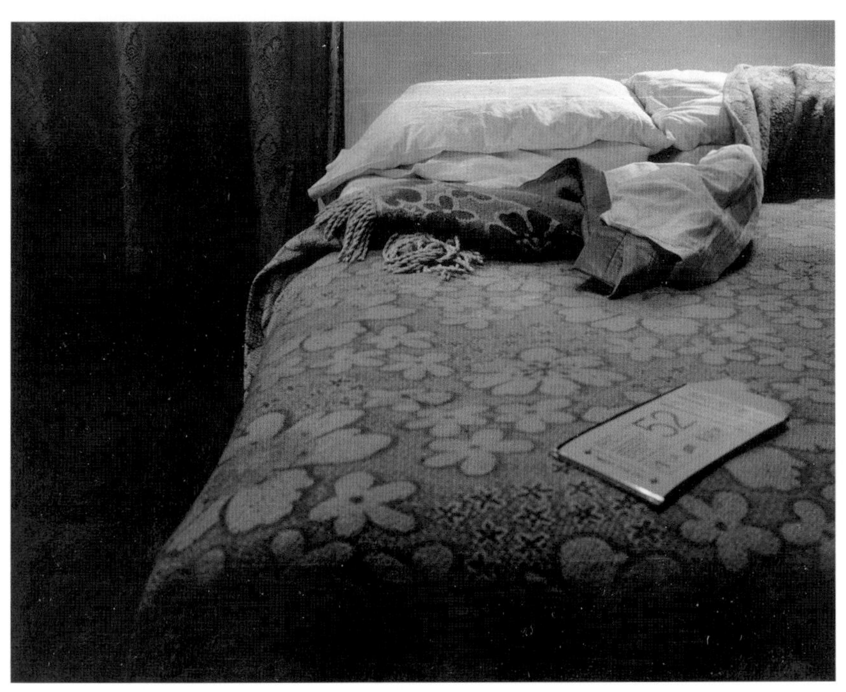

Plate 61. *Untitled*. 1973/75

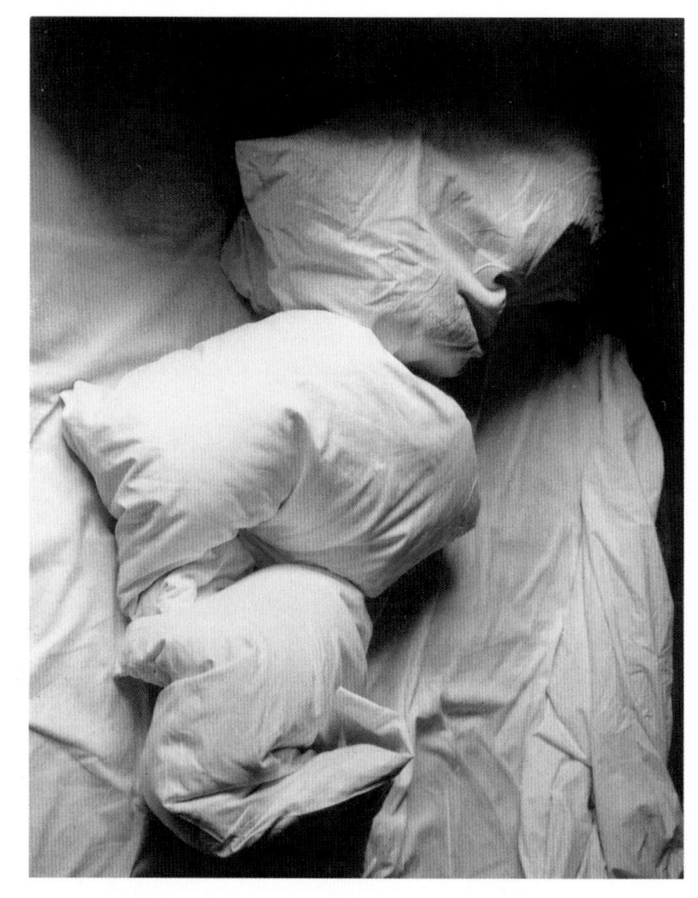

Plate 62. *Untitled*. 1973/75

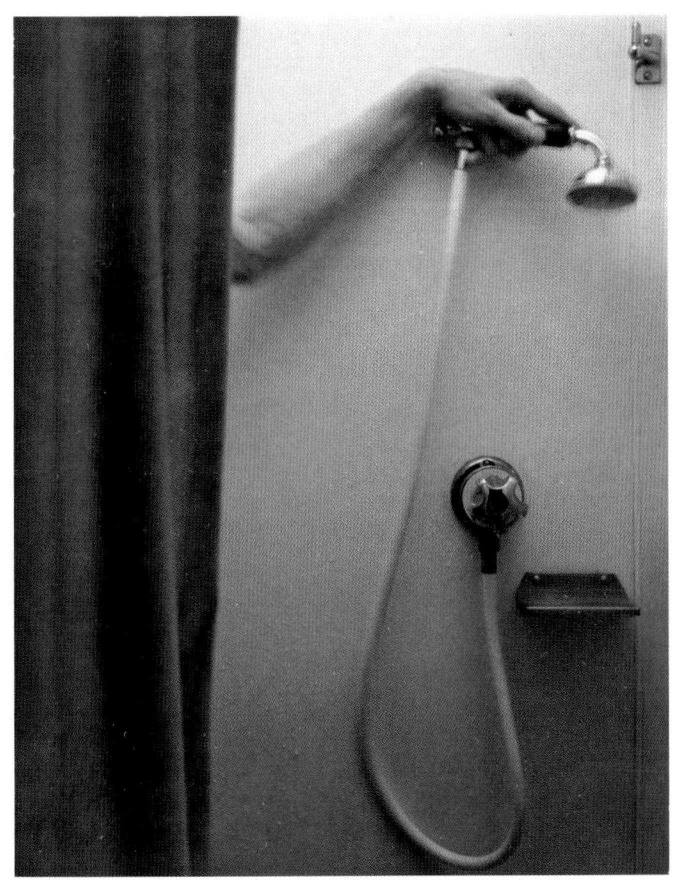

Plate 63. *Untitled (Constantine Hotel)*. 1973/75

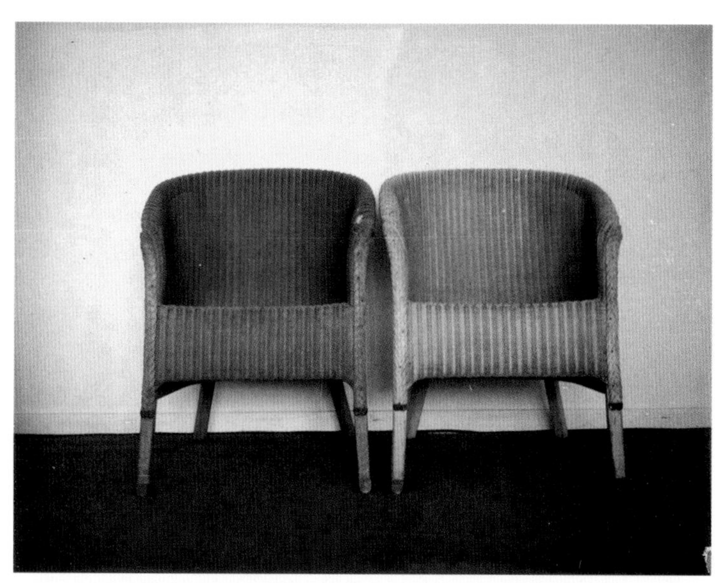

Plate 64. *Untitled*. 1970/73

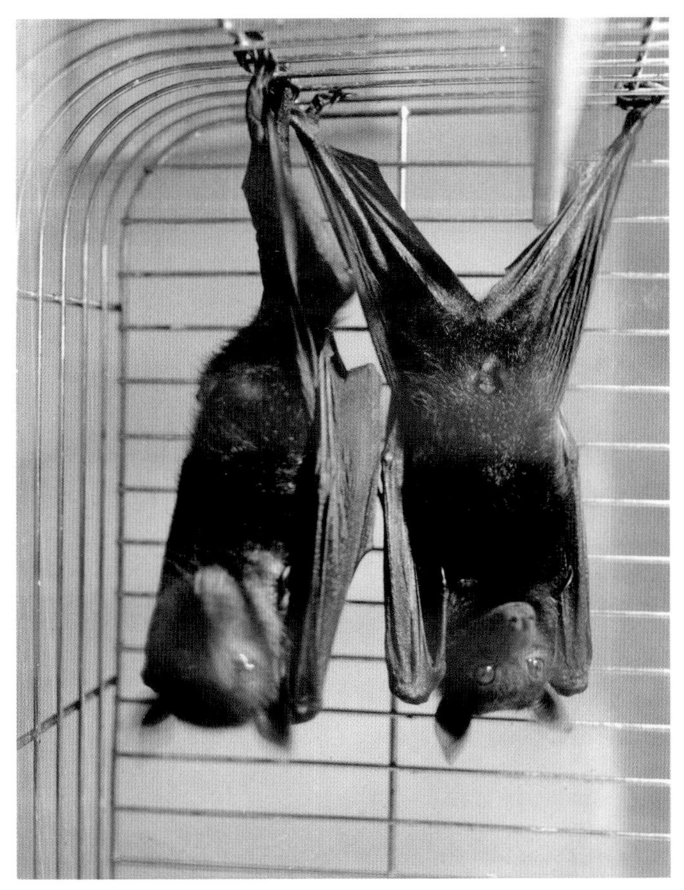

Plate 65. *Untitled (Helen Marden's Bats).* 1973/75

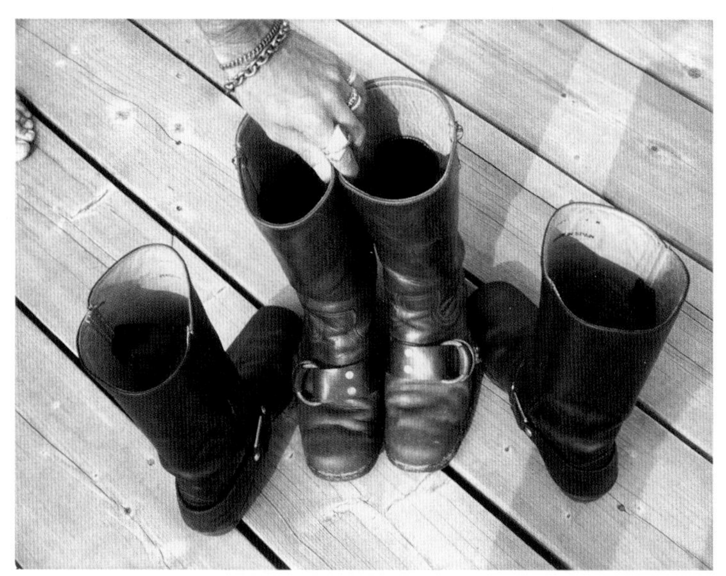

Plate 66. *Untitled*. 1970/73

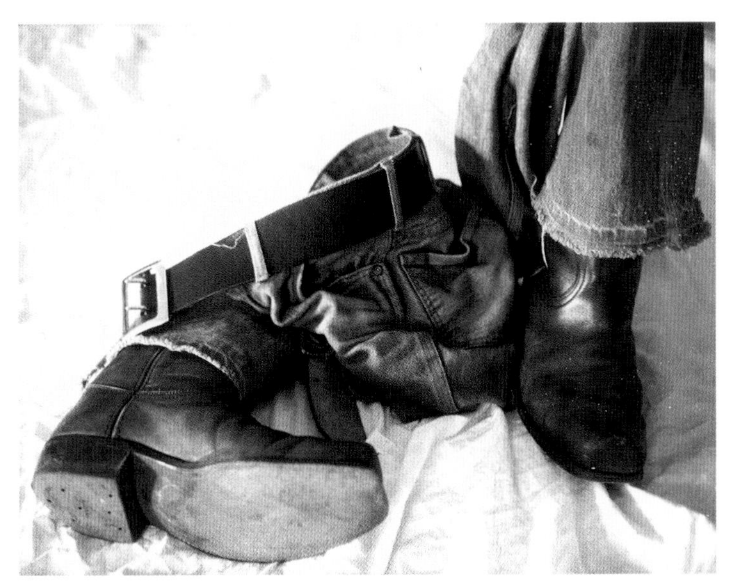

Plate 67. *Untitled*. 1970/73

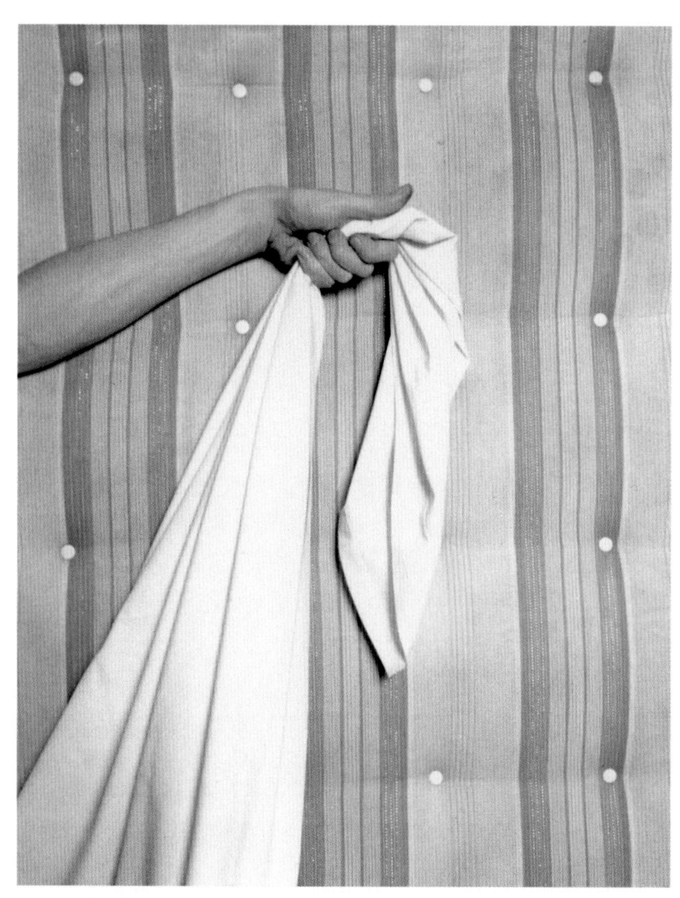

Plate 68. *Untitled*. 1973/75

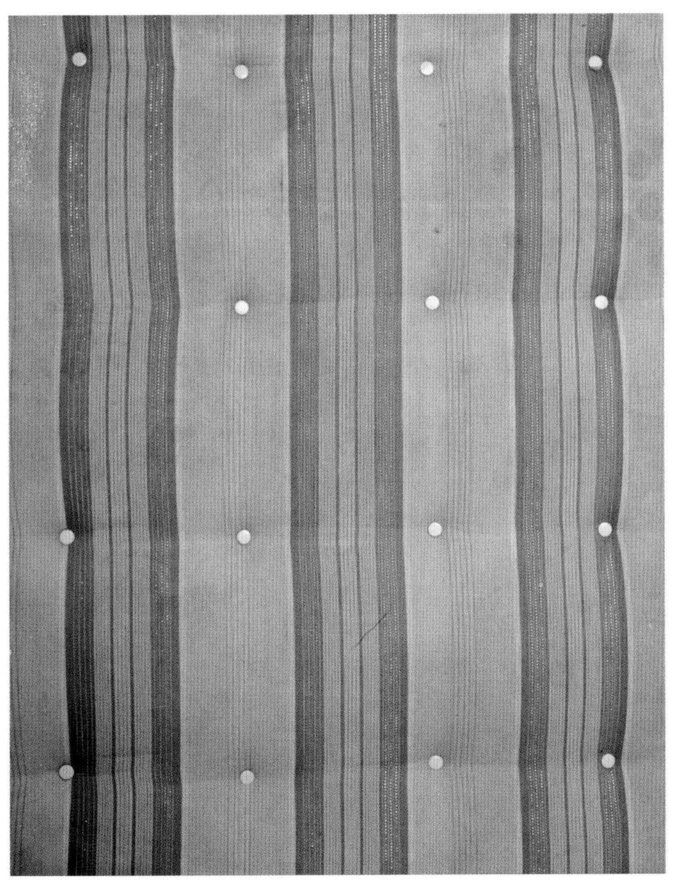

Plate 69. *Untitled*. 1973/75

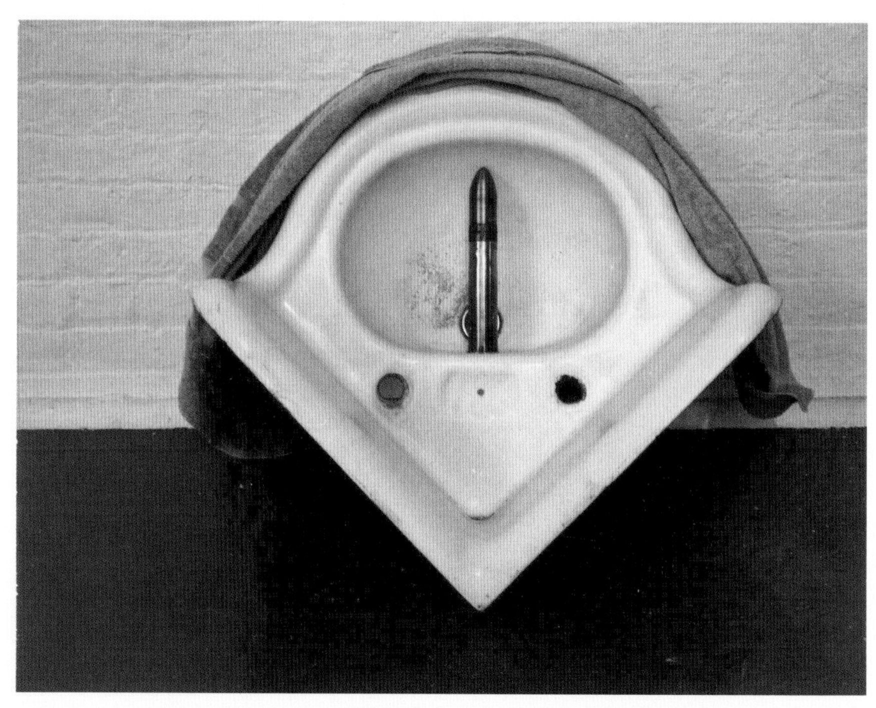

Plate 70. *Untitled*. 1973/75

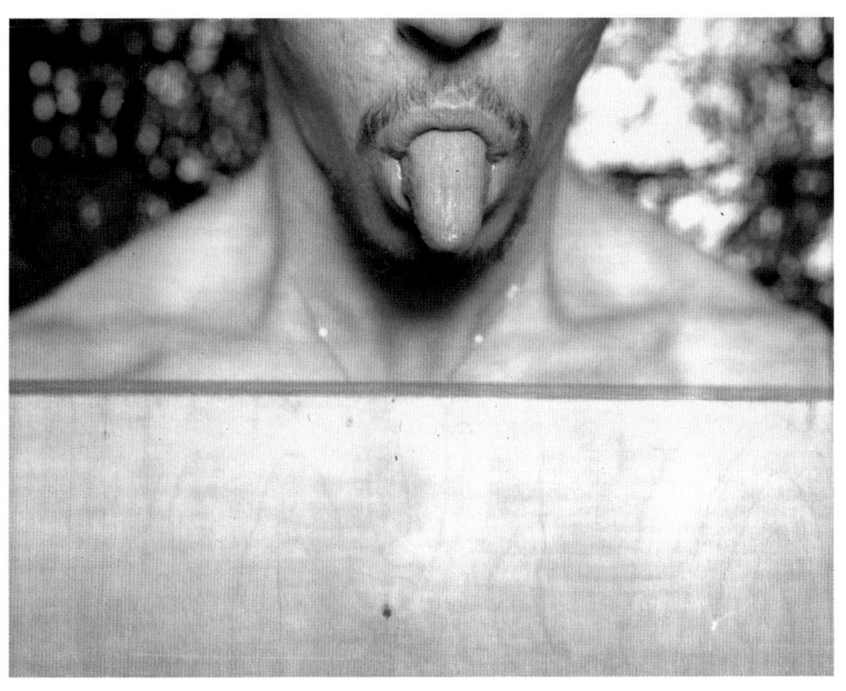

Plate 71. *Untitled (self-portrait)*. 1973/75

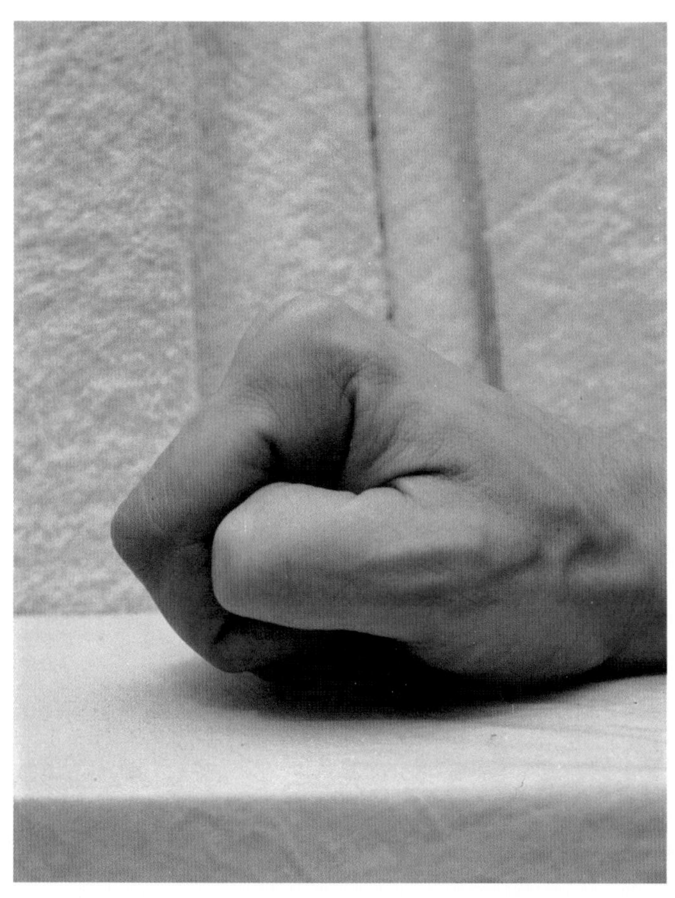

Plate 72. *Untitled*. 1973/75

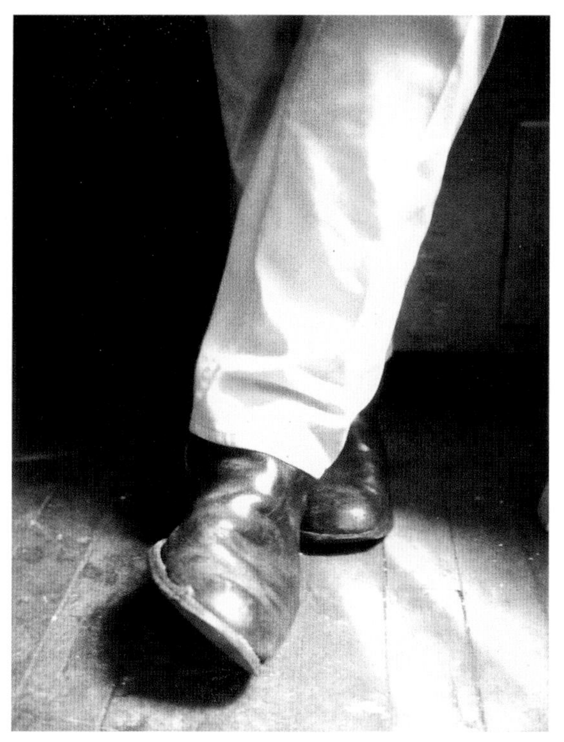

Plate 73. *Untitled*. 1970/73

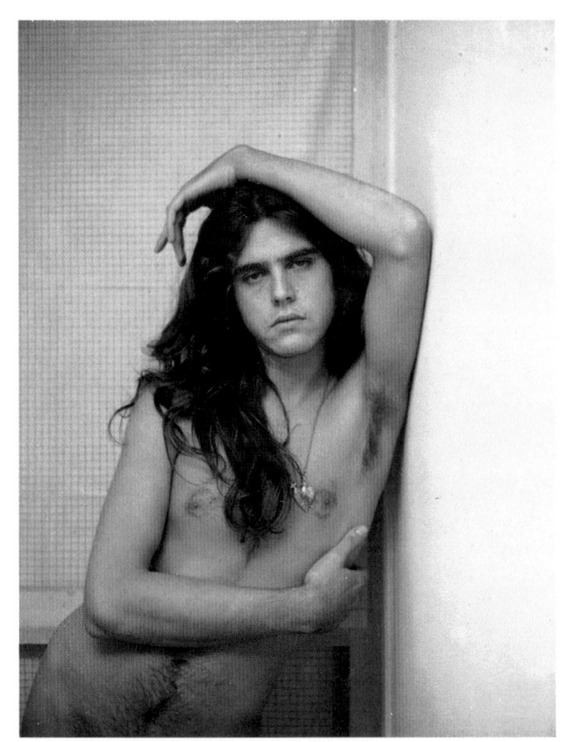

Plate 74. *Untitled (Jamie)*. 1970/73

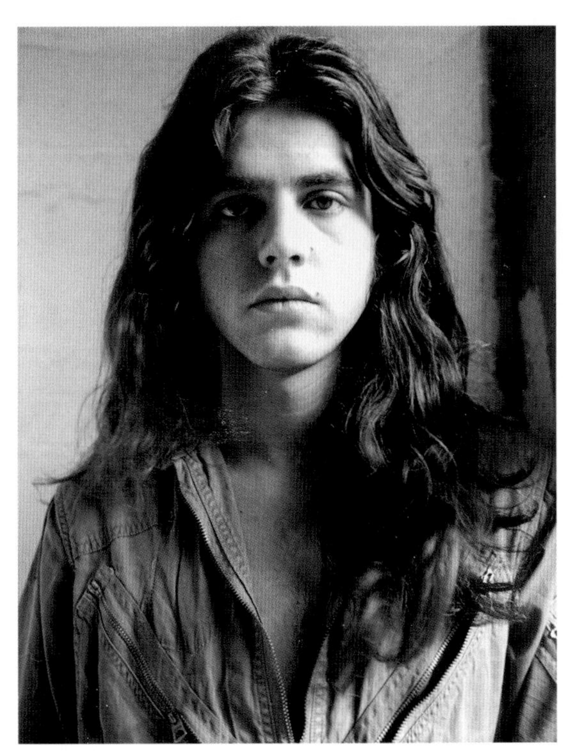

Plate 75. *Untitled (Jamie)*. 1970/73

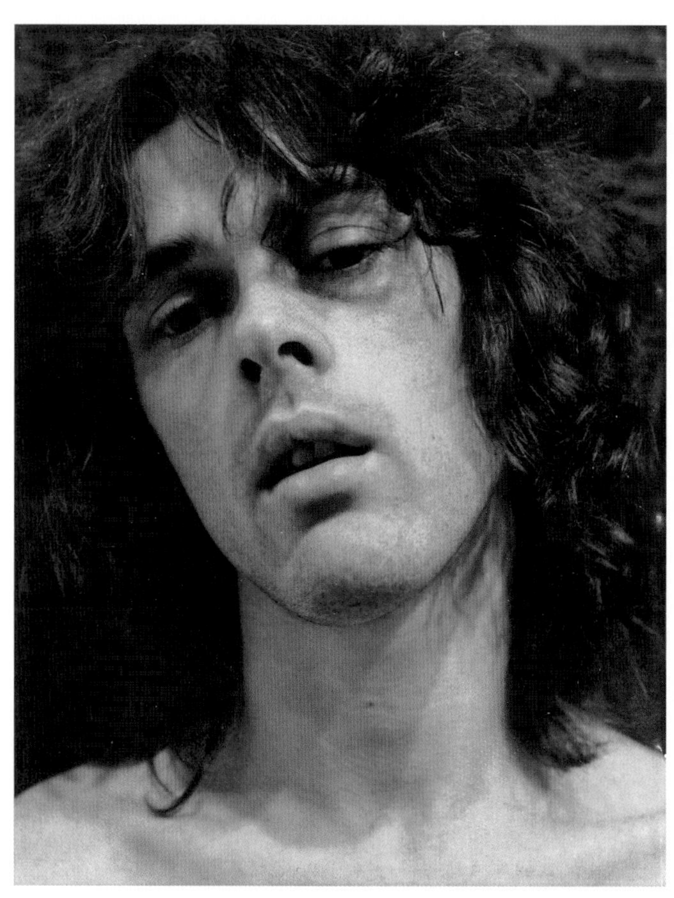

Plate 76. *Untitled (Michael)*. 1973/75

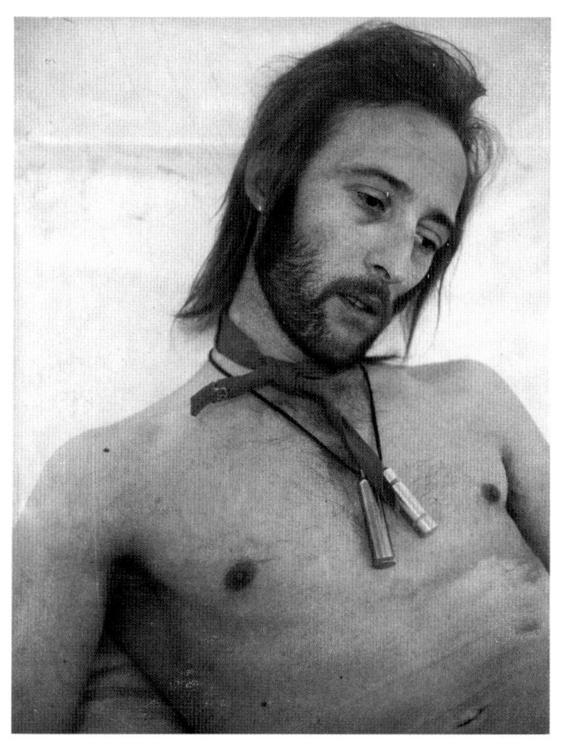

Plate 77. *Untitled*. 1970/73

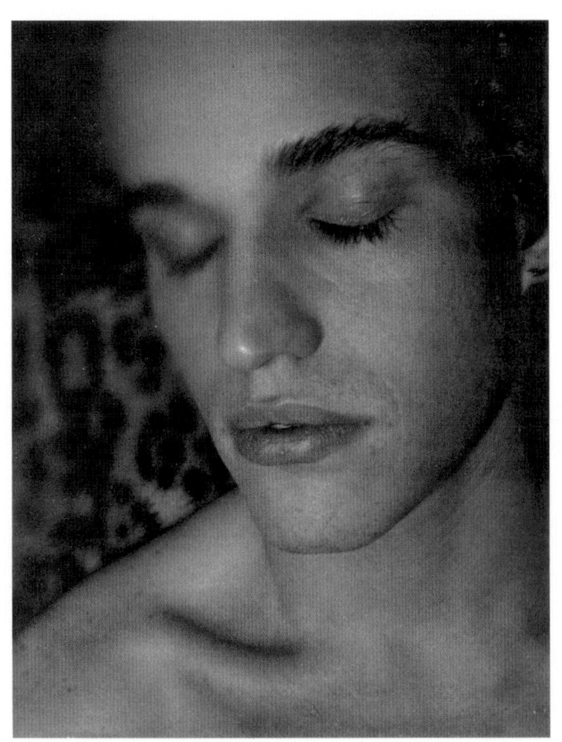

Plate 78. *Untitled (Jay Johnson, London)*. 1973

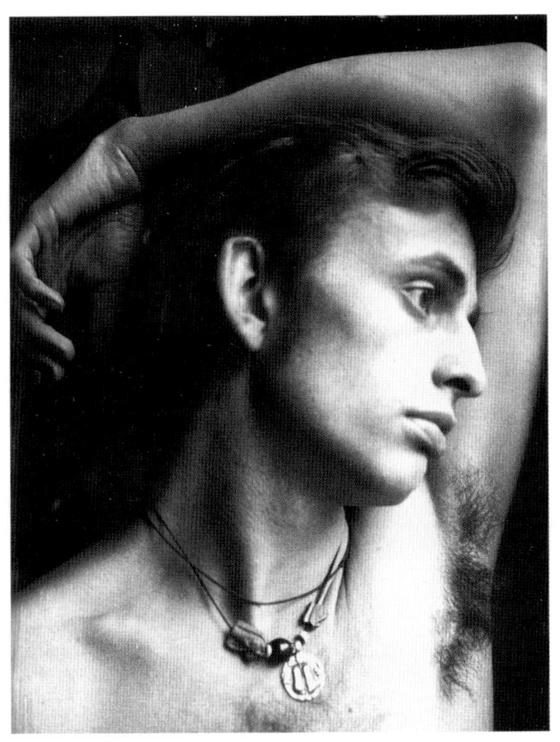

Plate 79. *Untitled (Nicholas Black, London)*. 1973

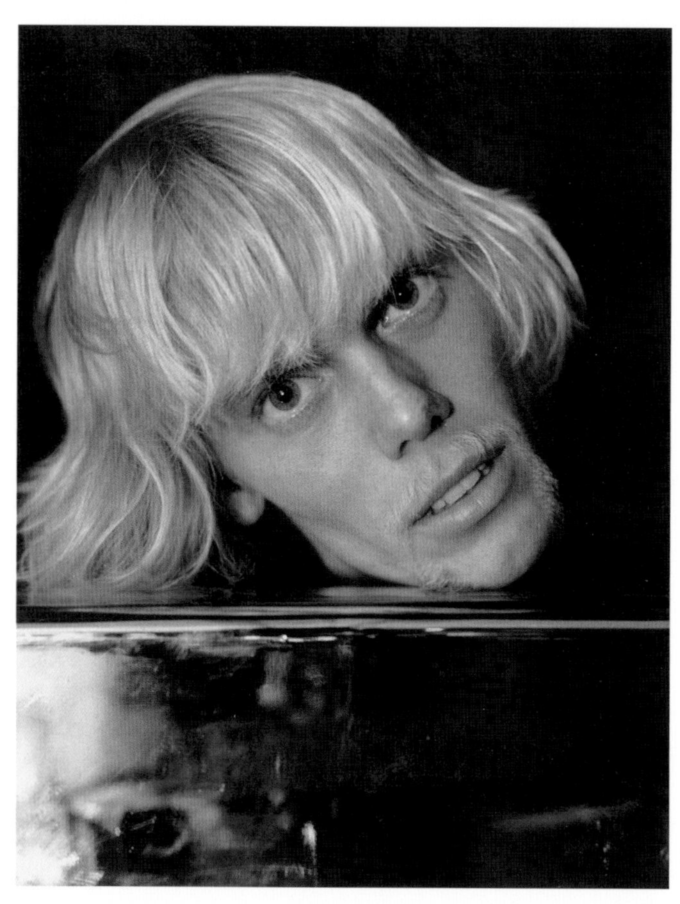

Plate 80. *Untitled (Randy)*. 1973/75

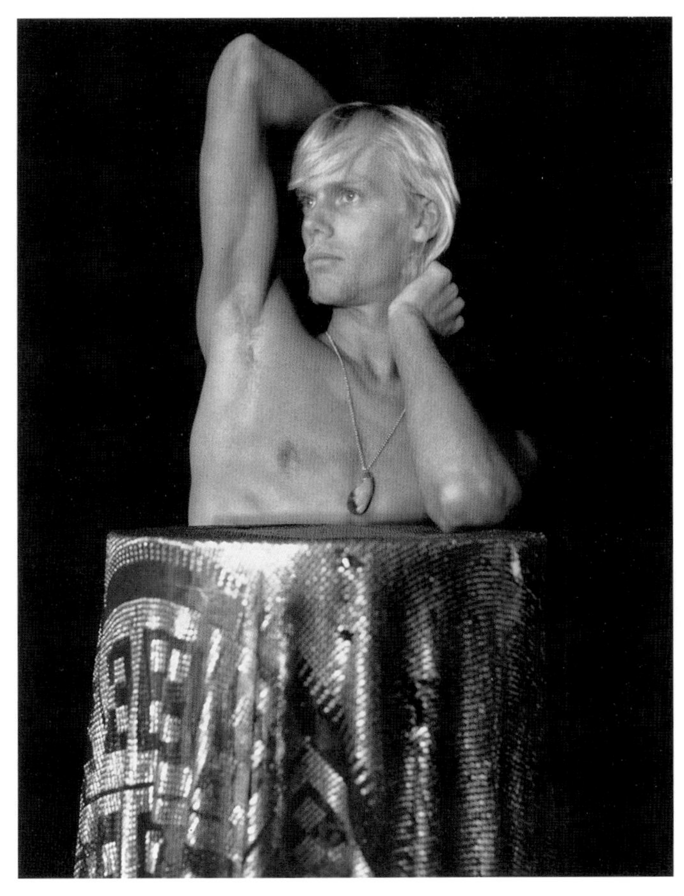

Plate 81. *Untitled (Randy)*. 1973/75

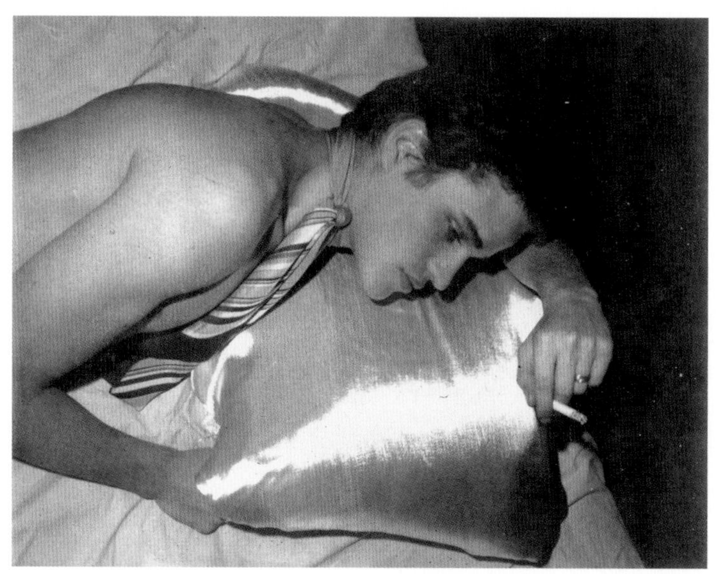

Plate 82. *Untitled (Jay Johnson)*. 1970

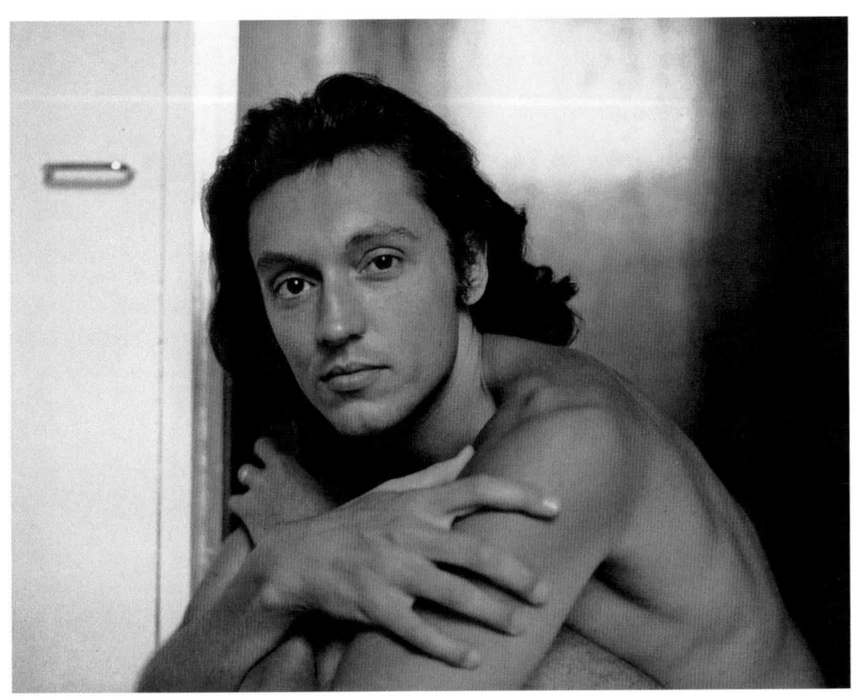

Plate 83. *Untitled (François)*. 1973/75

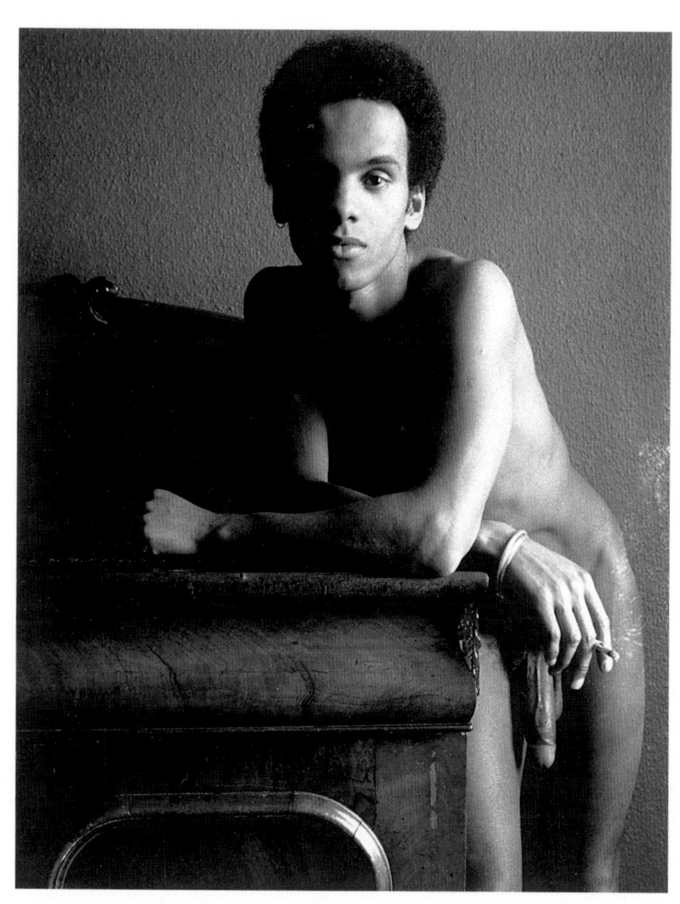

Plate 84. *Untitled (Stewart Foster)*. 1973/75

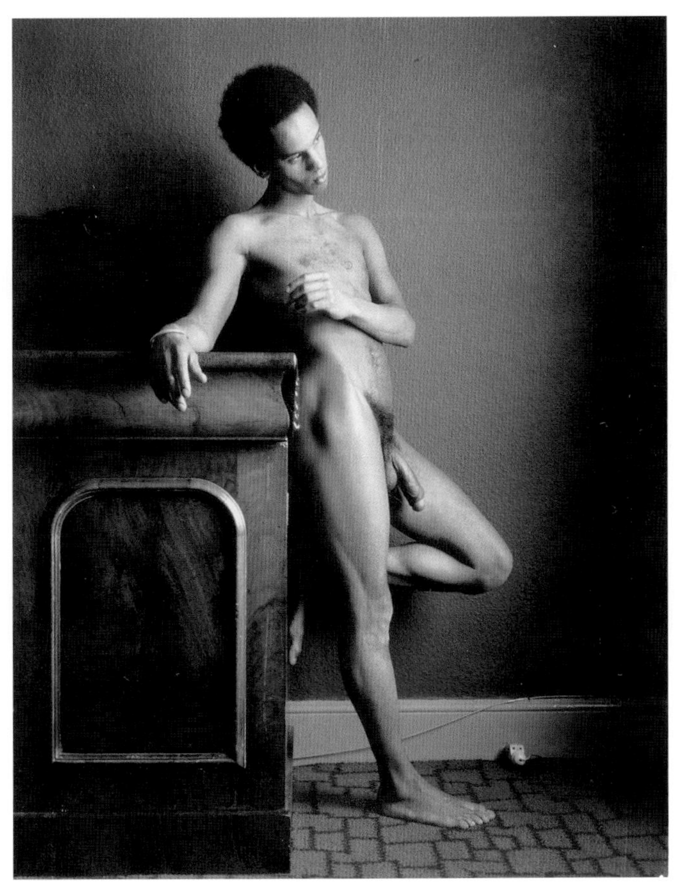

Plate 85. *Untitled (Stewart Foster)*, 1973/75

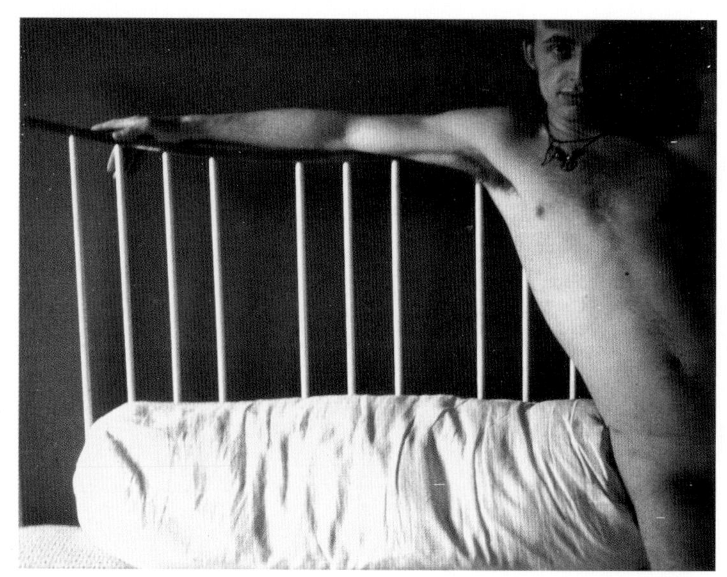

Plate 86. *Untitled (Nicholas, London)*. 1973

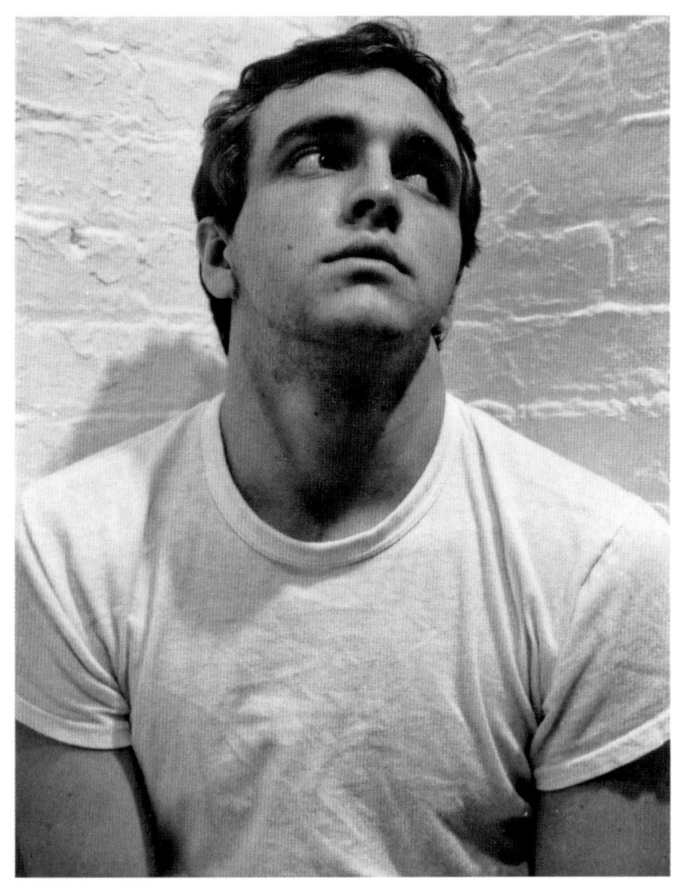

Plate 87. *Untitled*. 1973/75

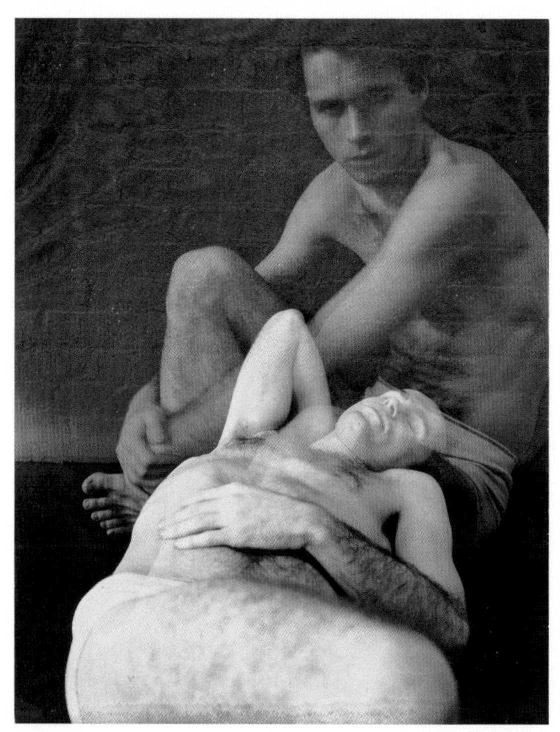

Plate 88. *Untitled*. 1973/75

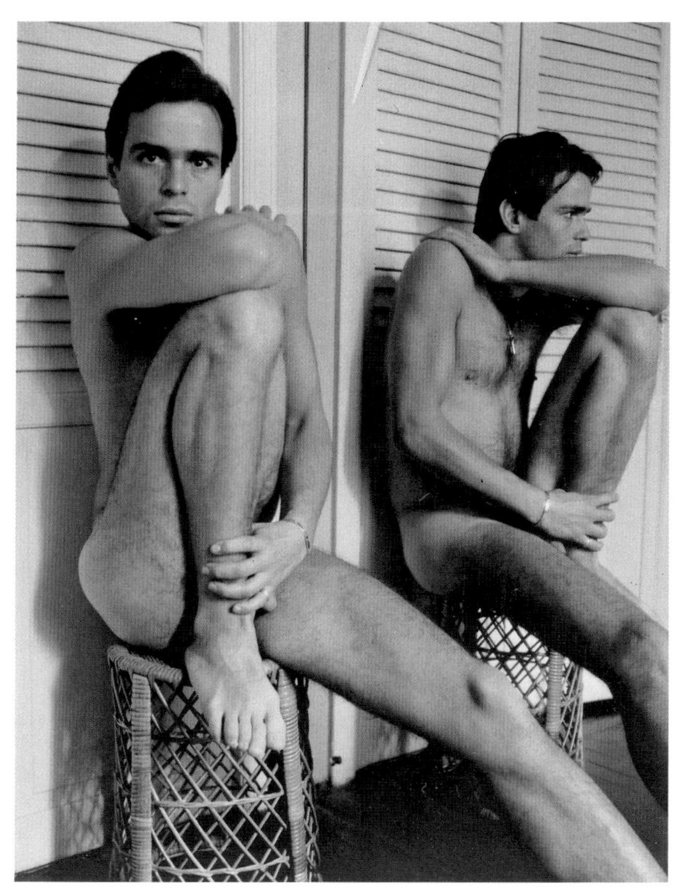

Plate 89. *Untitled (Boaz Mazor)*. 1973/75

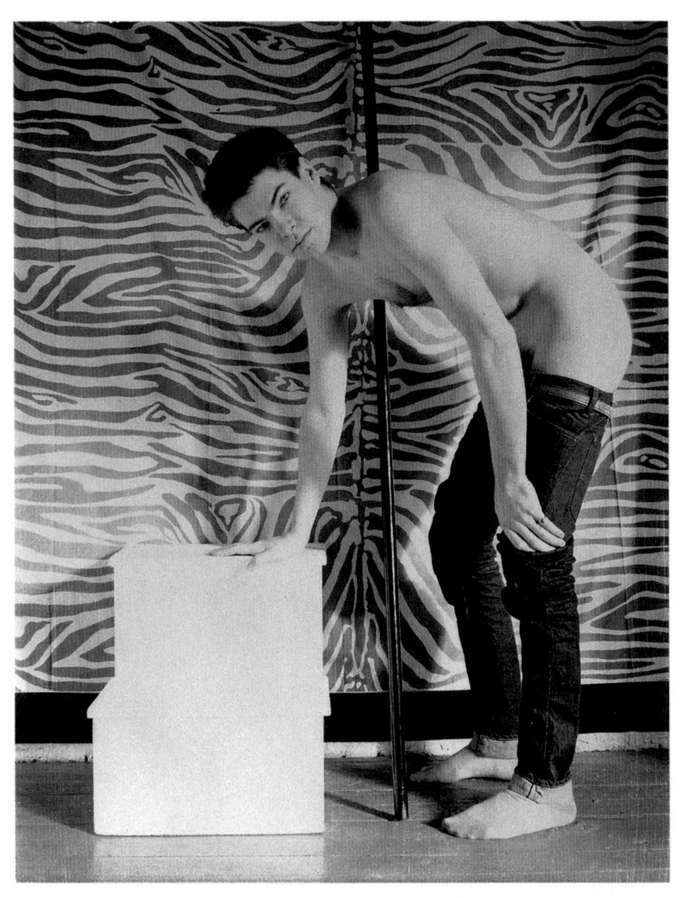

Plate 90. *Untitled*. 1973/75

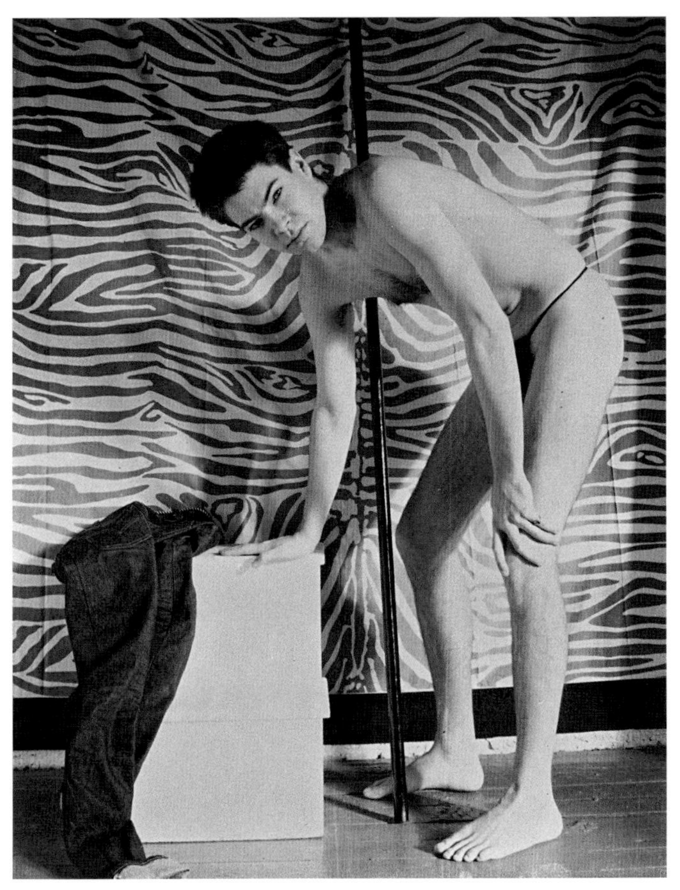

Plate 91. *Untitled*. 1973/75

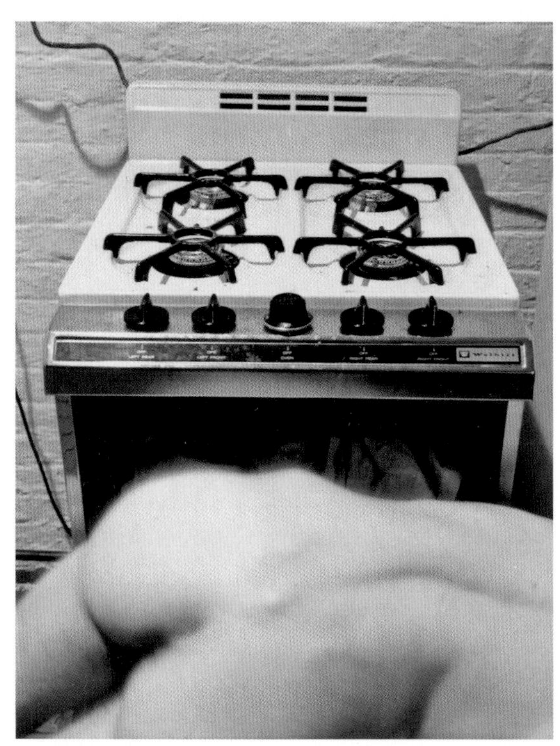

Plate 92. *Untitled*. 1970/73

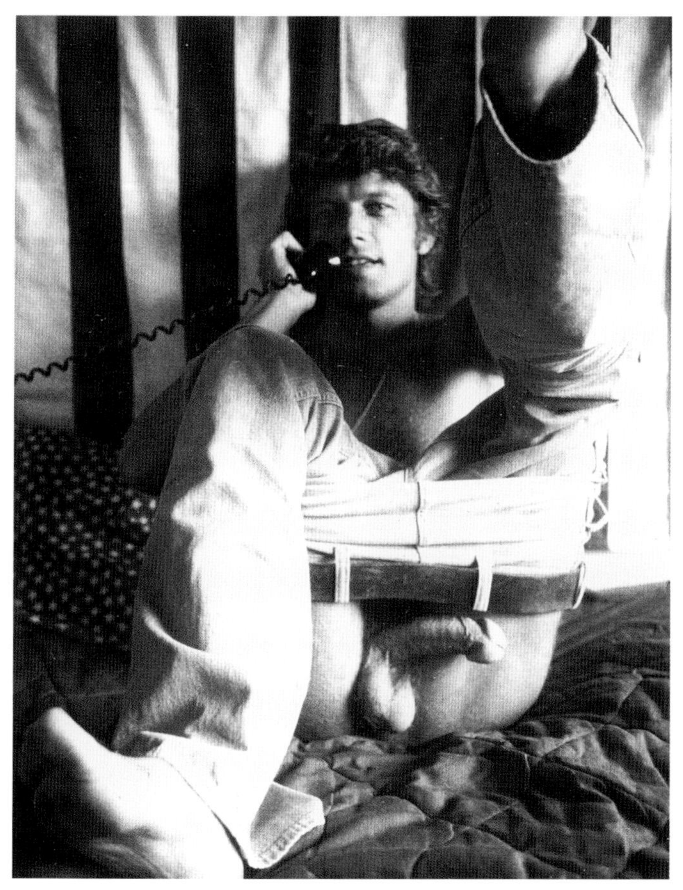

Plate 93. *Untitled*. 1973/75

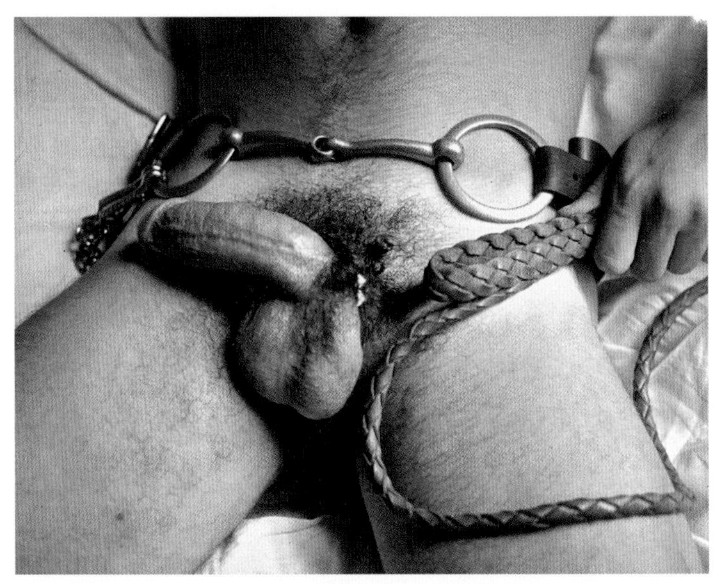

Plate 94. *Untitled*. 1970/73

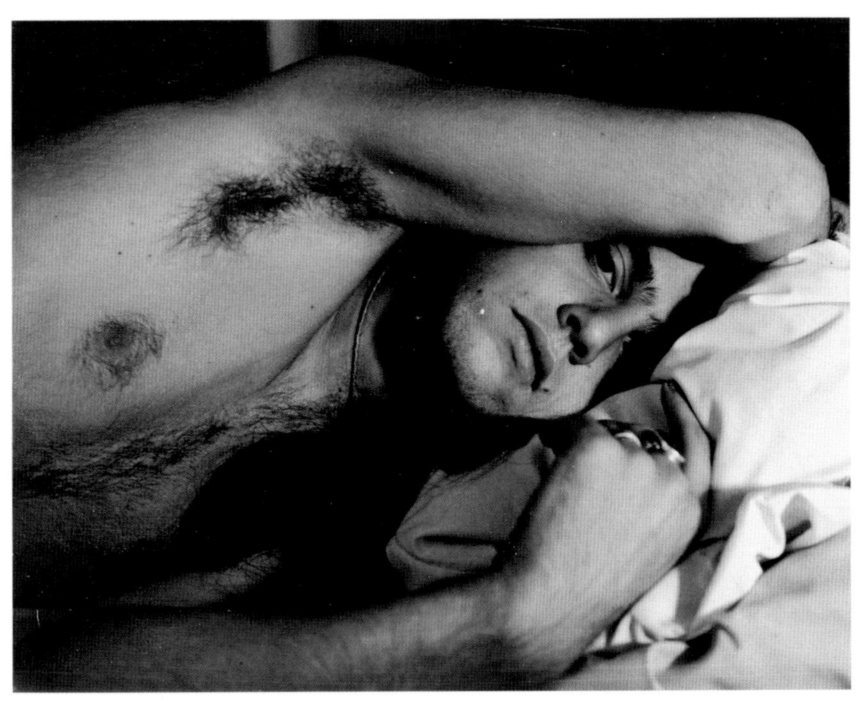

Plate 95. *Untitled (Jamie)*. 1973/75

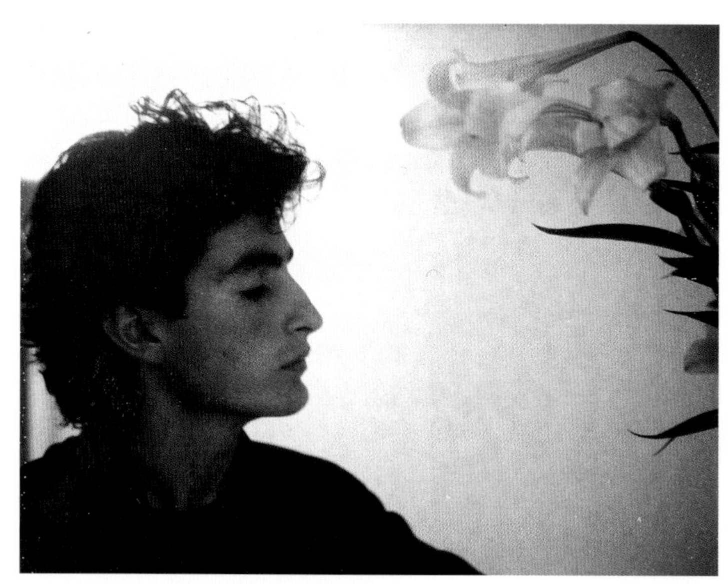

Plate 96. *Untitled (Enrique Maza)*. 1970/73

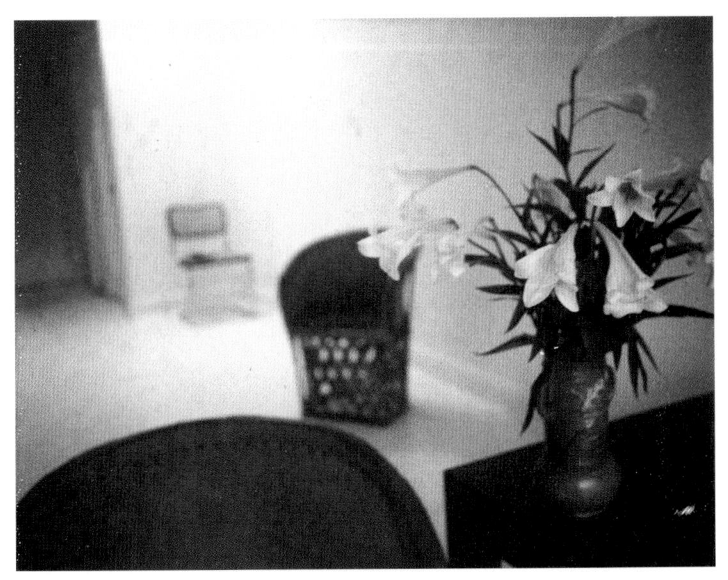

Plate 97. *Untitled*. 1970/73

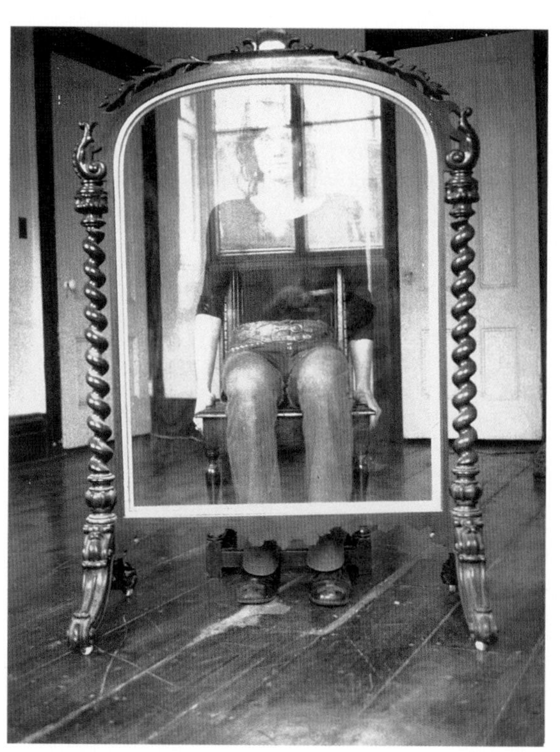

Plate 98. *Untitled (Eddie)*. 1973

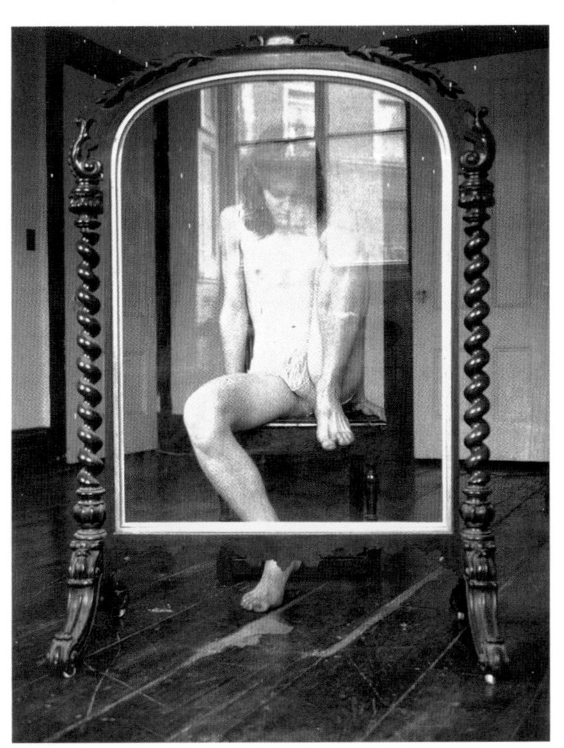

Plate 99. *Untitled (Eddie)*. 1973

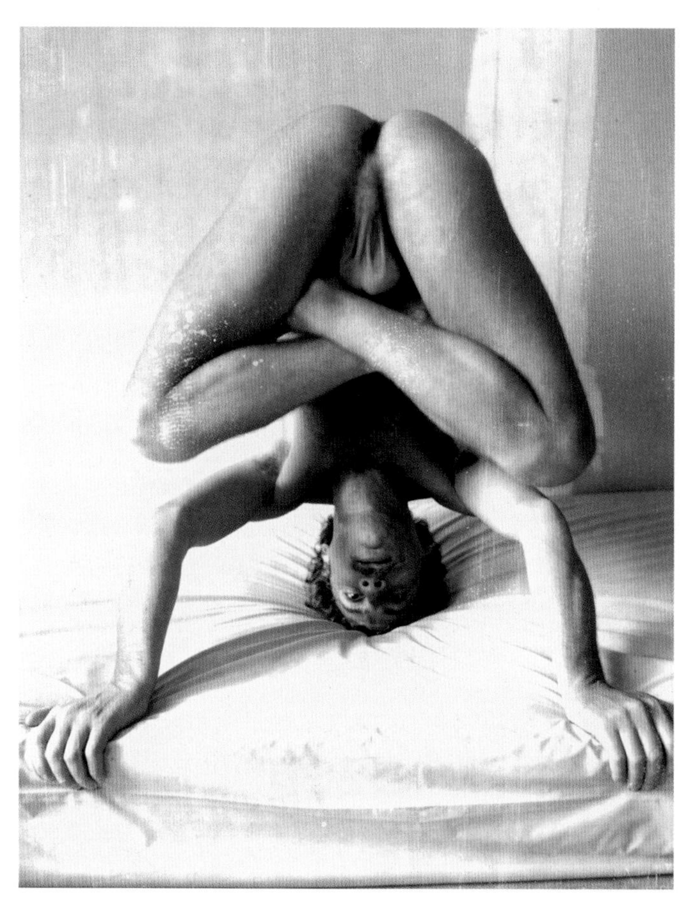

Plate 100. *Untitled*. 1973

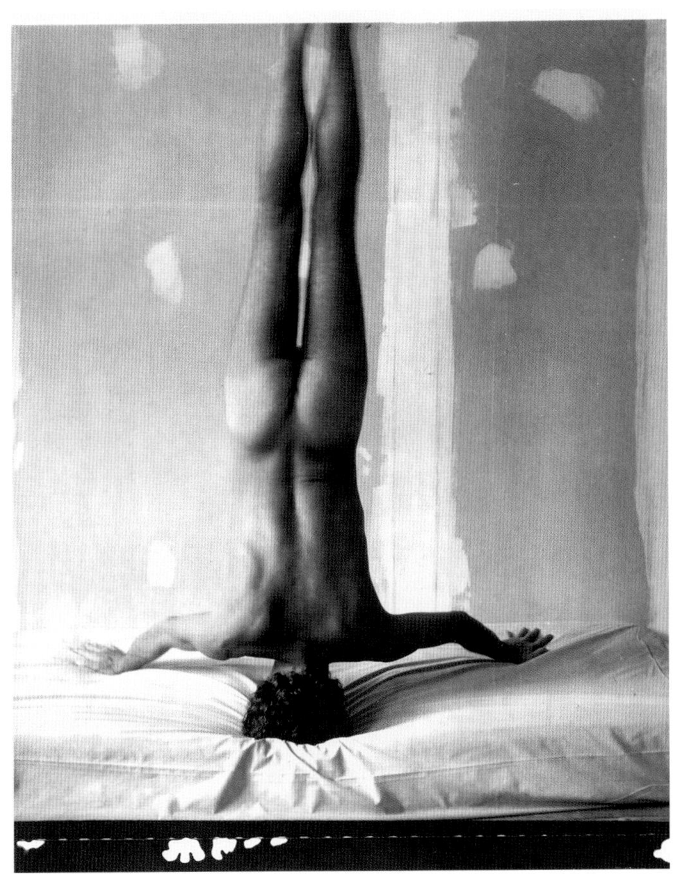

Plate 101. *Untitled*. 1973

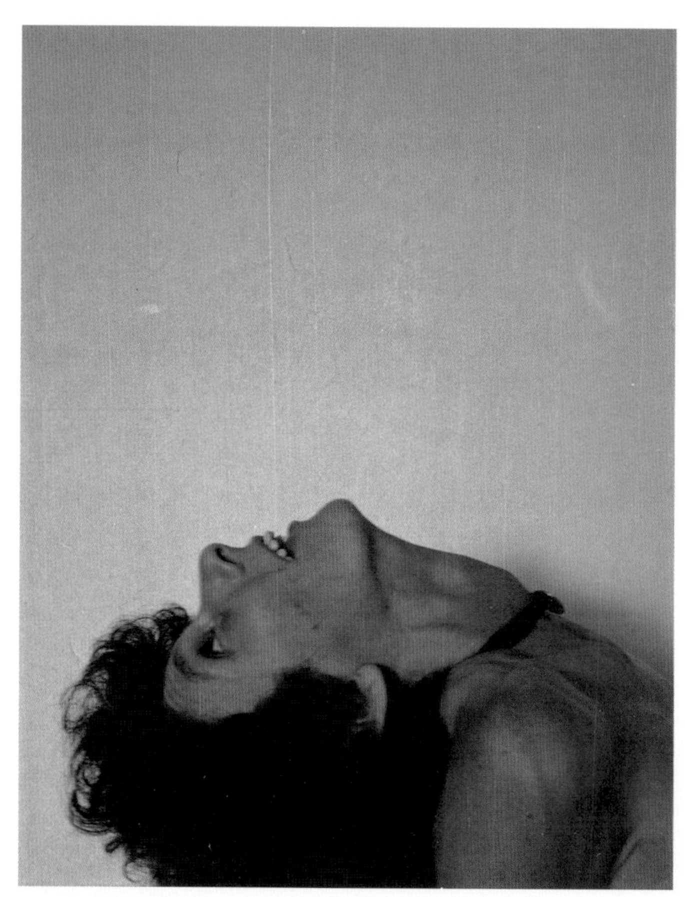

Plate 102. *Untitled*. 1973/75

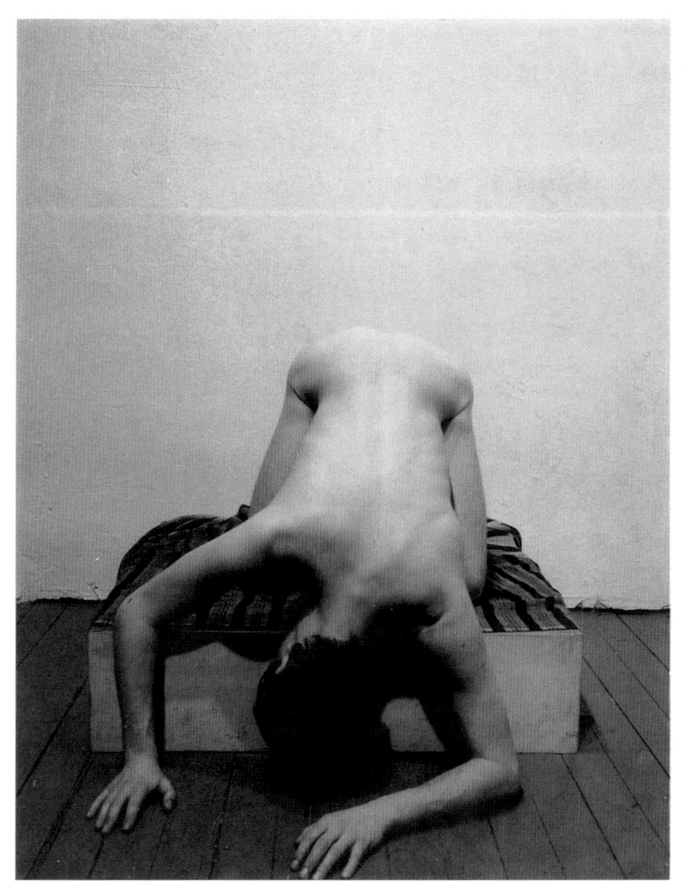

Plate 103. *Untitled*. 1973/75

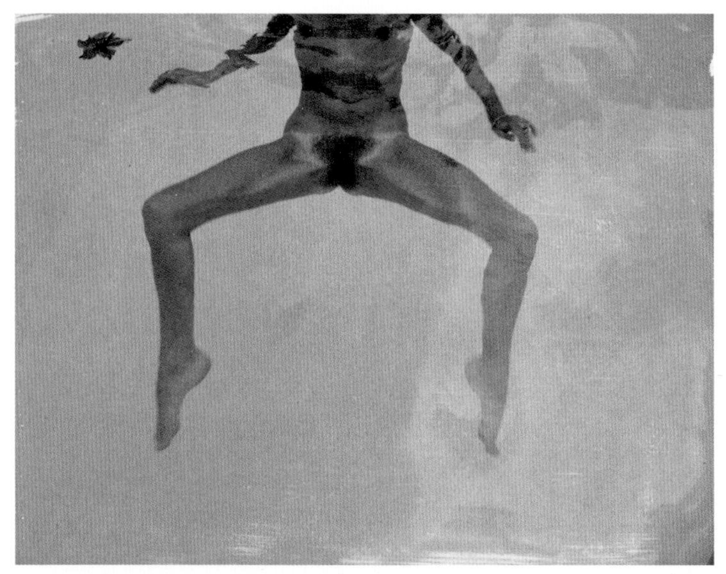

Plate 104. *Untitled*. 1970/73

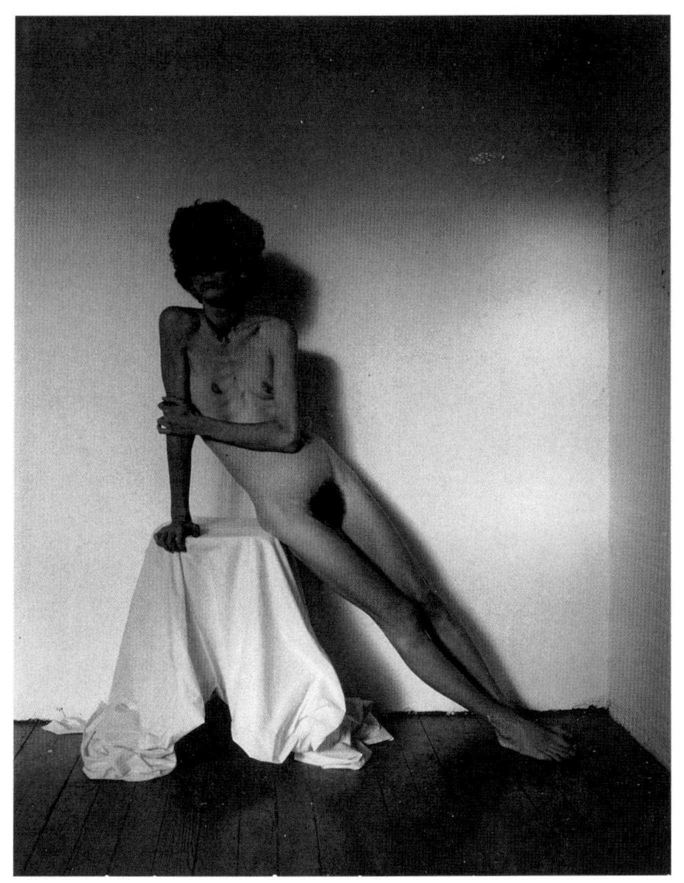

Plate 105. *Untitled (Diane)*. 1973/75

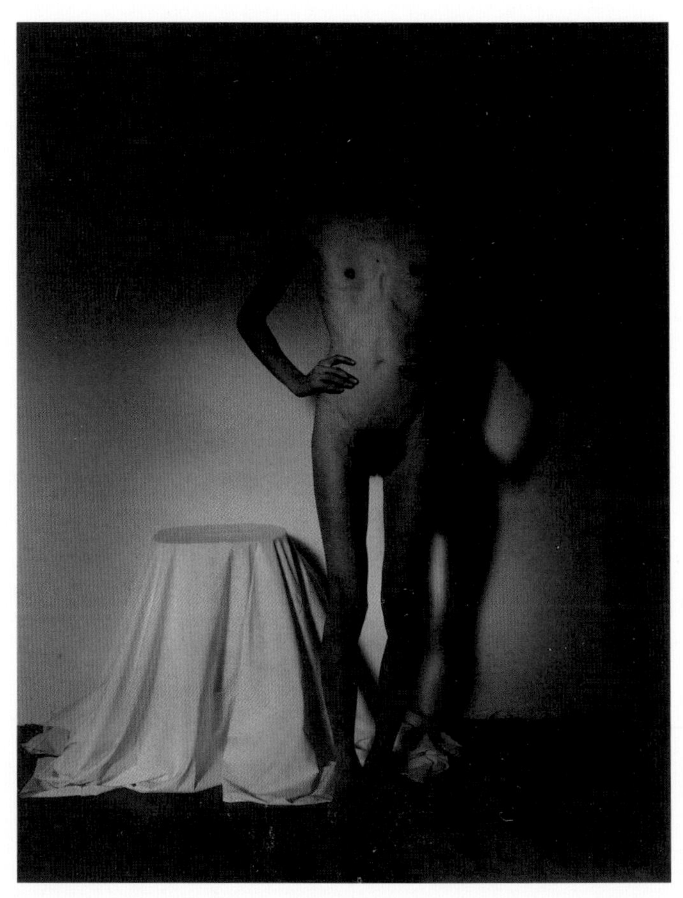

Plate 106. *Untitled (Diane)*. 1973/75

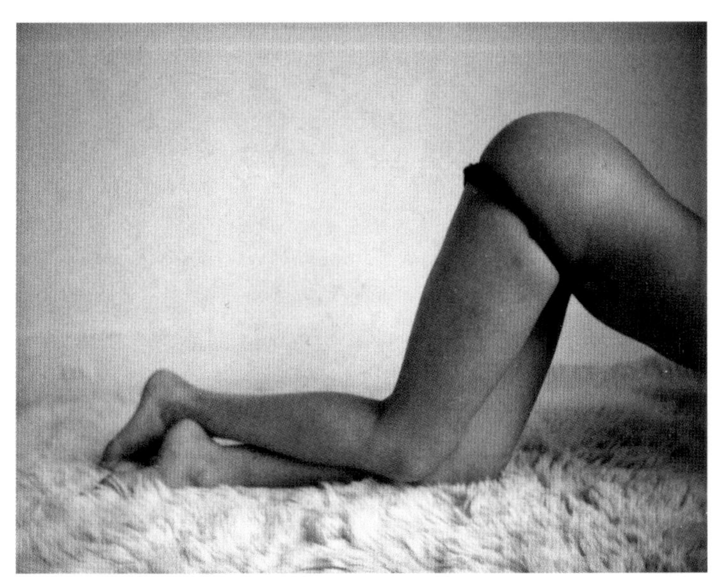

Plate 107. *Untitled (Lucy, Paris)*. 1971/73

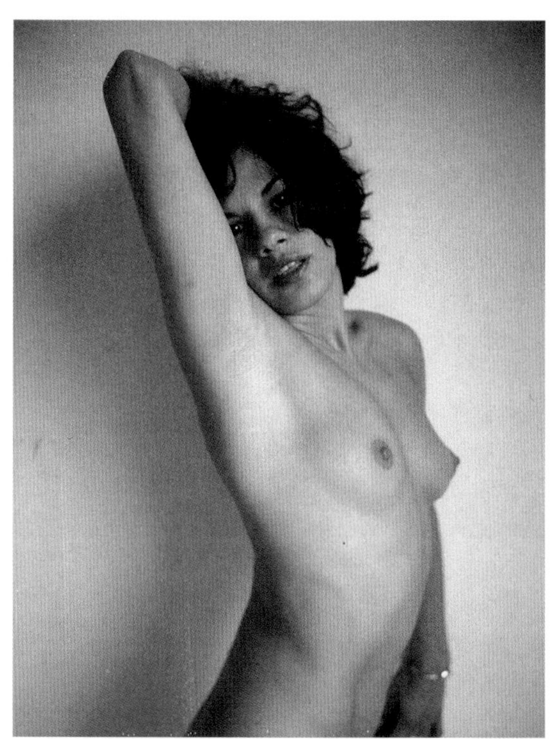

Plate 108. *Untitled (Lucy, Paris)*. 1971/73

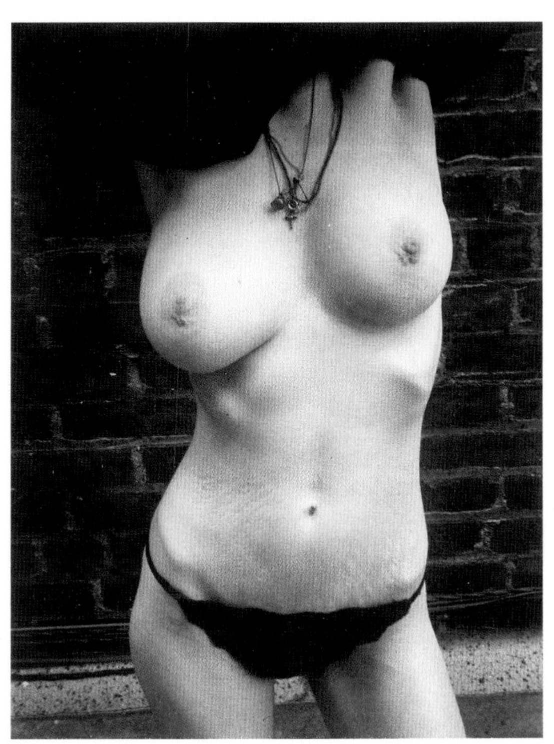

Plate 109. *Untitled*. 1970

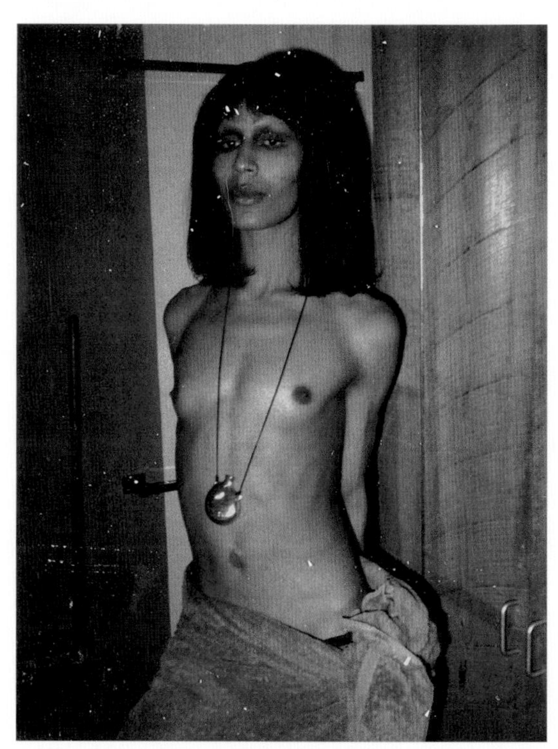

Plate 110. *Untitled*. 1970/73

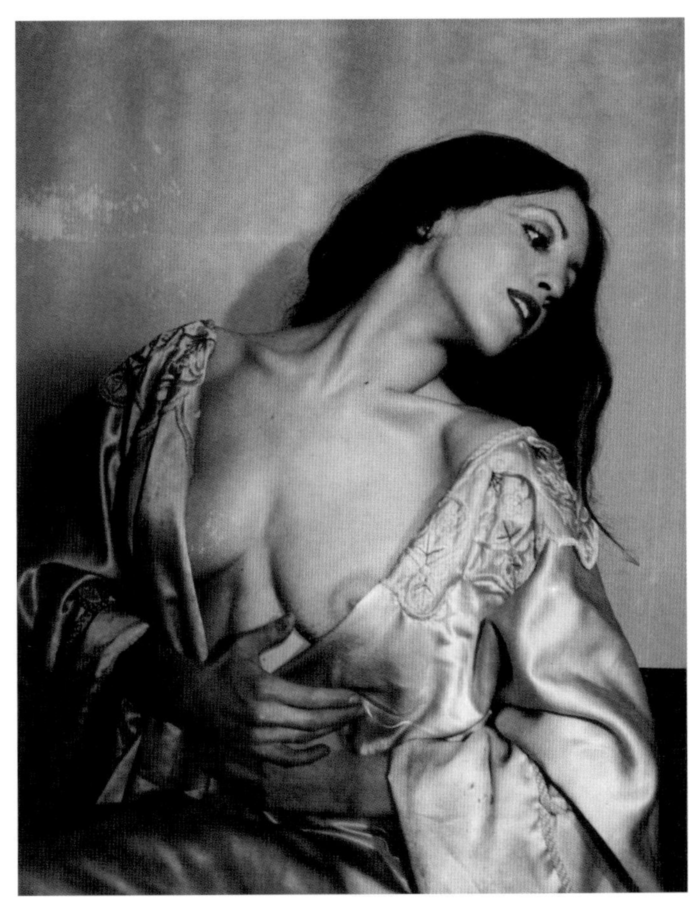

Plate 111. *Untitled*. 1973/75

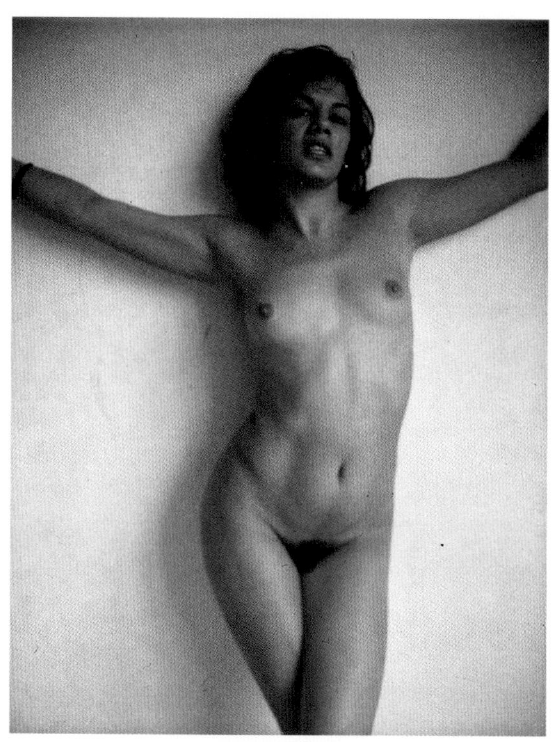

Plate 112. *Untitled (Lucy, Paris)*. 1971/73

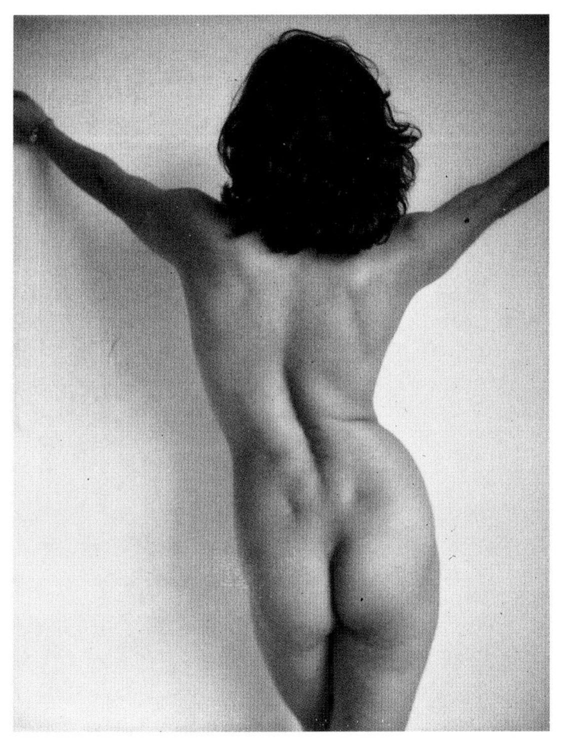

Plate 113. *Untitled (Lucy, Paris)*. 1971/73

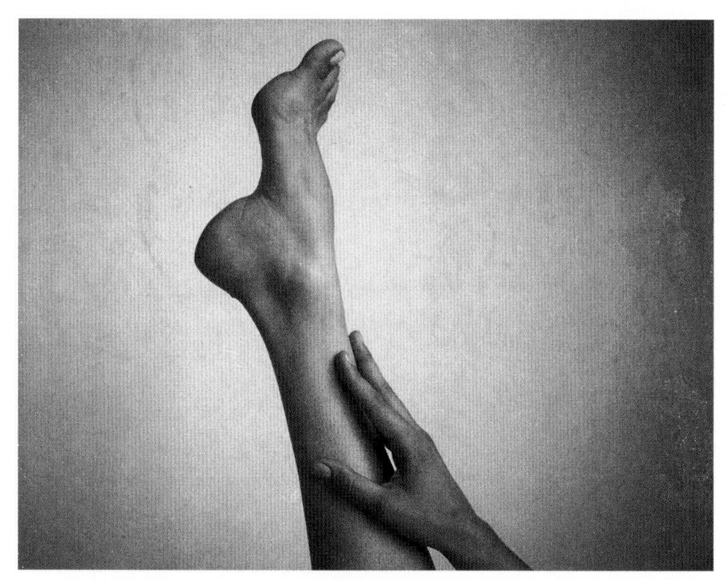

Plate 114. *Untitled (Lucy, Paris).* 1971/73

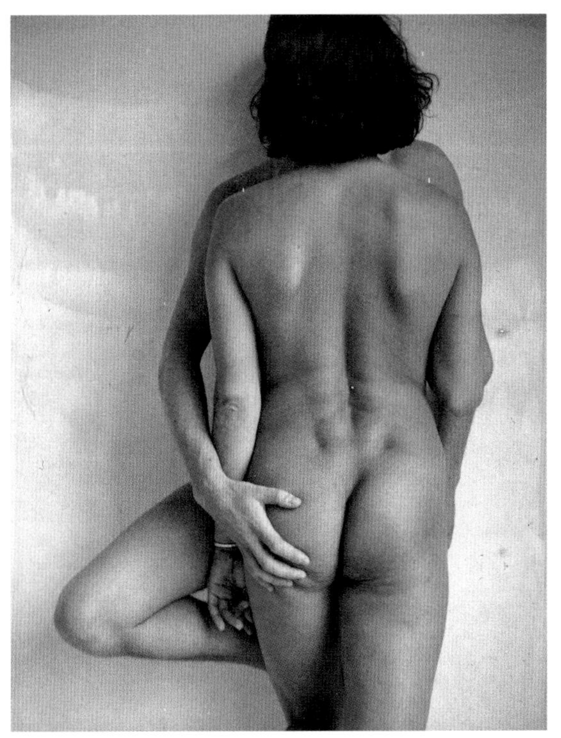

Plate 115. *Untitled (Lucy and Fred, Paris)*. 1971/73

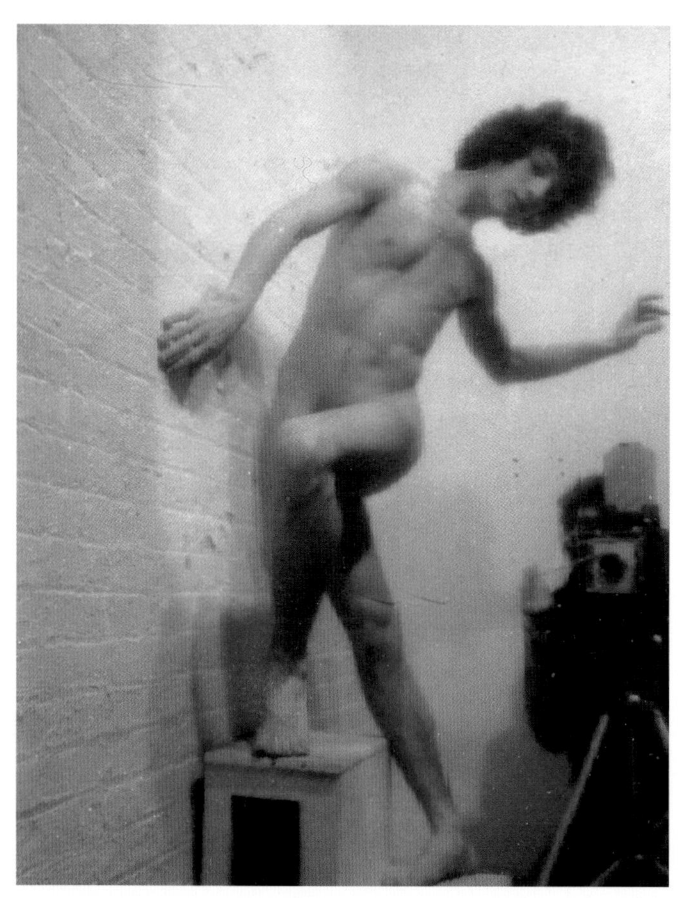

Plate 116. *Untitled (The Dancer)*. 1974

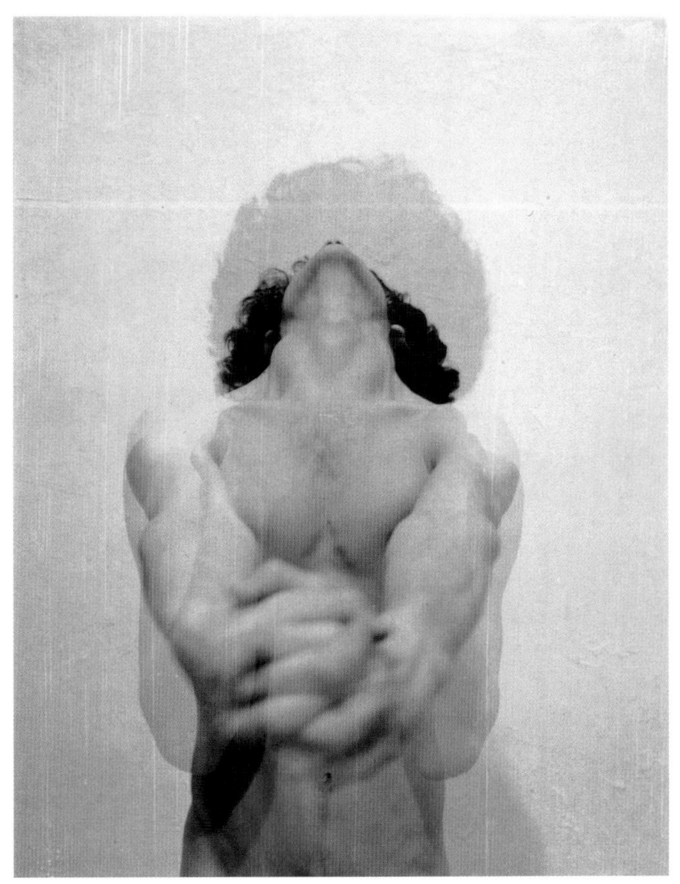

Plate 117. *Untitled (The Dancer)*. 1974

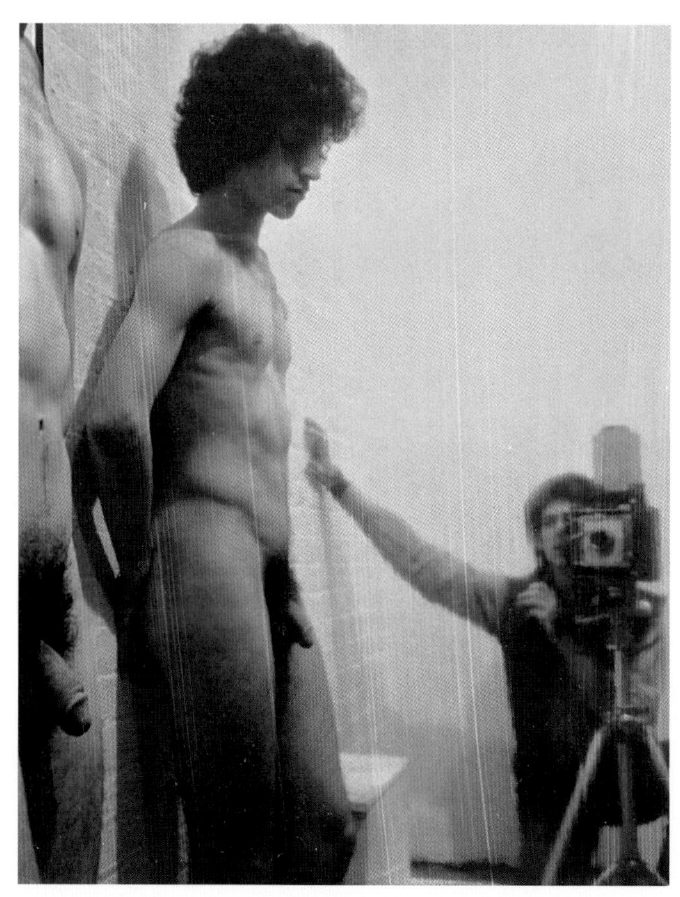

Plate 118. *Untitled (The Dancer)*. 1974

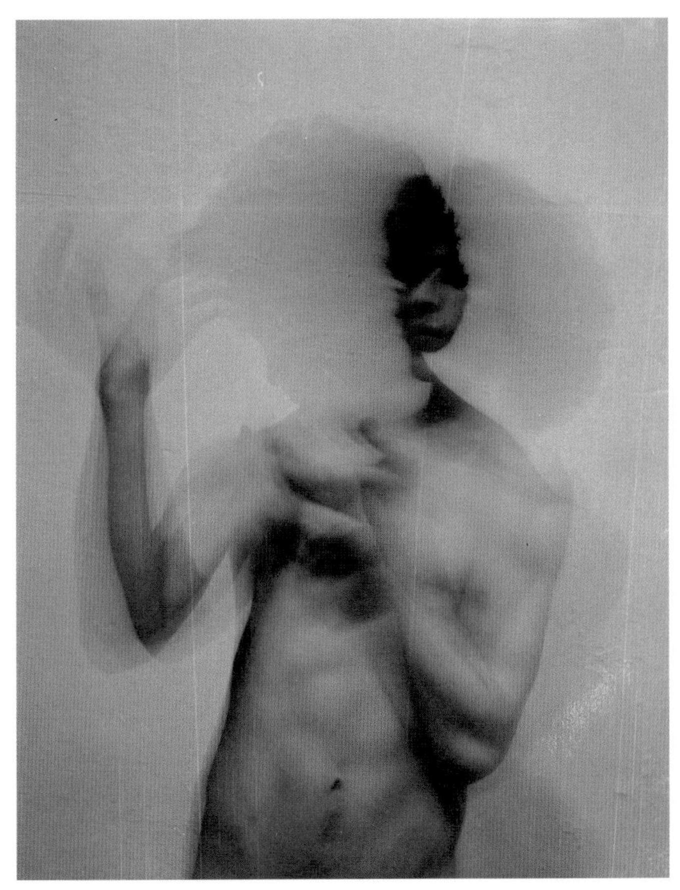

Plate 119. *Untitled (The Dancer)*. 1974

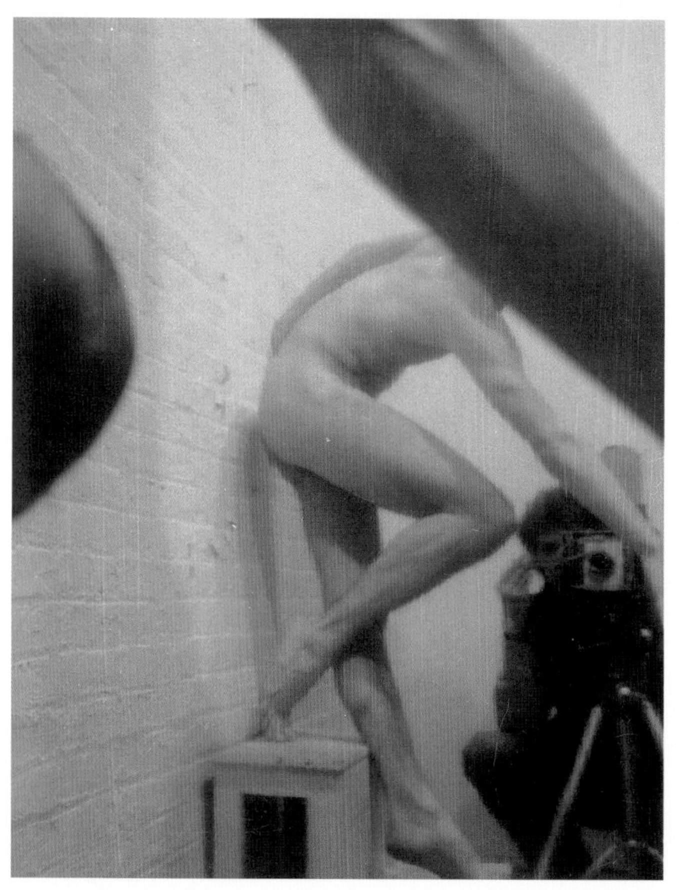

Plate 120. *Untitled (The Dancer)*. 1974

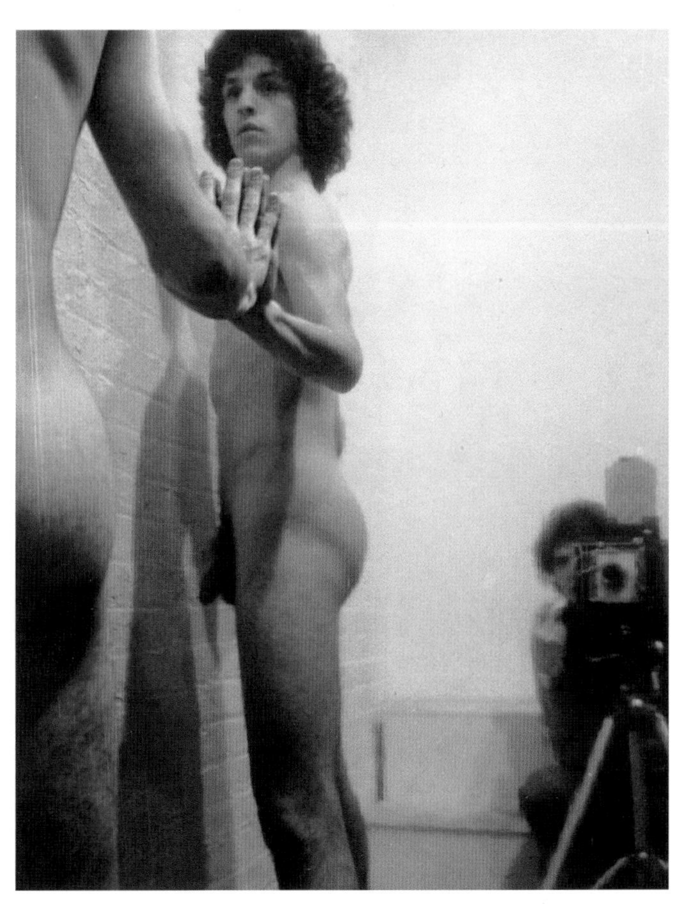

Plate 121. *Untitled (The Dancer)*. 1974

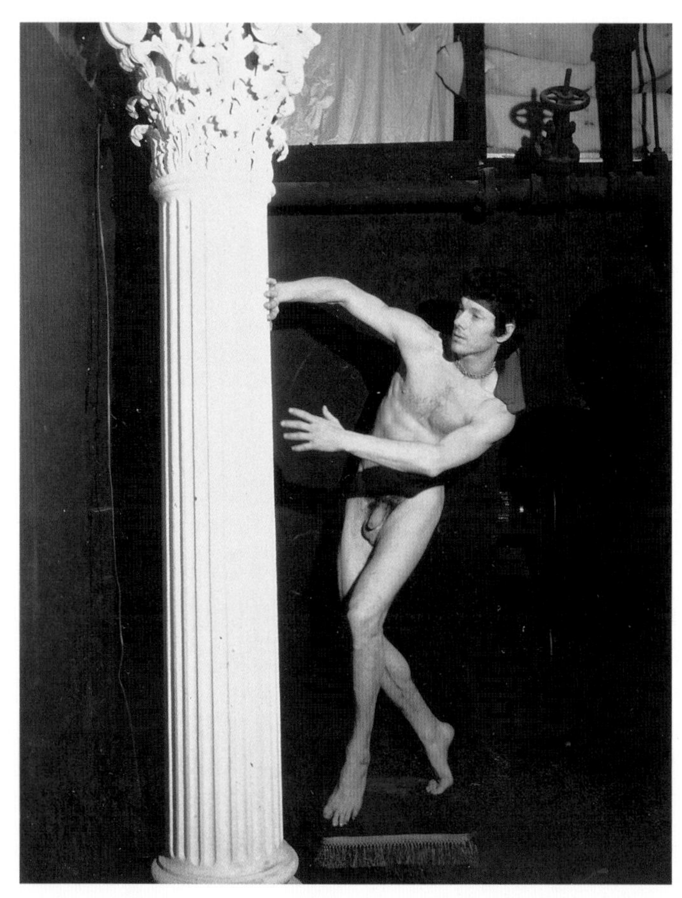

Plate 122. *Untitled (Gyles Fontaine)*. 1974

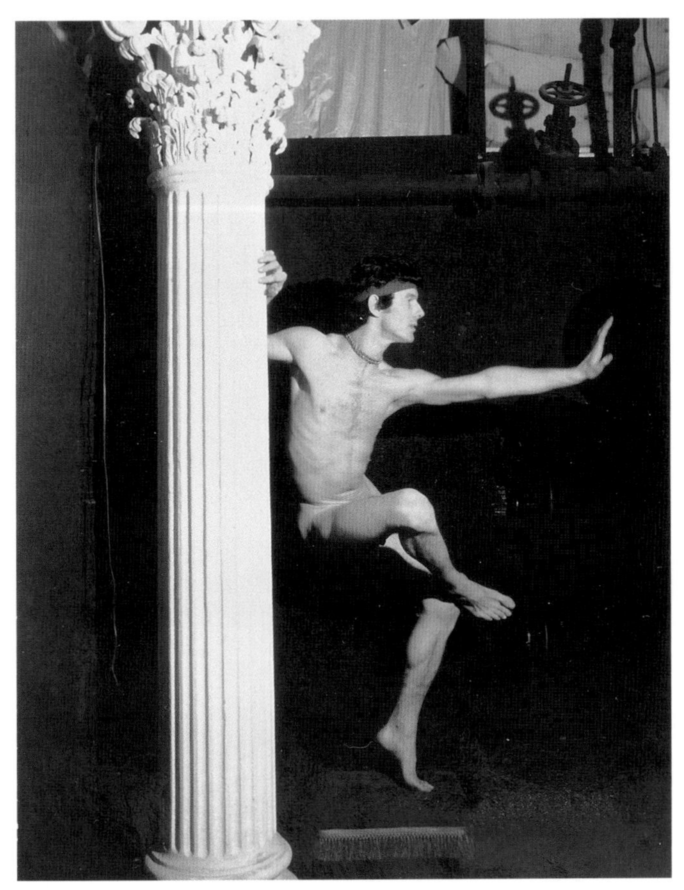

Plate 123. *Untitled (Gyles Fontaine)*. 1974

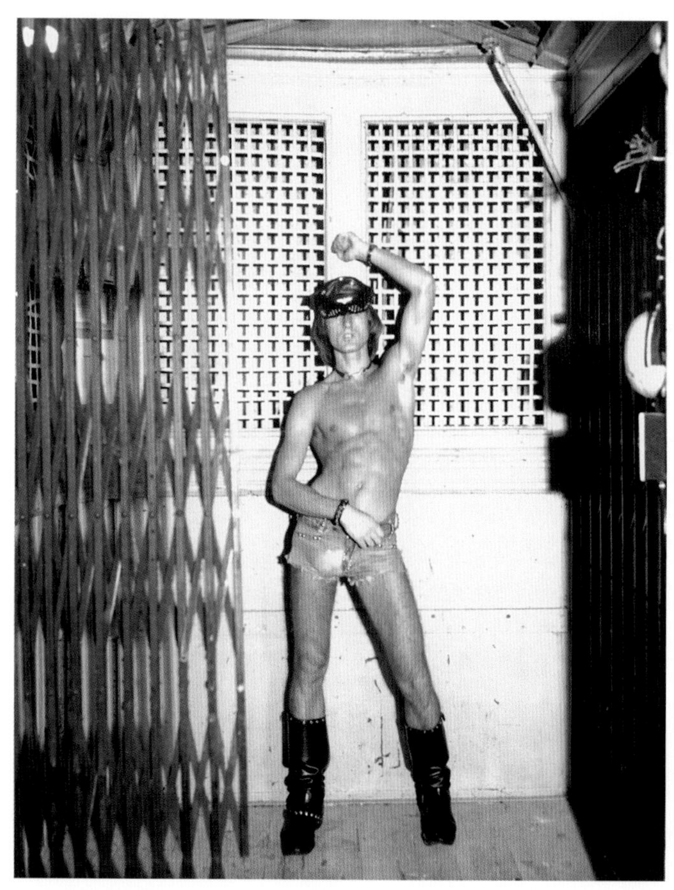

Plate 124. *Untitled (Peter Berlin)*. 1974

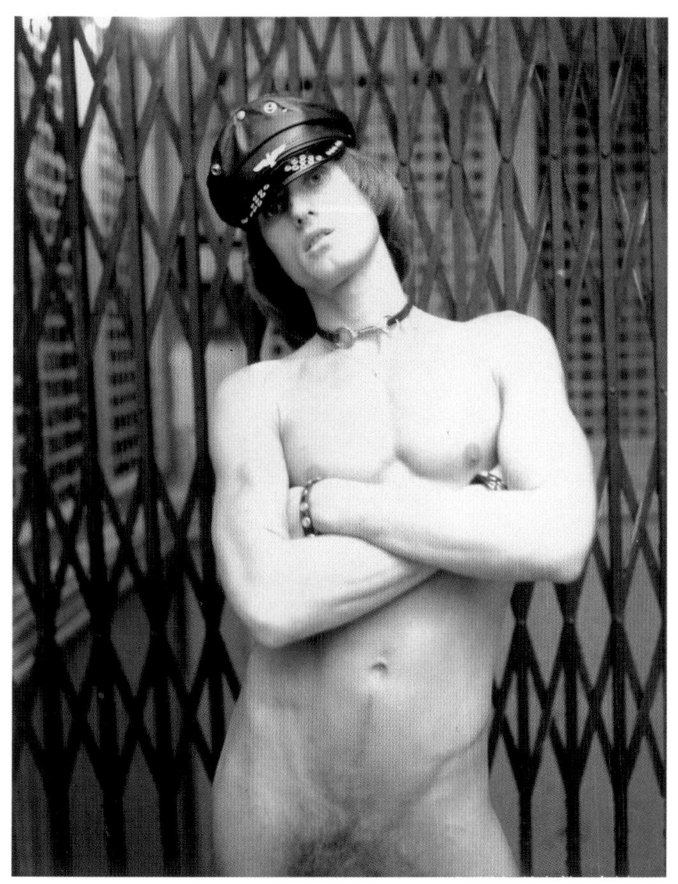

Plate 125. *Untitled (Peter Berlin)*. 1974

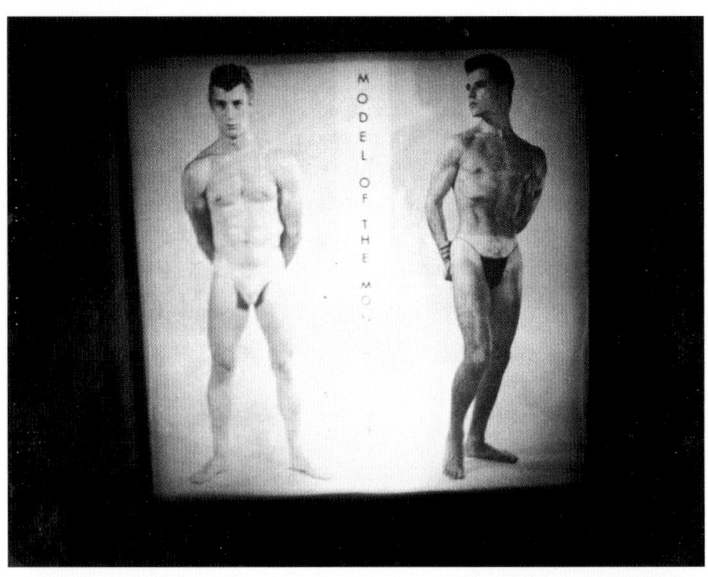

Plate 126. *Untitled*. 1970/73

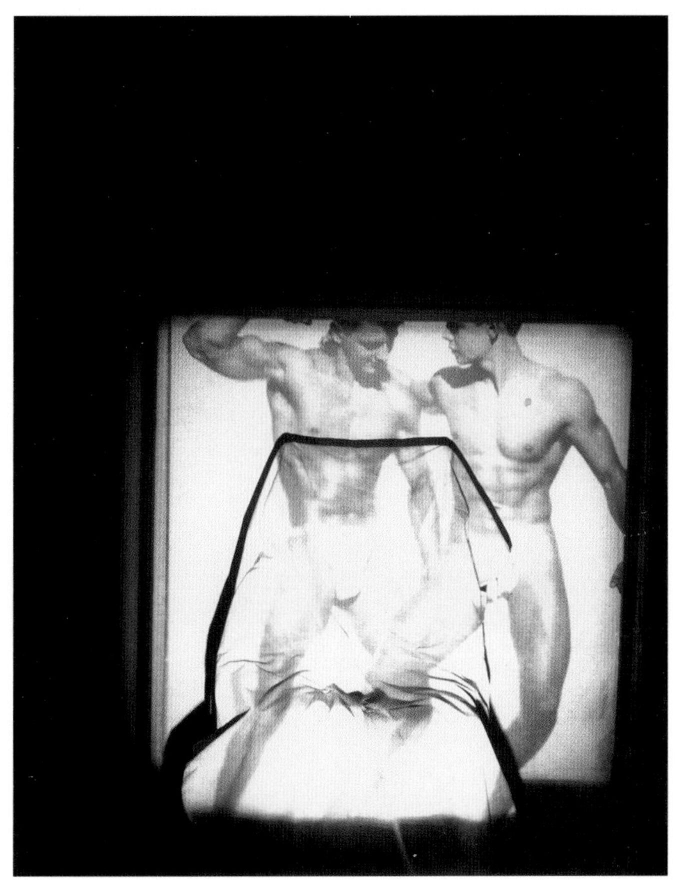

Plate 127. *Untitled*. 1973/75

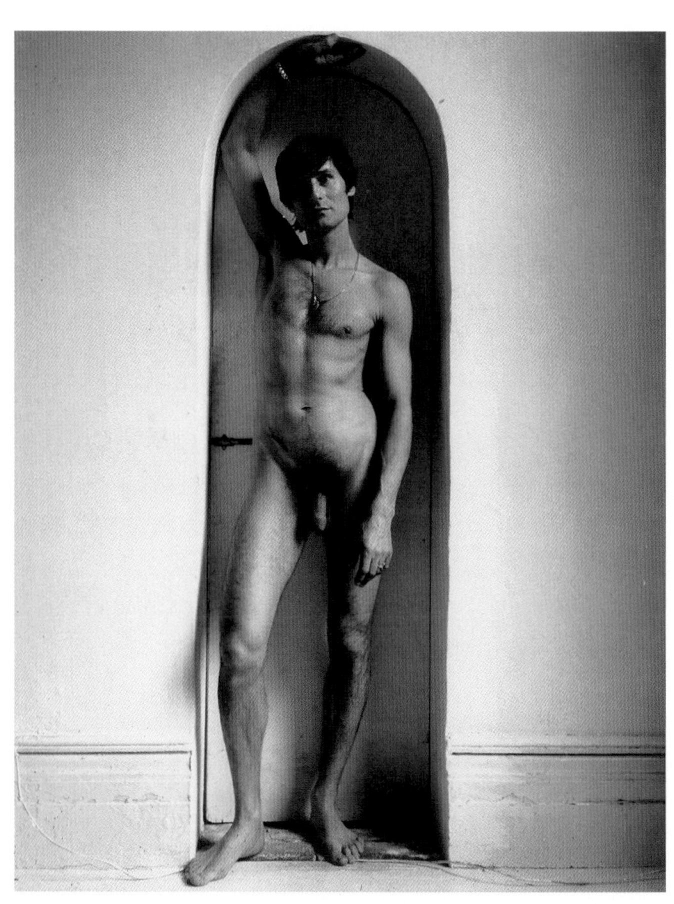

Plate 128. *Untitled (Manfred)*. 1974

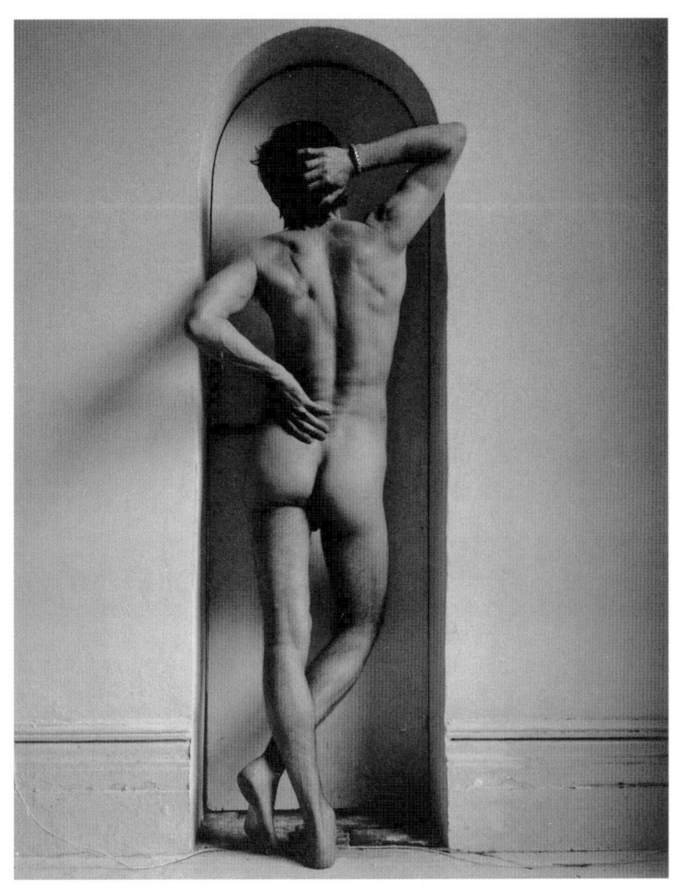

Plate 129. *Untitled (Manfred)*. 1974

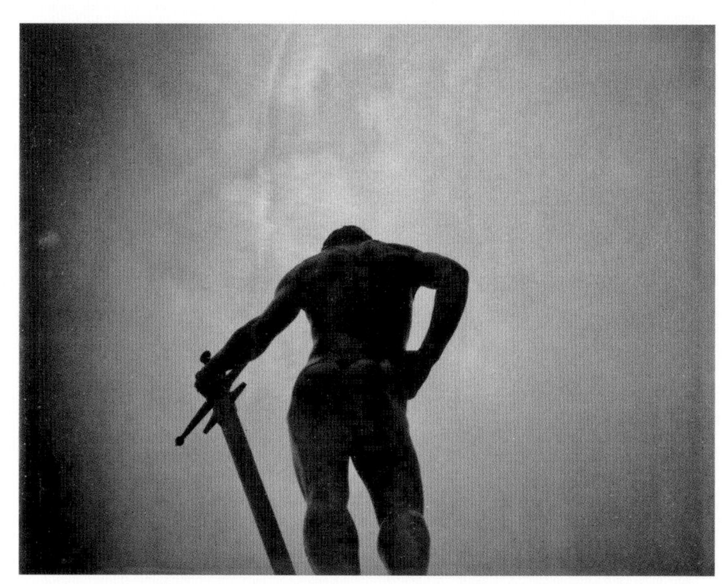

Plate 130. *Untitled*. 1970/73

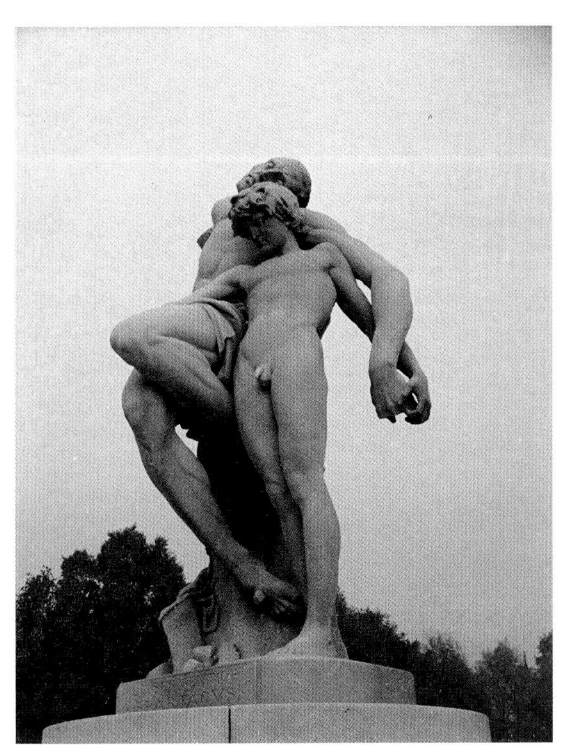

Plate 131. *Untitled (La Serpentine).* 1971

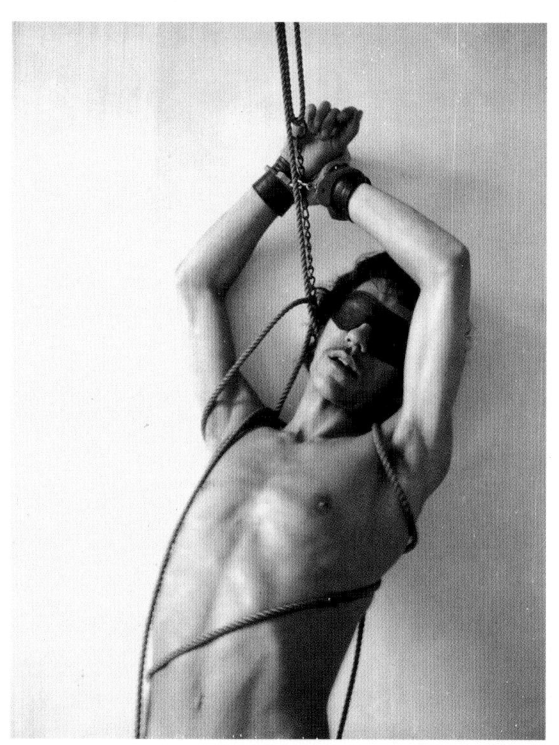

Plate 132. *Untitled*. 1970/73

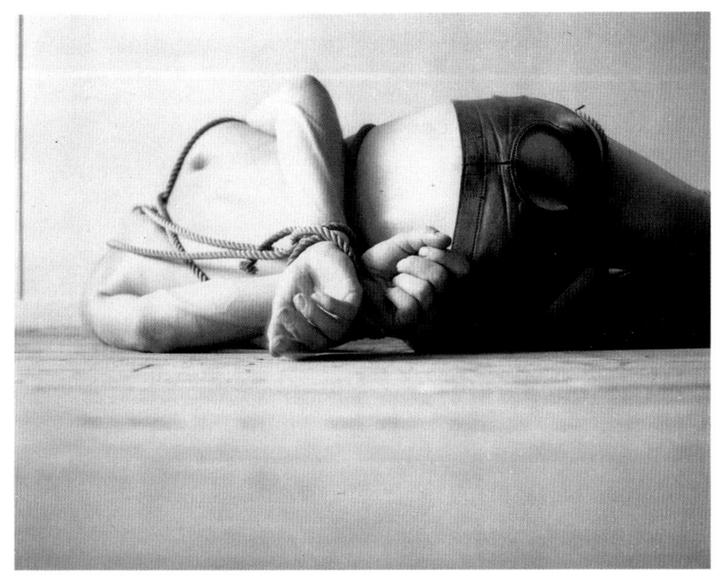

Plate 133. *Untitled*. 1970/73

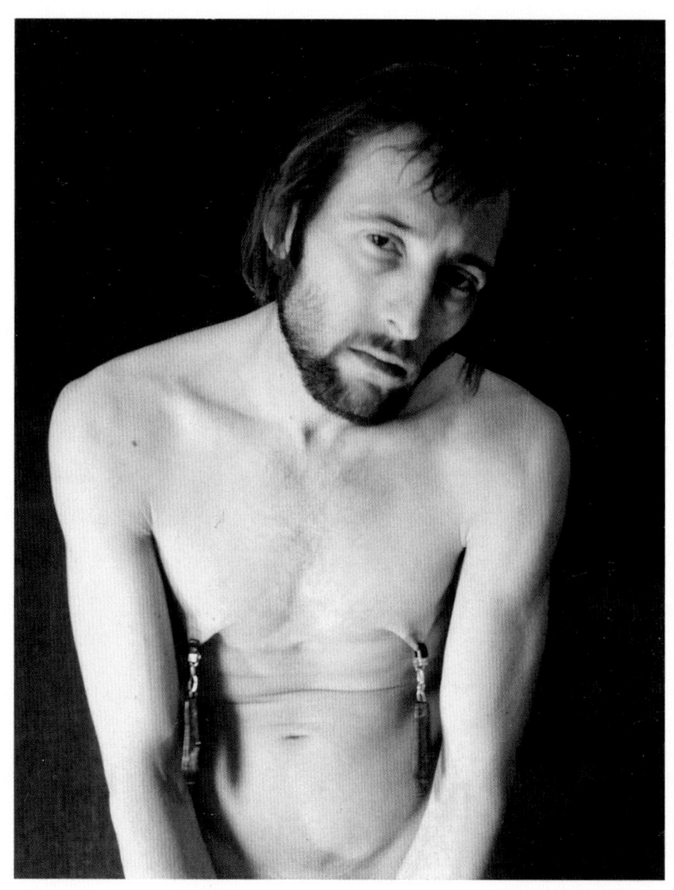

Plate 134. *Untitled*. 1973/75

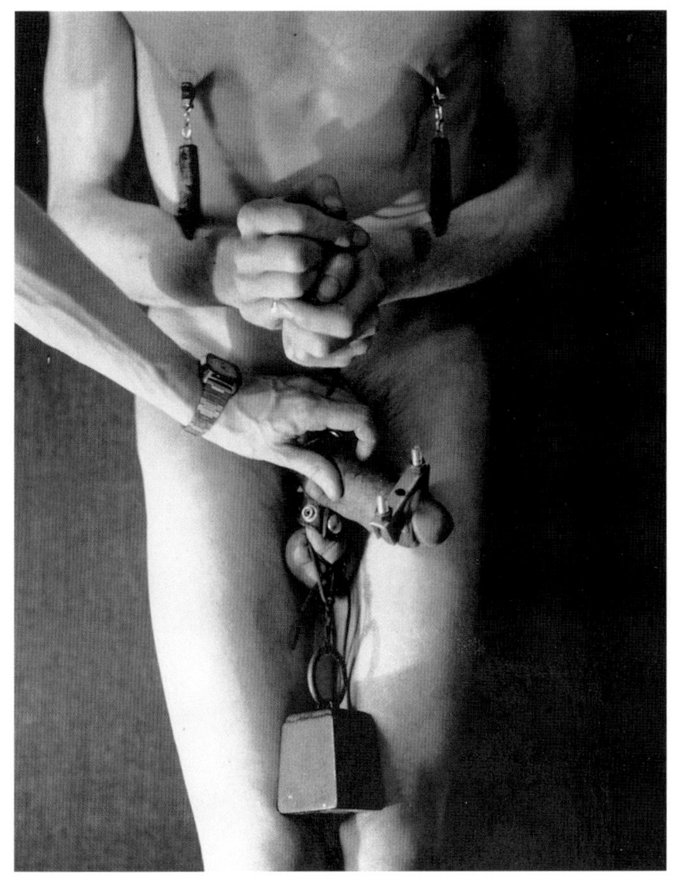

Plate 135. *Untitled*. 1973/75

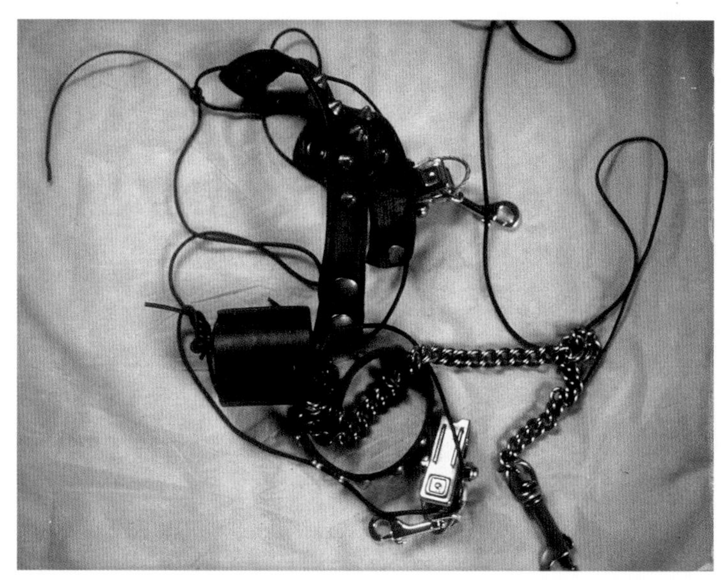

Plate 136. *Untitled*. 1970/73

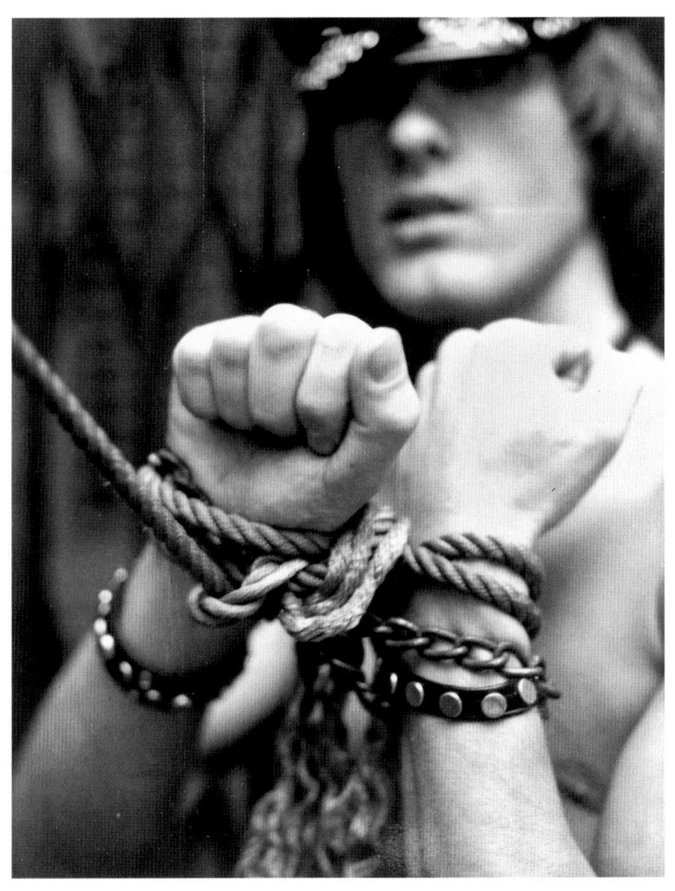

Plate 137. *Untitled (Peter Berlin)*. 1973/75

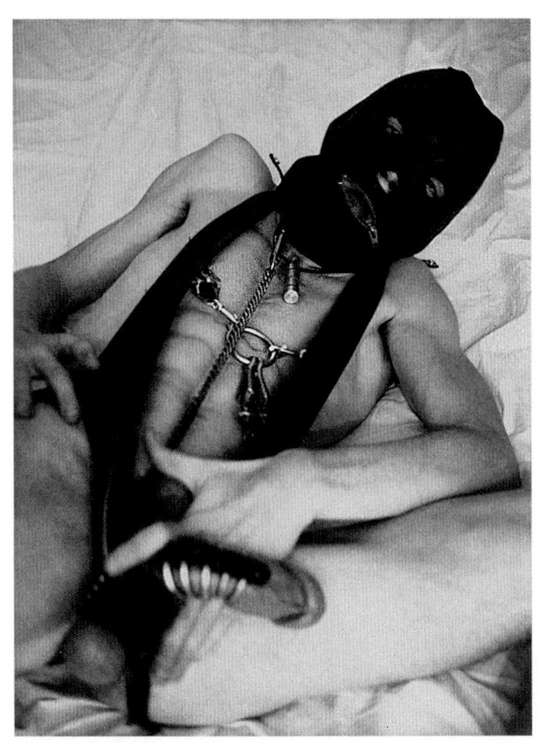

Plate 138. *Untitled (self-portrait).* 1970/73

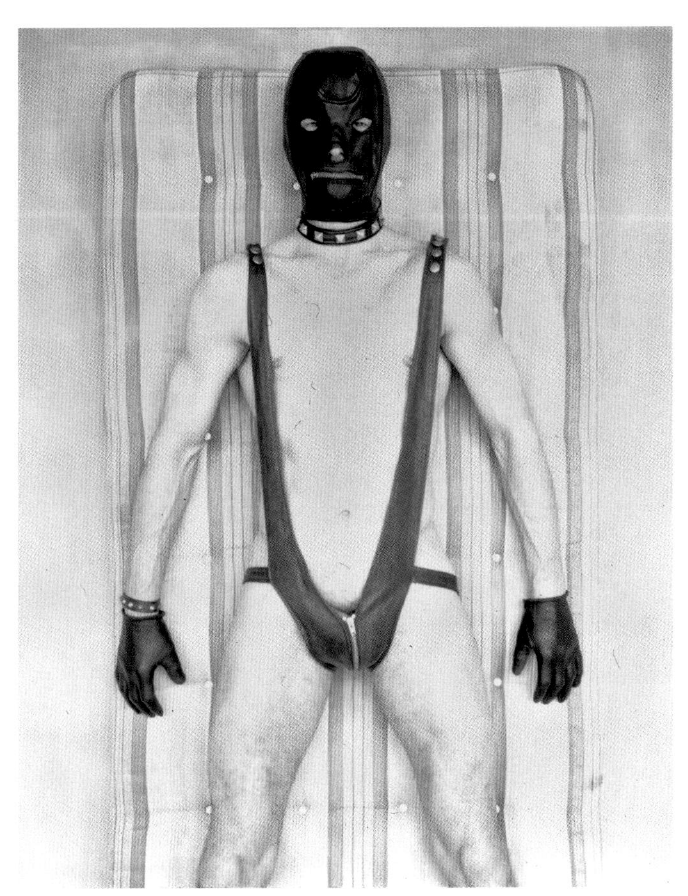

Plate 139. *Untitled*. 1973/75

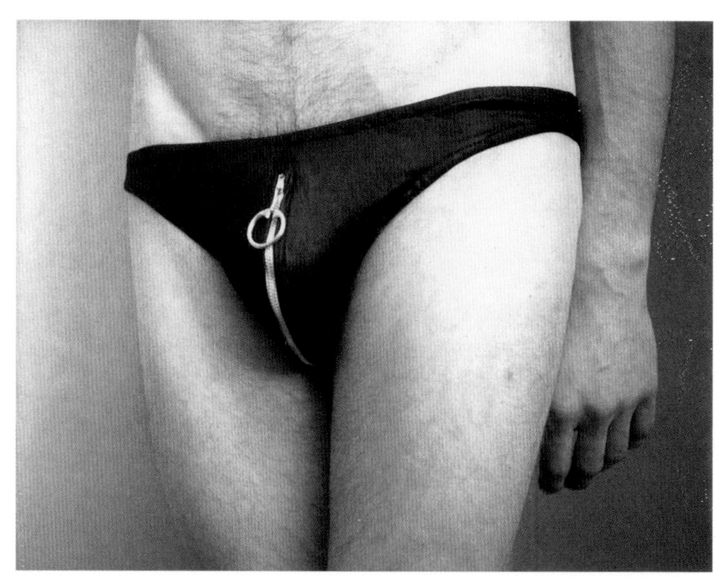

Plate 140. *Untitled*. 1973

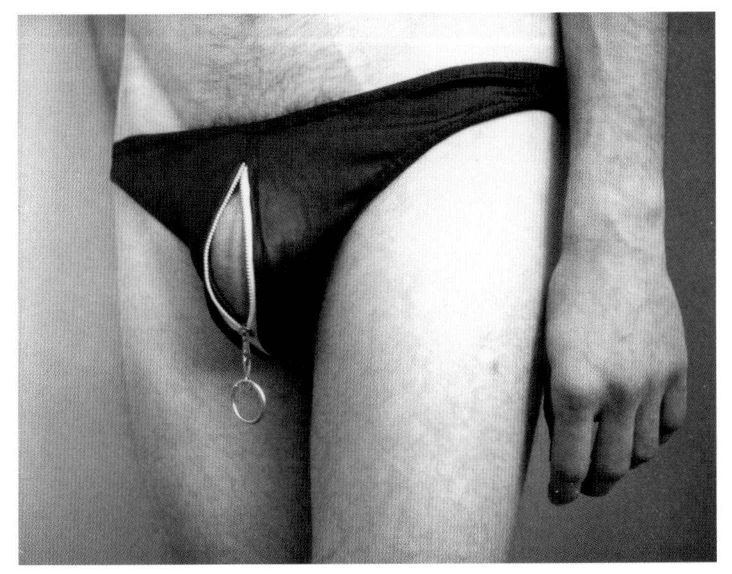

Plate 141. *Untitled*. 1973

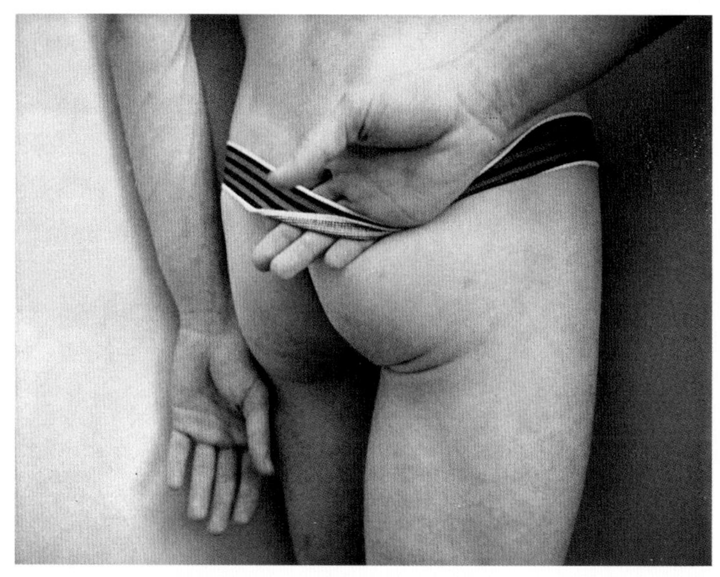

Plate 142. *Untitled*. 1973

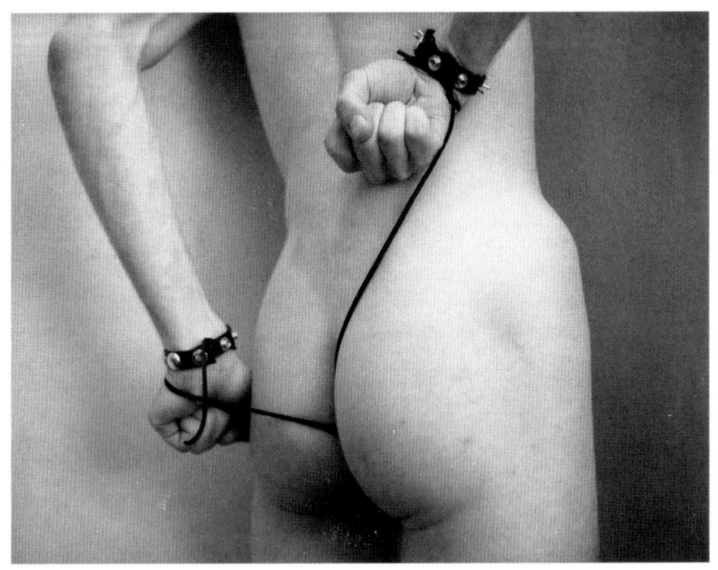

Plate 143. *Untitled*. 1973

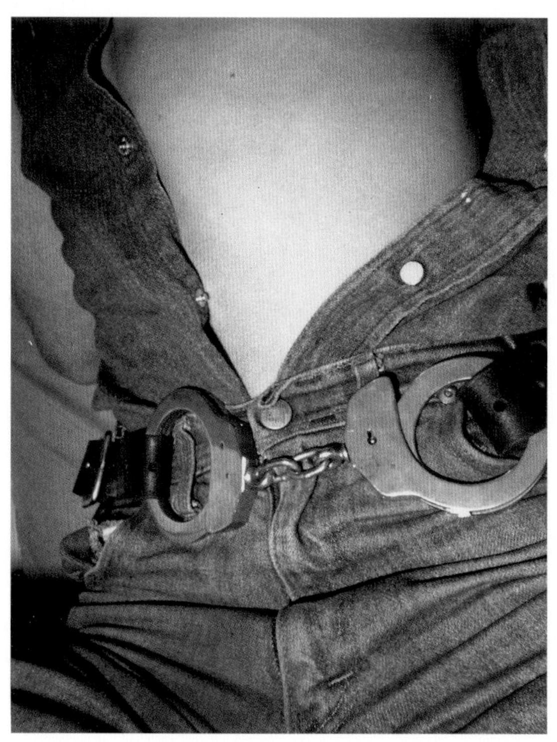

Plate 144. *Untitled (self-portrait)*. 1972

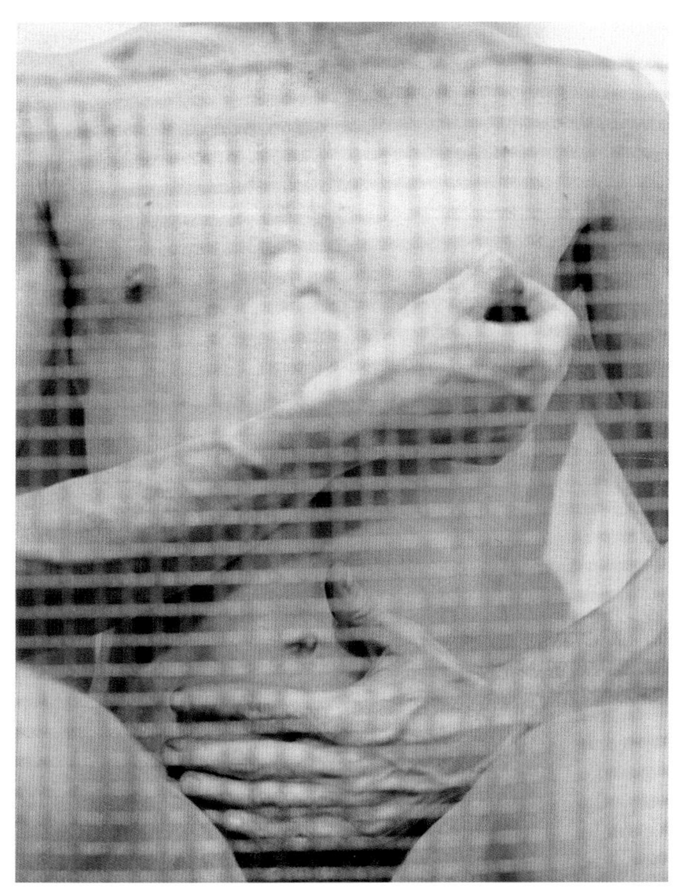

Plate 145. *Untitled*. 1973/75

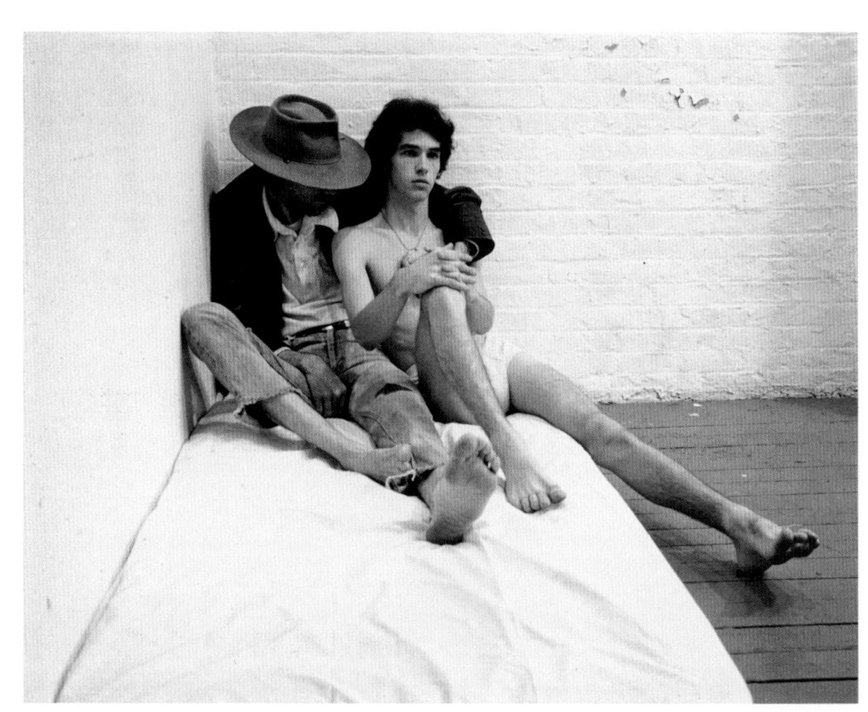

Plate 146. *Untitled (Charles and Jim).* 1973

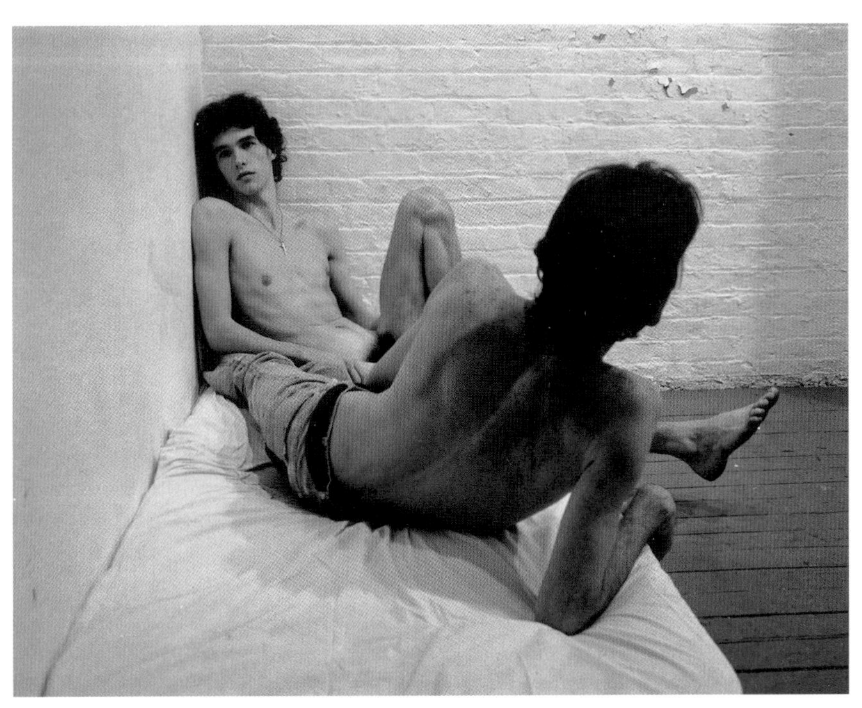

Plate 147. *Untitled (Charles and Jim)*. 1973

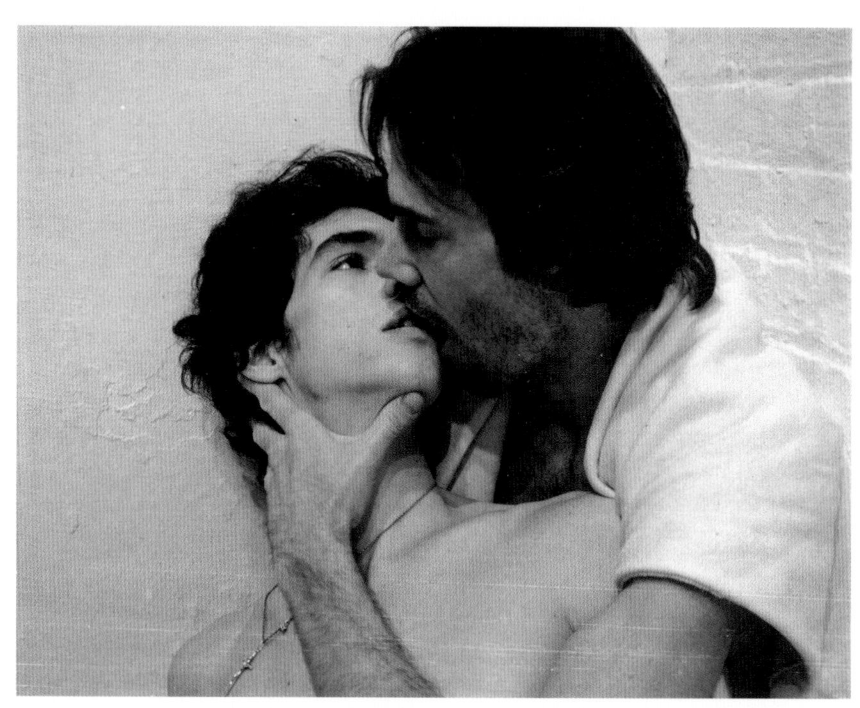

Plate 148. *Untitled (Charles and Jim)*. 1973

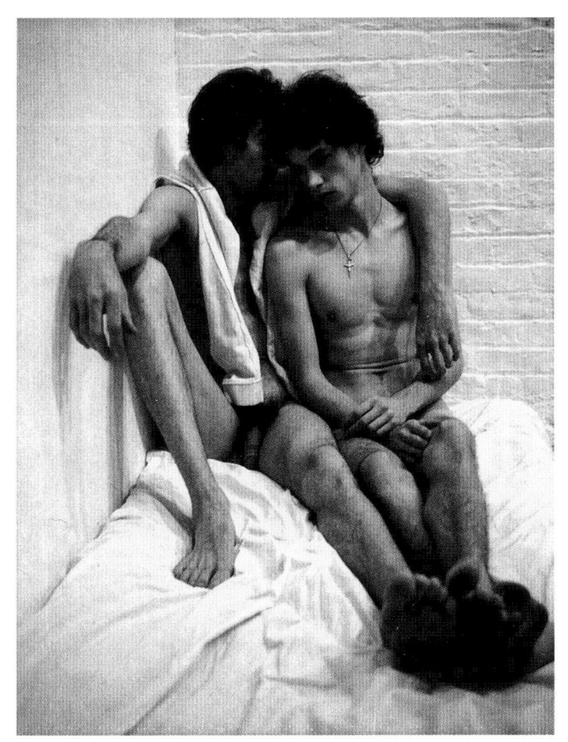

Plate 149. *Untitled (Charles and Jim).* 1973

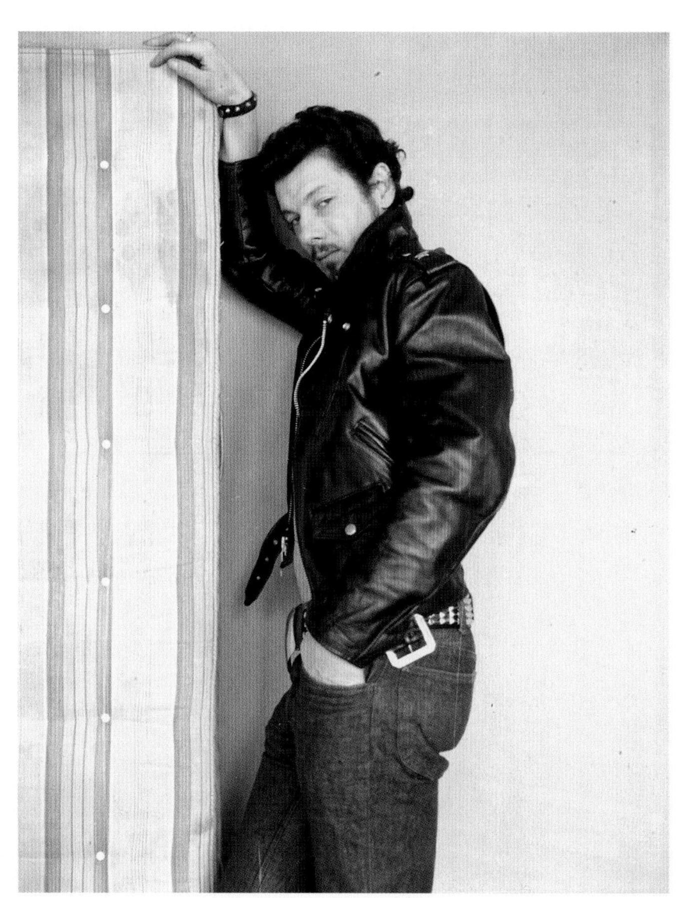

Plate 150. *Untitled (Gyles Fontaine)*. 1973/75

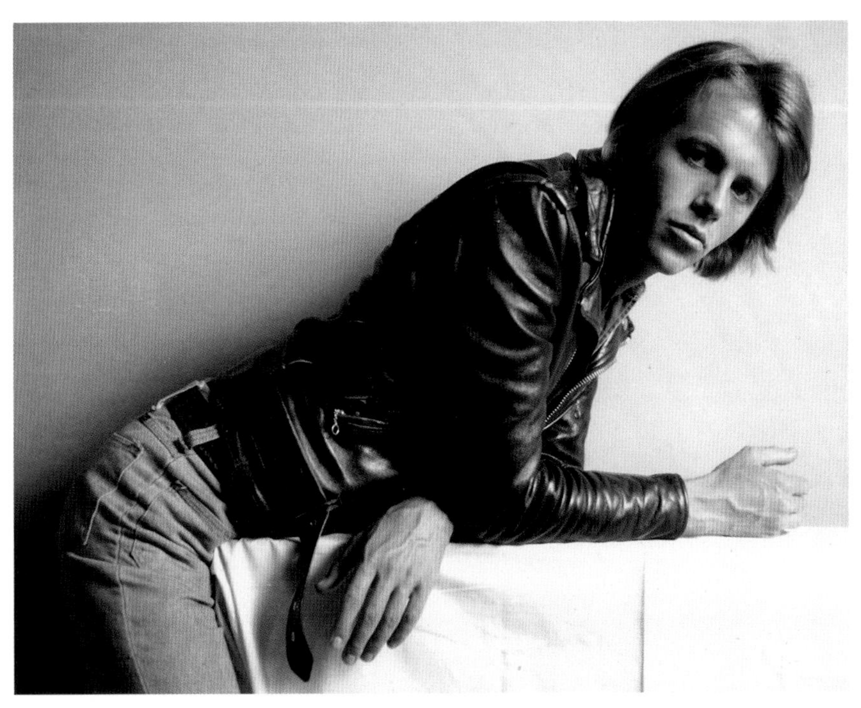

Plate 151. *Untitled*. 1973/75

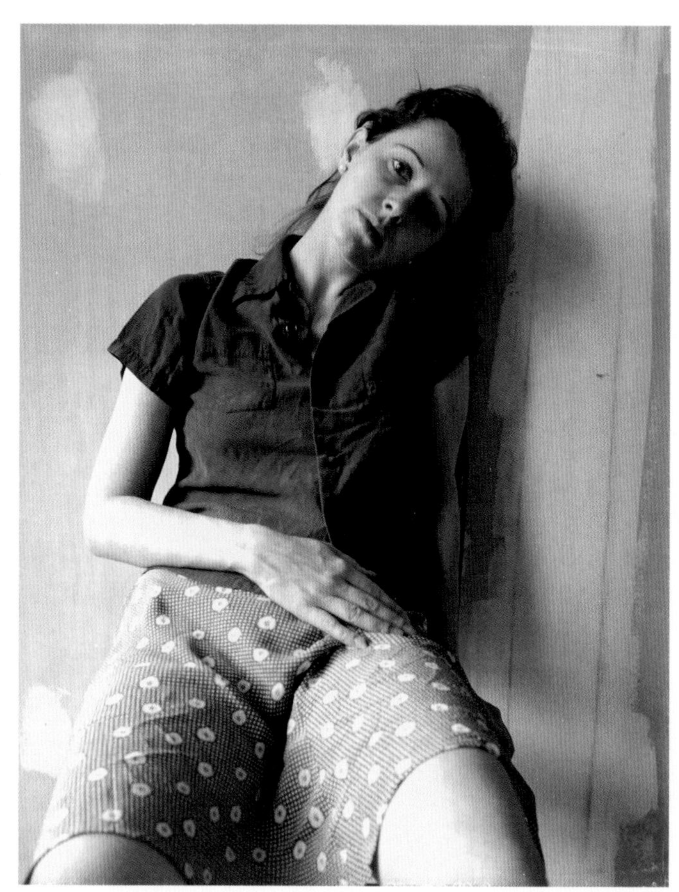

Plate 152. *Untitled (Judy Linn)*. 1973/75

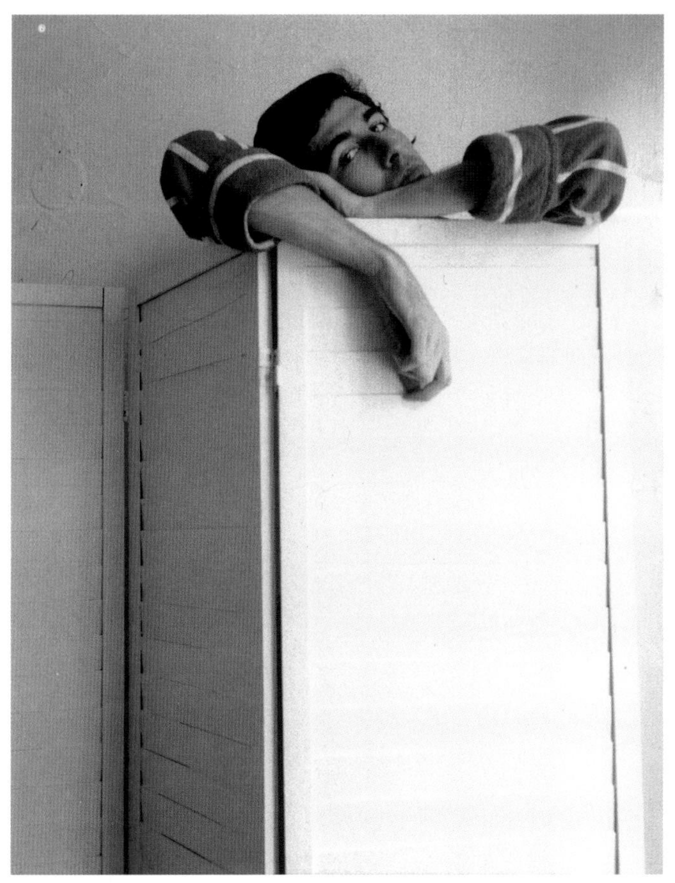

Plate 153. *Untitled (David Croland)*. 1973

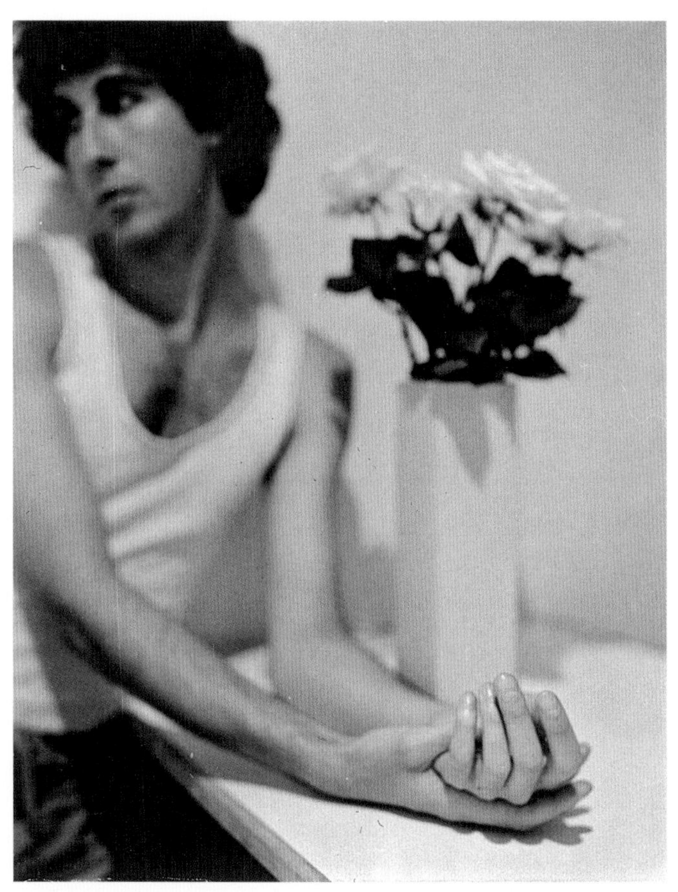

Plate 154. *Untitled (David Croland)*. 1973

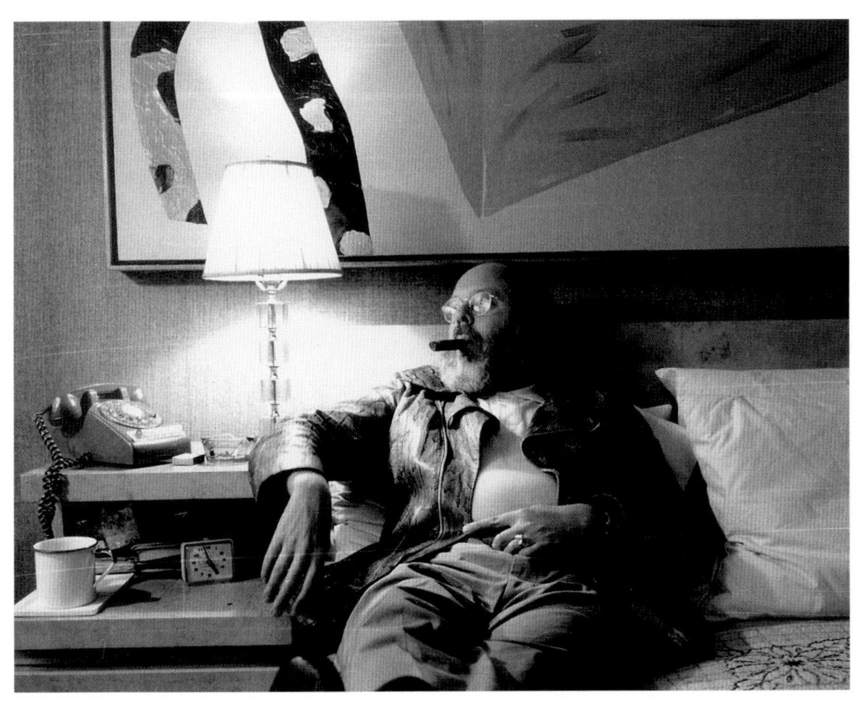

Plate 155. *Untitled (Henry Geldzahler)*. 1973

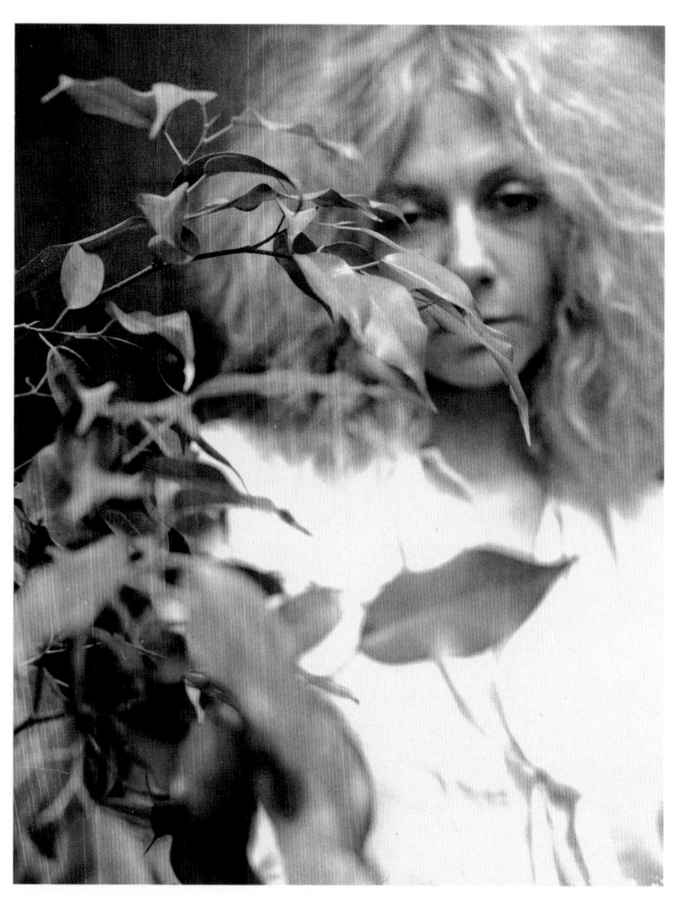

Plate 156. *Untitled (Helen Marden)*. 1973/75

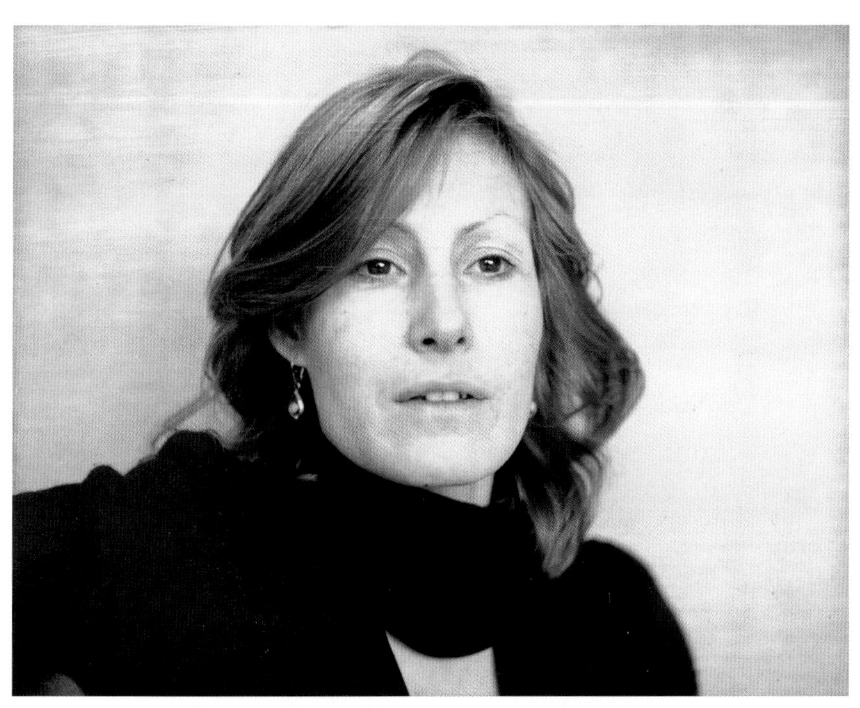

Plate 157. *Untitled (Clarissa Dalrymple)*. 1973/75

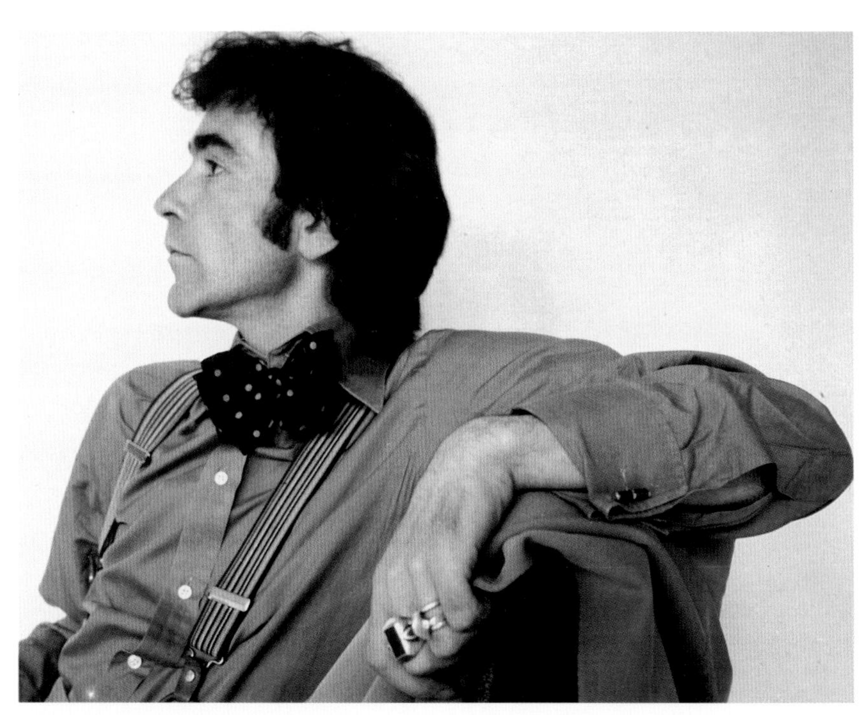

Plate 158. *Untitled (Ozzie Clark)*. 1973/75

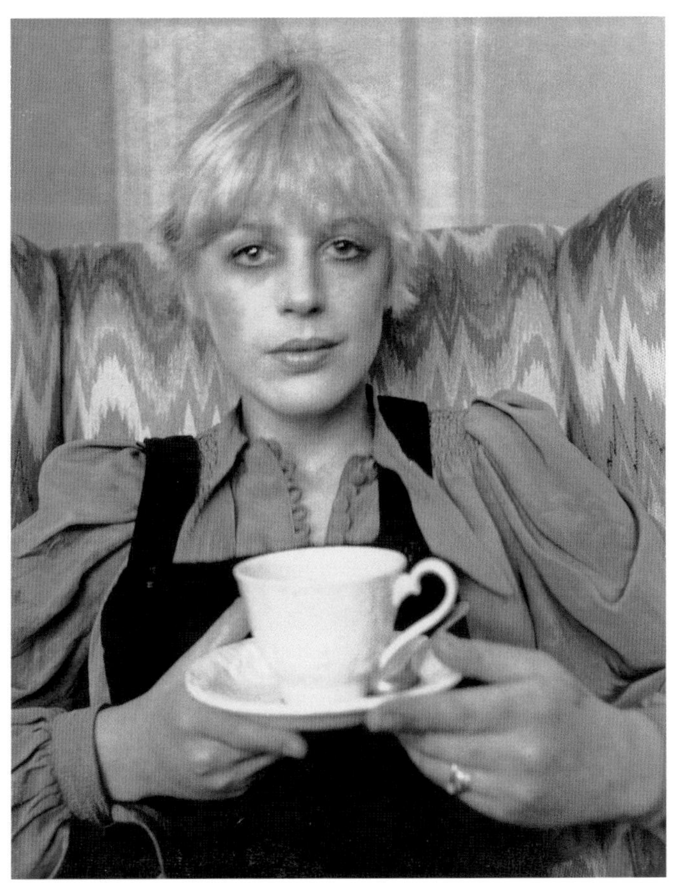

Plate 159. *Untitled (Marianne Faithfull)*. 1974

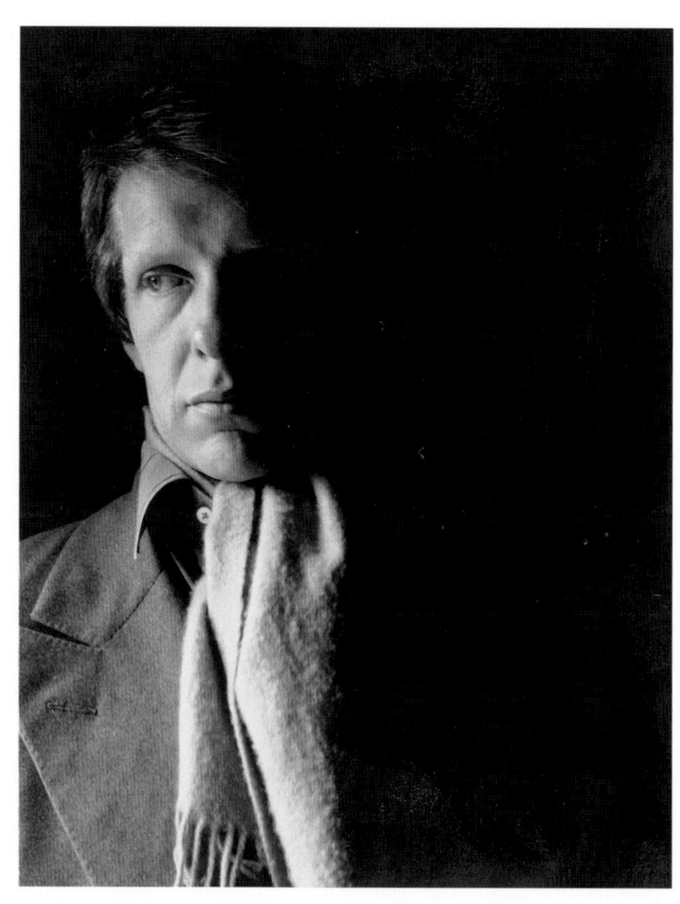

Plate 160. *Untitled (Christopher Gibbs)*. 1974

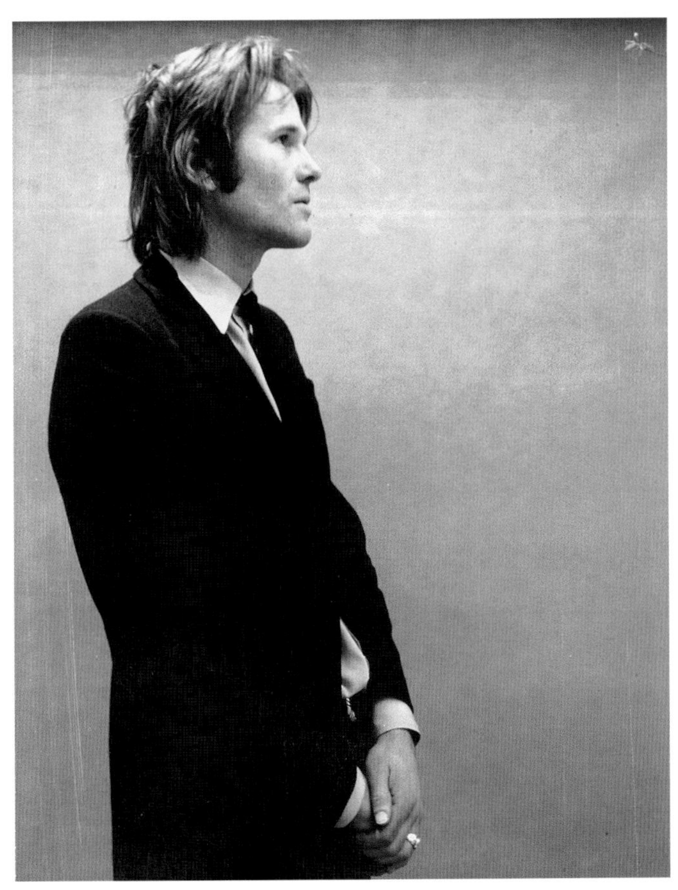

Plate 161. *Untitled (Michael Ranney)*. 1973/75

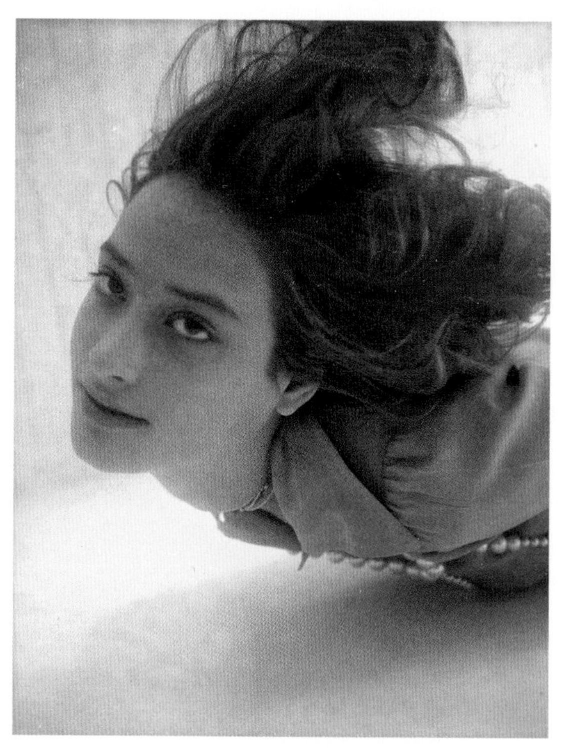

Plate 162. *Untitled (Nicky Weymouth)*. 1973

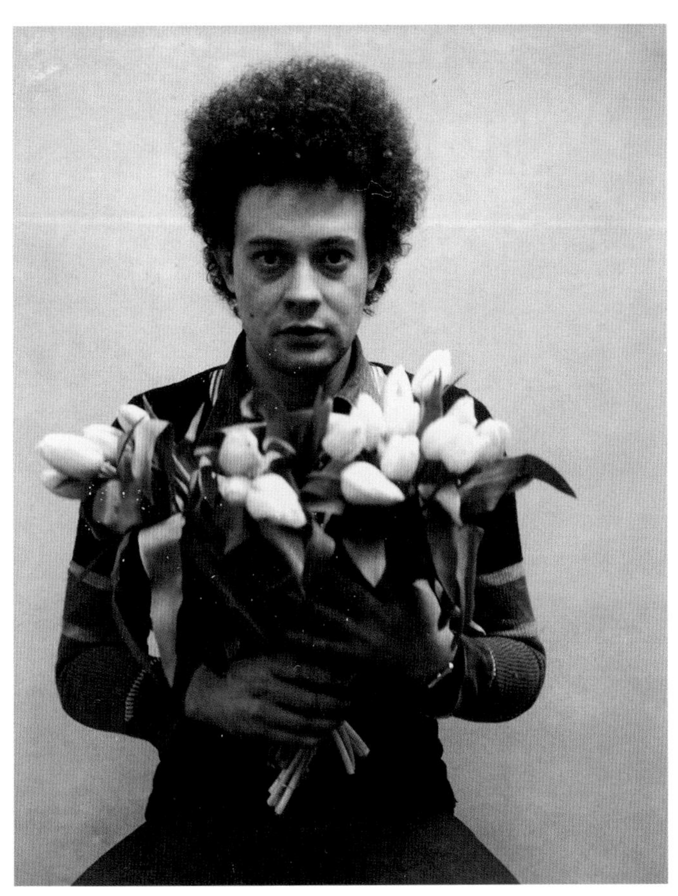

Plate 163. *Untitled (Nigel Weymouth)*. 1973/75

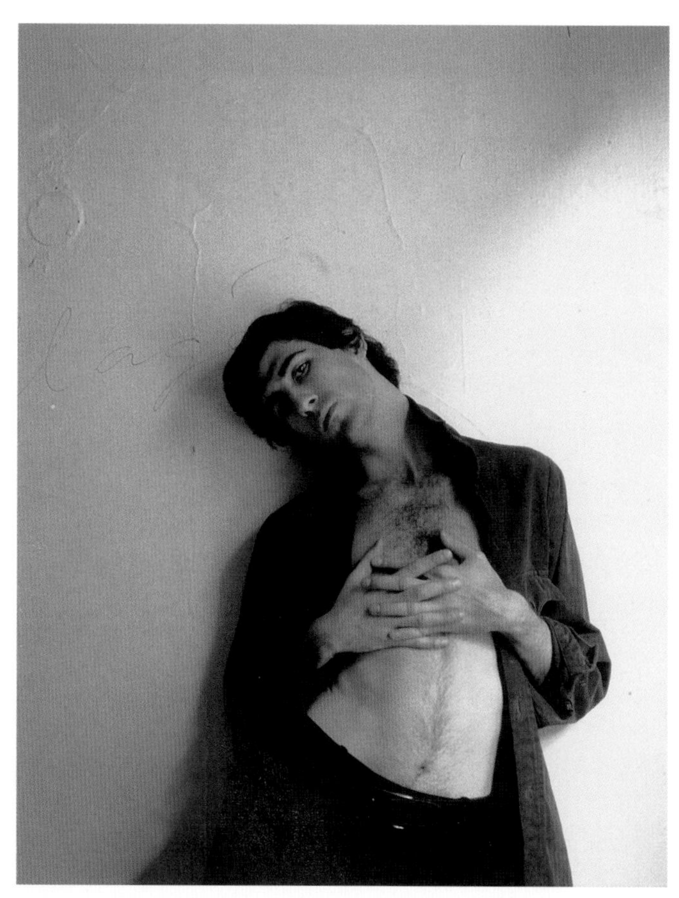

Plate 164. *Untitled (David Croland)*. 1973

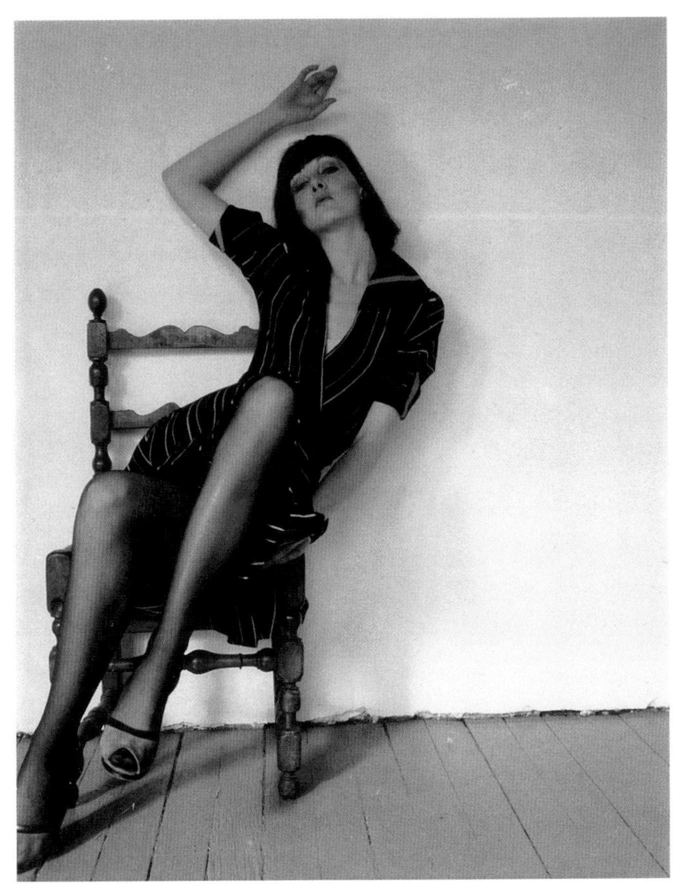

Plate 165. *Untitled (Nancy Nortia)*. 1973/75

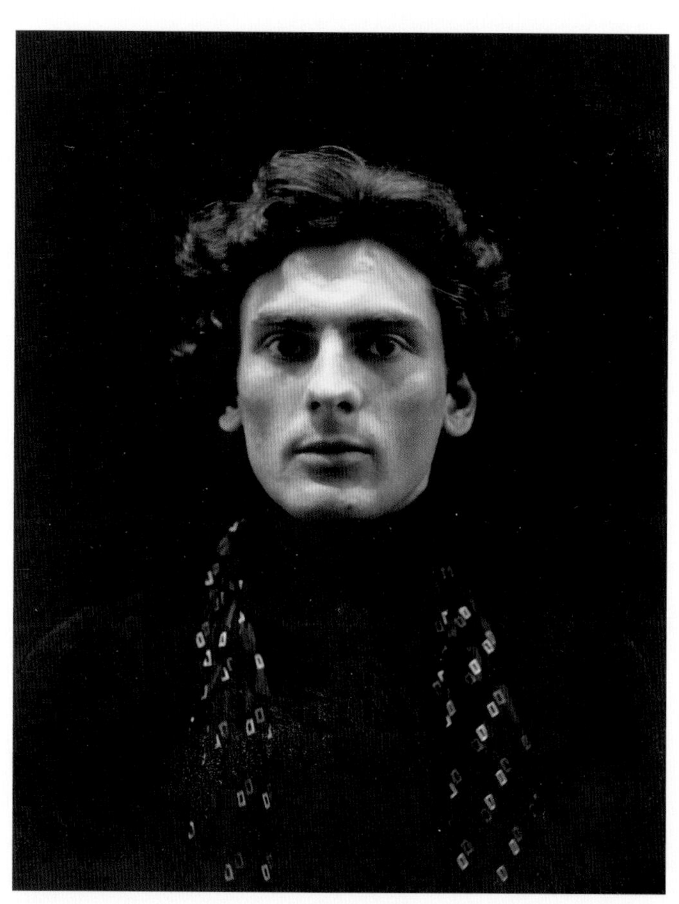

Plate 166. *Untitled*. 1973/75

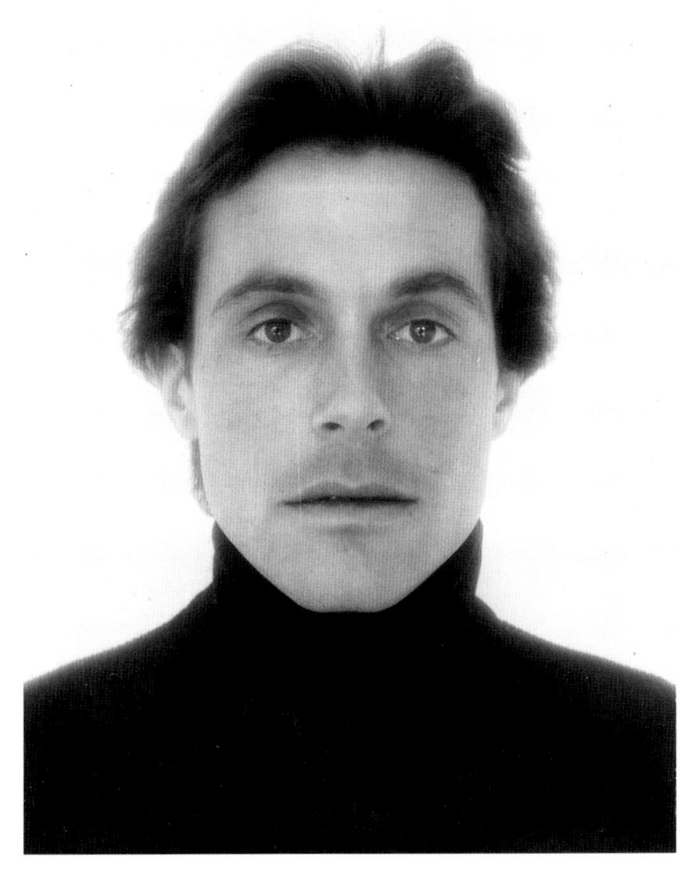

Plate 167. *Untitled (Lars Kampmann)*. 1973/75

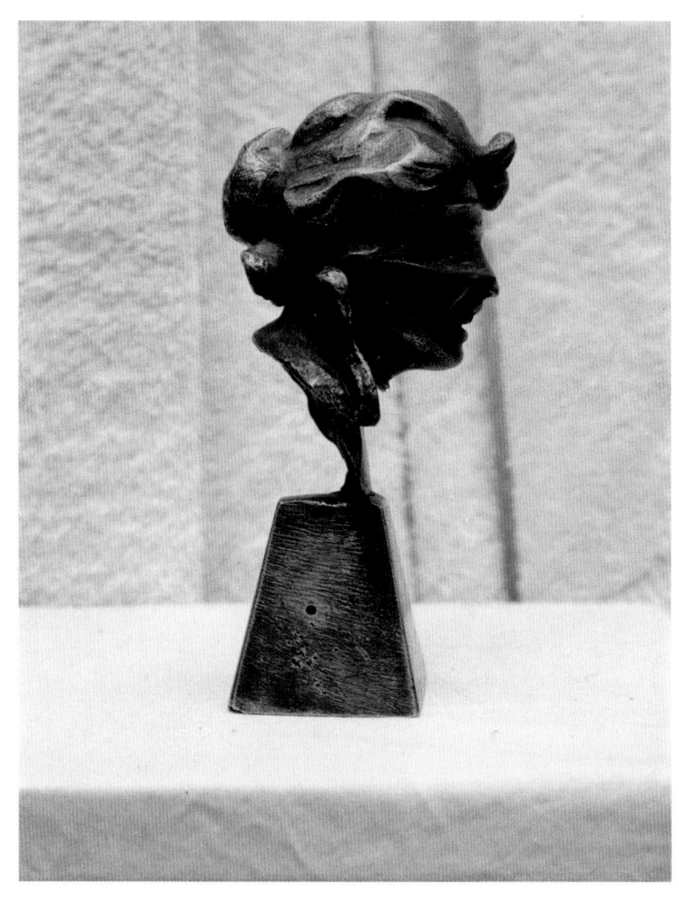

Plate 168. *Untitled*. 1973/75

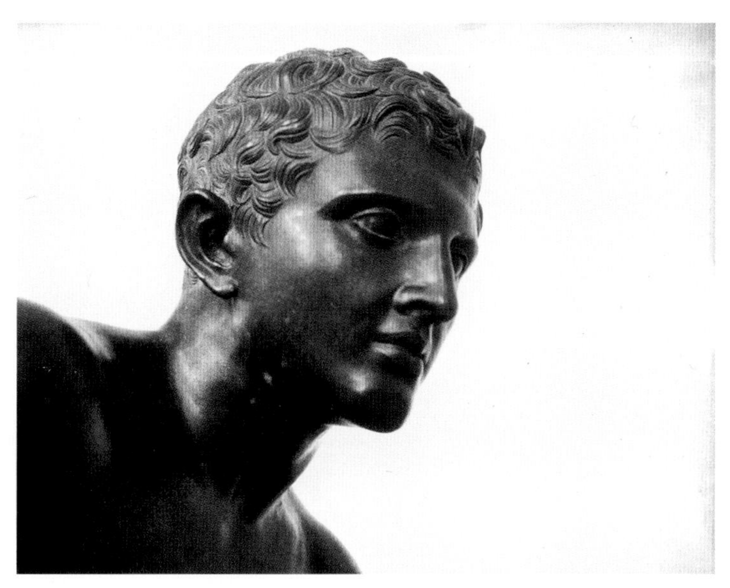

Plate 169. *Untitled*. 1970/73

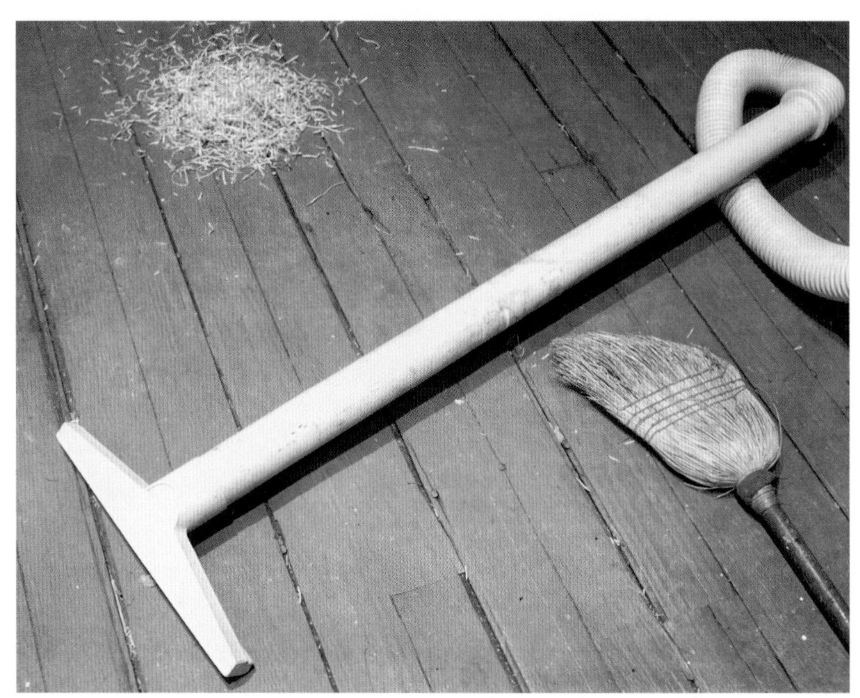

Plate 170. *Untitled*. 1973/75

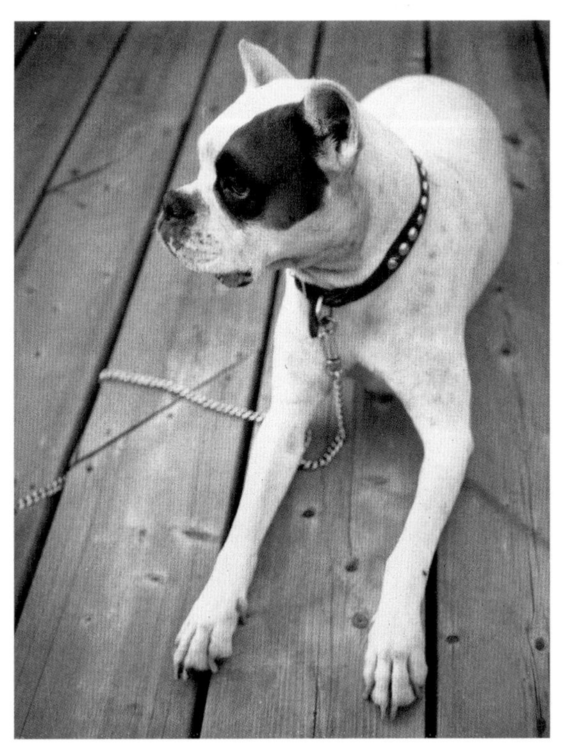

Plate 171. *Untitled*. 1970/73

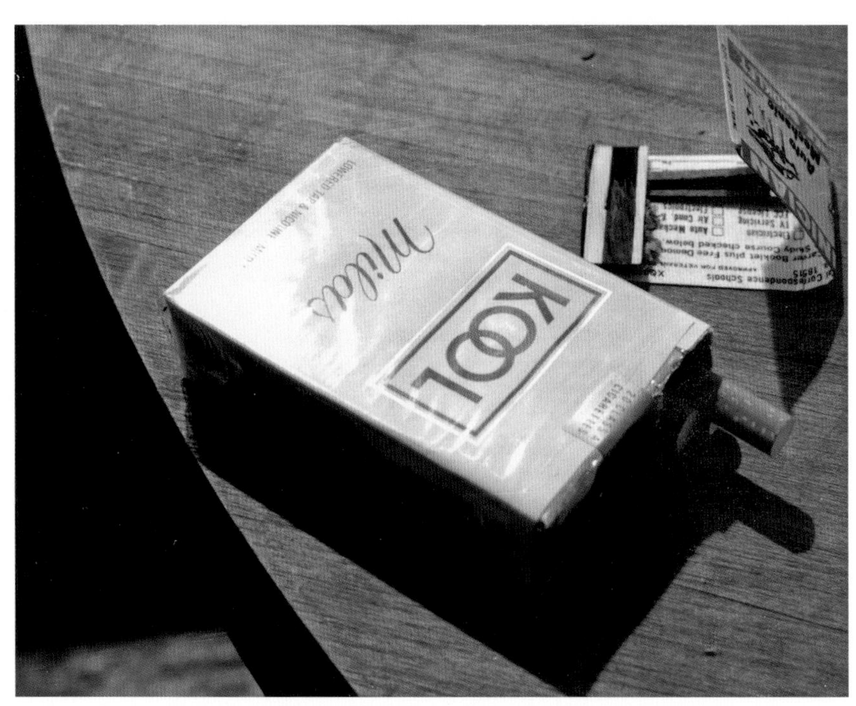

Plate 172. *Untitled*. 1975

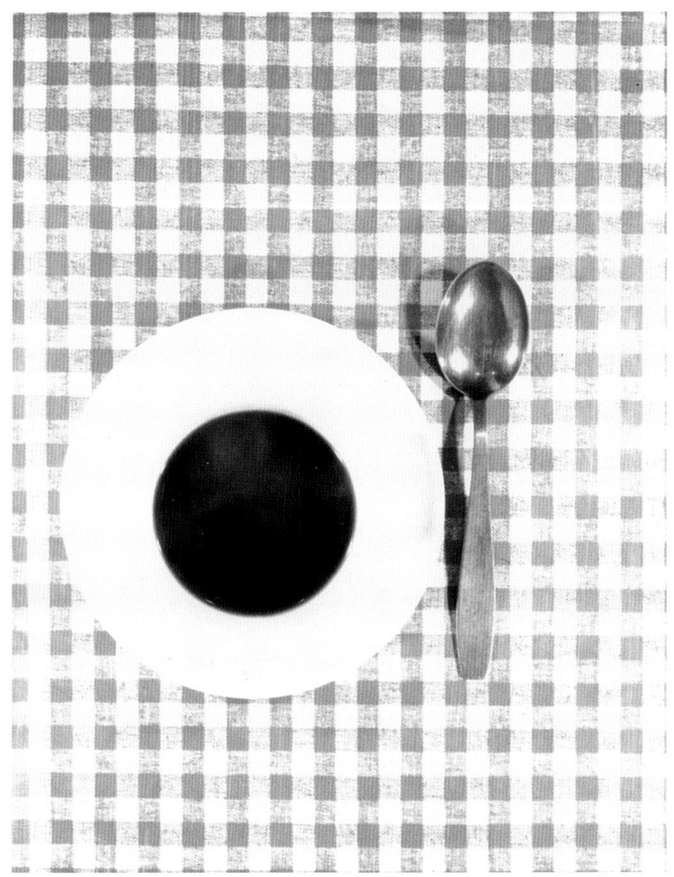

Plate 173. *Untitled*. 1973/75

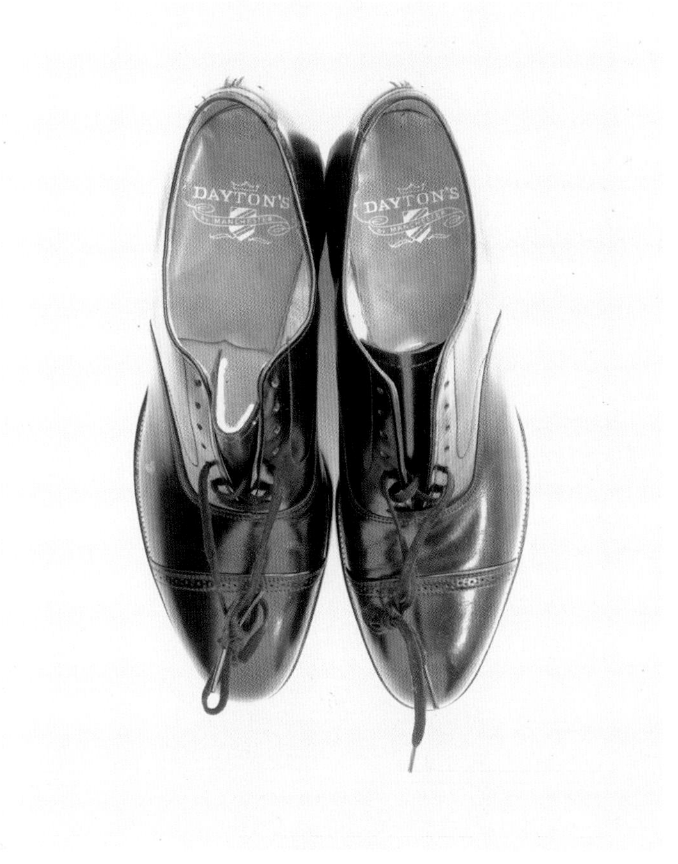

Plate 174. *Untitled*. 1974

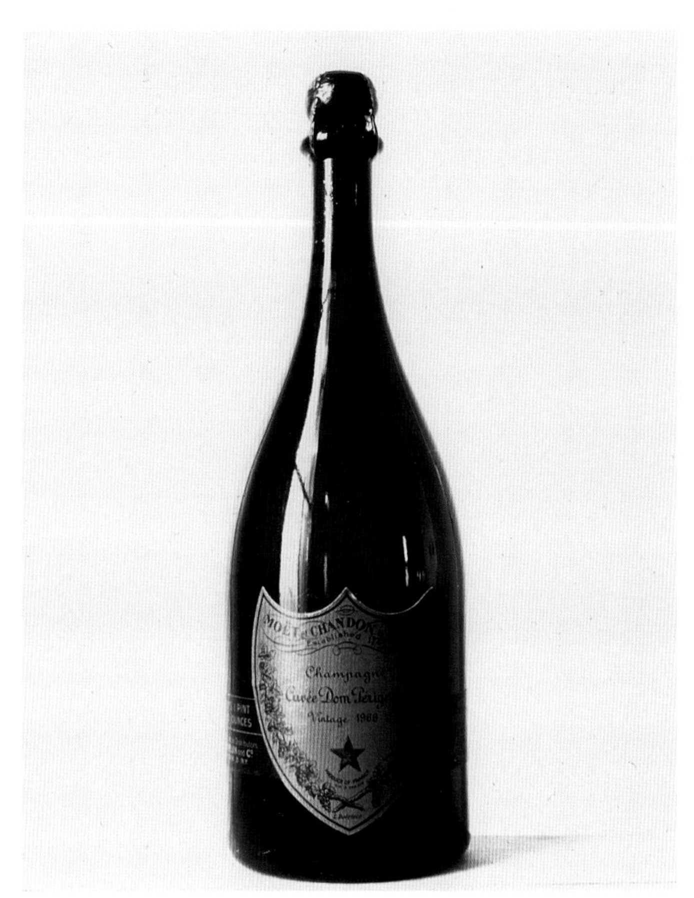

Plate 175. *Untitled*. 1974

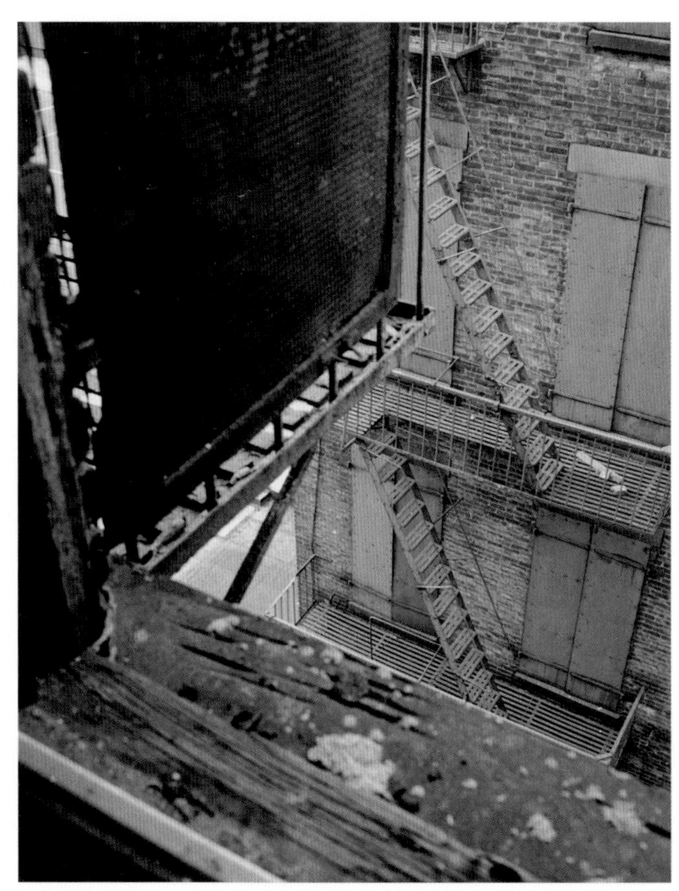

Plate 176. *Untitled (Bond Street)*. 1973/75

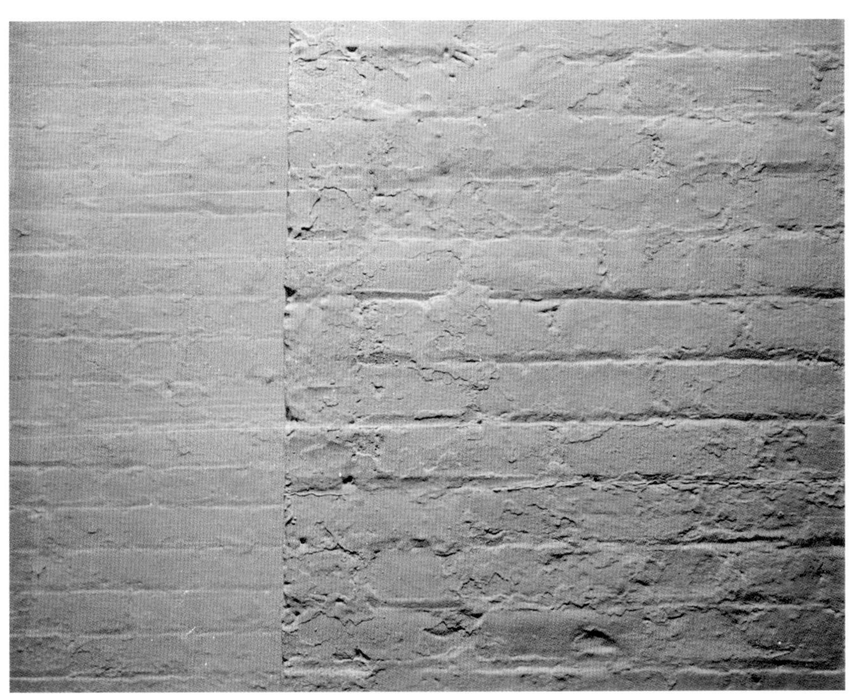

Plate 177. *Untitled*. 1973/75

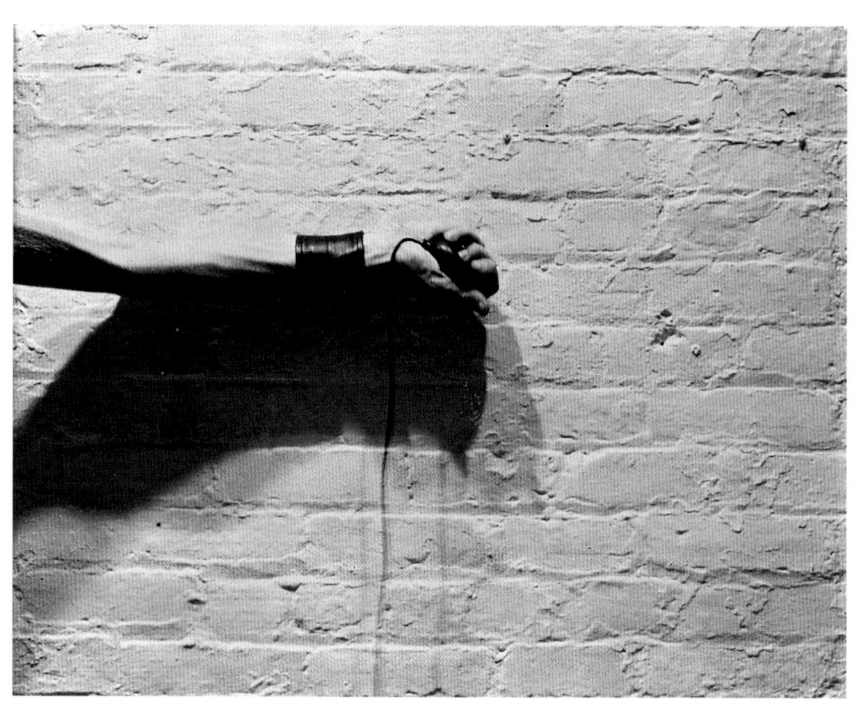

Plate 178. *Untitled (self-portrait).* 1973/75

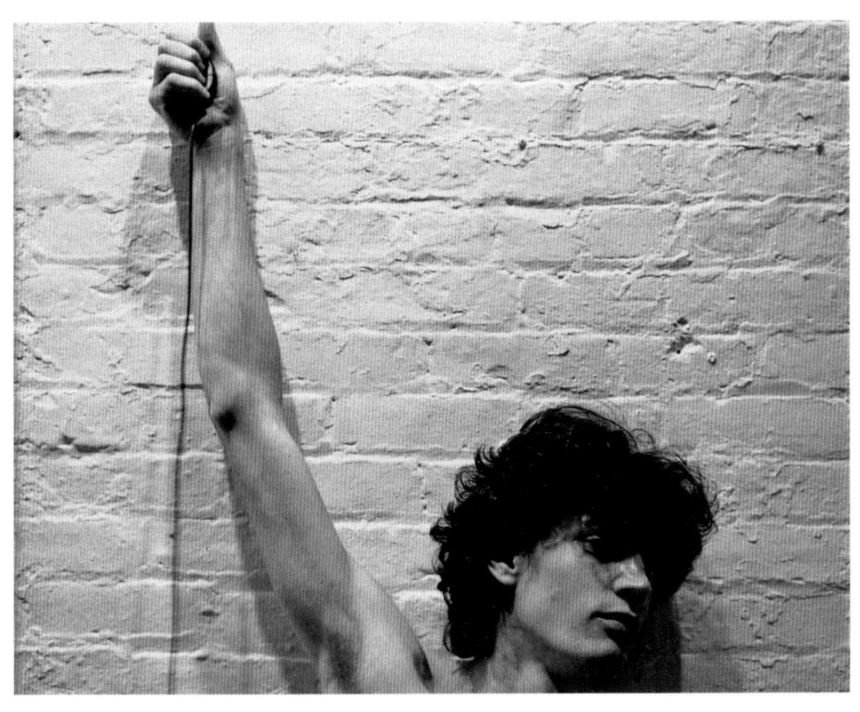

Plate 179. *Untitled (self-portrait)*. 1973/75

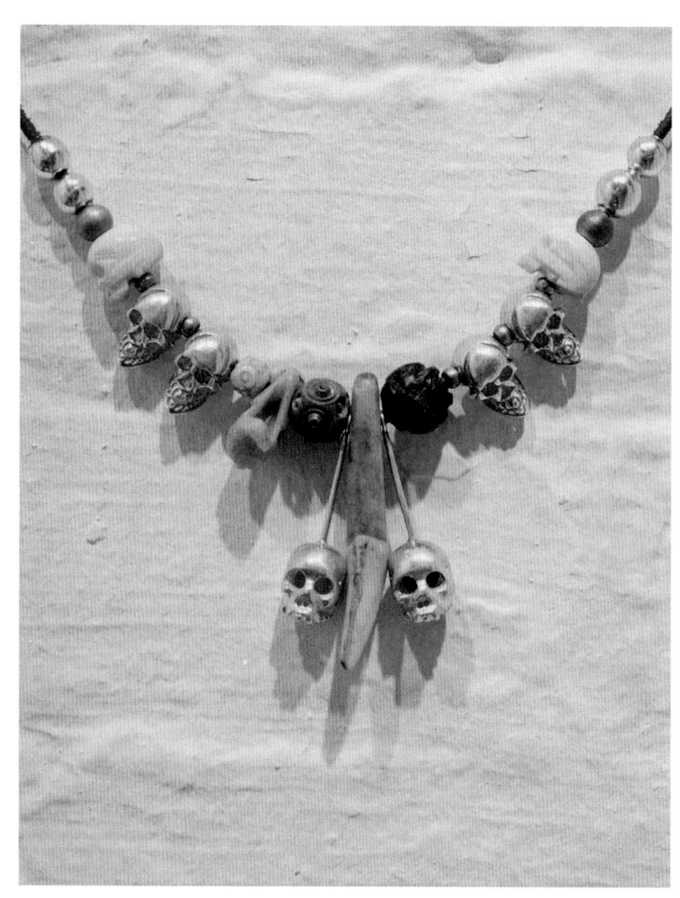

Plate 180. *Untitled*. 1973/75

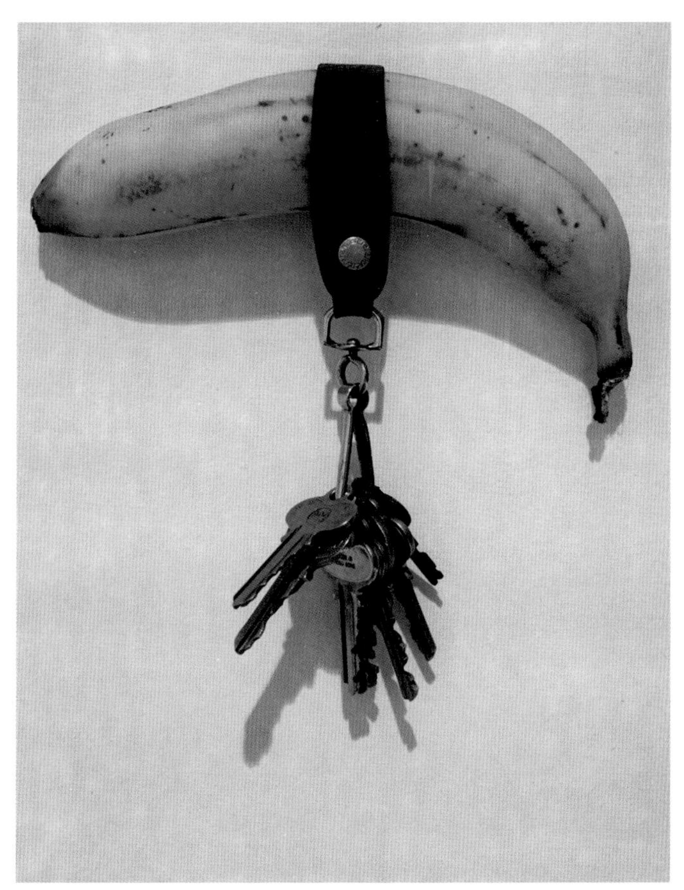

Plate 181. *Untitled*. 1973/75

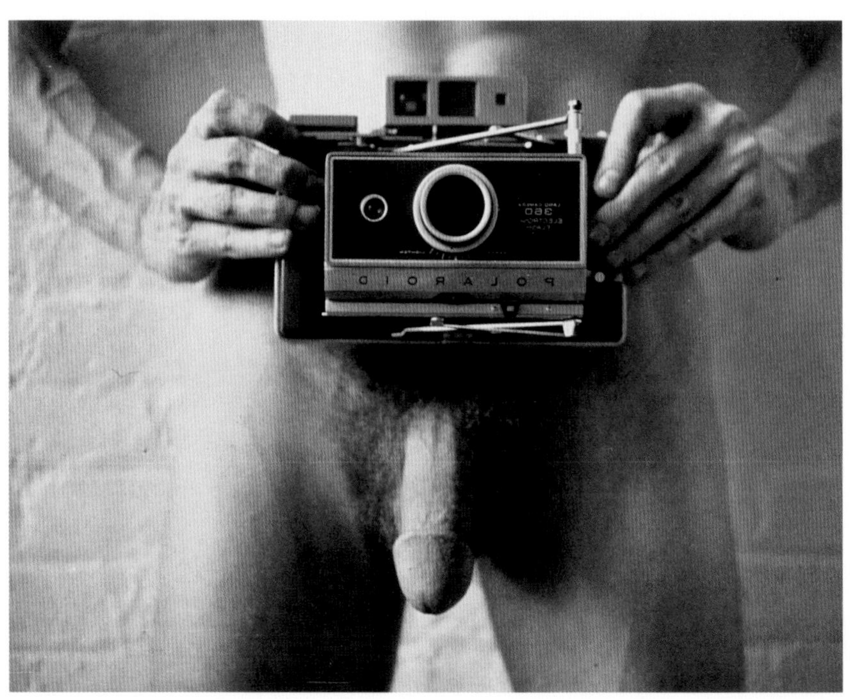

Plate 182. *Untitled (self-portrait)*. 1973

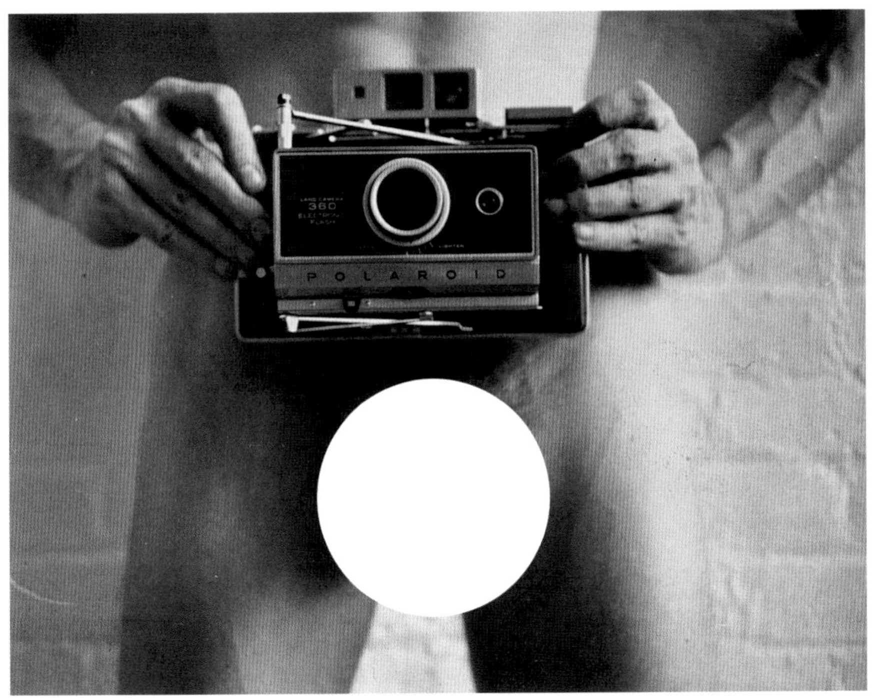

ROBERT MAPPLETHORPE

Plate 183. Invitation to Light Gallery opening, January 6, 1973

Essay Notes

1. Robert Mapplethorpe, quoted in Ingrid Sischy, "A Society First," in Richard Marshall, *Robert Mapplethorpe* (New York: Whitney Museum of American Art and New York Graphic Society Books, and Boston: Little, Brown and Company, 1988), p. 81.

2. Patricia Morrisroe, *Robert Mapplethorpe: A Biography* (New York: Da Capo Press, 1997), p. 27.

3. The photograph albums of Mapplethorpe's father, Harry, which are now owned by Robert's younger brother, Edward, show that he mostly photographed family members and neighborhood events.

4. Mapplethorpe, quoted in Sischy, "A Society First," p. 82.

5. On gay life in New York in the years before the Stonewall Inn incident, see George Chauncey, *Gay New York: Gender, Urban Culture, and the Making of the Gay Male World 1890–1940* (New York: Basic Books, 1994).

6. See Thomas Waugh, *Hard to Imagine: Gay Male Eroticism in Photography and Film from Their Beginnings to Stonewall* (New York: Columbia University Press, 1996).

7. Mapplethorpe told Morrisroe about a particularly memorable exercise in which a pledge was ordered to tie one end of a rope around his penis and the other around a brick, then throw the brick across the room. *A Biography*, p. 31.

8. Ibid., pp. 38–39.

9. Patti Smith, conversation with the author, September 9, 2006.

10. See Morrisroe, *A Biography,* p. 18.

11. Mapplethorpe, quoted in ibid.

12. See Eleanor Heartney, *Postmodern Heretics: The Catholic Imagination in Contemporary Art* (New York: Midmarch Arts Press, 2004), pp. 1–15.

13. Mapplethorpe left Pratt in June of 1969, one credit shy of graduating (he had failed a class earlier that year). He and Smith moved to the Chelsea Hotel the following month. See ibid., pp. 60–63.

14. Mapplethorpe, quoted in ibid, p. 87.

15. Smith often asked Mapplethorpe to photograph her for her own album and book covers, such as her 1973 book of poetry *WITT* and her 1975 album *Horses*.

16. Smith, conversation with the author.

17. Smith, in ibid., and Mapplethorpe's first boyfriend, David Croland, who was the subject of a later emulsion-transfer, have vividly described Mapplethorpe using this process. Croland, conversation with the author, July 11, 2006.

18. The play opened on April 29, 1971, at American Place Theater, New York, and starred both Smith and Sam Shepard. Morrisroe, *A Biography,* p. 94.

19. The Polaroid Model 360 camera used black and white positive/negative film or color film that yielded a $2\frac{7}{8}$-by-$3\frac{3}{4}$-inch image on a $3\frac{1}{4}$-by-$4\frac{1}{4}$-inch sheet. Mapplethorpe used this format until 1973, when he acquired a Graflex and affixed to it a Polaroid back. That camera also took positive/negative film and produced a $3\frac{1}{2}$-by-$4\frac{1}{2}$-inch image on a $4\frac{1}{8}$-by-$5\frac{1}{8}$-inch sheet. Since friends and associates remember that Mapplethorpe stopped using the Model 360 camera when he bought the Graflex, I believe the smaller prints were made from 1970 to 1973 and the larger prints from 1973 to 1975, when Mapplethorpe began to work with a Hasselblad camera and ceased to use Polaroid cameras and film in any regular way.

20. Croland, conversation with the author.

21. Ibid.

22. Mapplethorpe, quoted in Janet Kardon, *Robert Mapplethorpe: The Perfect Moment* (Philadelphia: Institute of Contemporary Art, University of Pennsylvania, 1988), p. 23.

23. The sculpture, by Charles Sargeant Jagger, was made in 1921–25. Picturing wounded and exhausted soldiers, it is not a heroic portrayal of war.

24. Morrisroe, *A Biography*, pp. 108–9.

25. See Richard Saul Wurman, *Polaroid Access: Fifty Years* (Access Press, Ltd., 1989), n.p. The first Polaroid camera (Model 95) was sold on November 26, 1947, for $89.50.

26. See Barbara Hitchcock, *The Polaroid Book: Selections from the Polaroid Collections of Photography* (Cologne: Taschen, 2005).

27. Smith, conversation with the author.

28. In earlier decades, color photographs were made almost exclusively for commercial purposes. The rare exceptions include photographs by Elliot Porter and Ernst Haas.

29. See *Andy Warhol: Photography* (Hamburg: Kunsthalle; Pittsburgh: The Andy Warhol Museum; and Thalwill and Zurich: Stemmle Publishers, 1999), pp. 157–60.

30. Mapplethorpe, in the television documentary *Robert Mapplethorpe* (BBC Television, 1988).

31. Mapplethorpe, quoted in Anne Horton, *Robert Mapplethorpe 1986* (Berlin: Galerie Raab; and Cologne: Kicken-Pauseback, 1986), n.p.

32. Kirk Varnedoe, *Modern Portraits: The Self and Others* (New York: Wildenstein, 1976), p. xix.

33. See Morrisroe, *A Biography,* p. 119.

34. See ibid, p. 118.

35. Mapplethorpe and Wagstaff regularly attended photography auctions in London and Paris starting in 1973. The first photography auction in New York, at Sotheby's, did not take place until 1975.

36. Of the numerous studies of the nude in nineteenth- and twentieth-century art, I found particularly relevant to this project Linda Nochlin's *Representing Women* (New York: Thames & Hudson, 1999) and Abigail Solomon-Godeau's *Male Trouble: A Crisis in Representation* (London: Thames & Hudson, 1999).

37. See Jonathan Miller, *On Reflection* (London: National Gallery, 1998).

38. See *Photographs from the Collection of Robert Mapplethorpe* (New York: Sotheby's, 1982) and *The Collection of Robert Mapplethorpe* (New York: Christie's, 1989). These auctions took place on Monday, May 24, 1982, and Tuesday, October 3, 1989, respectively. Also see *A Book of Photographs from the Collection of Sam Wagstaff* (New York: Gray Press, 1978).

39. See Eadweard Muybridge, *Animal Locomotion* (1887), eleven volumes containing 781 collotype plates of humans, animals, and birds in motion.

40. See *Girl sitting on her bed with her shirt off, NYC* (1968), in *Diane Arbus Revelations* (New York: Random House, 2003), p. 235.

41. See *A Book of Photographs from the Collection of Sam Wagstaff*, p. 126.

42. Mapplethorpe, quoted in Kardon, *The Perfect Moment*, p. 25.

43. See Waugh, *Hard to Imagine*, pp. 176–85.

44. Eugen Sandow was one of the most popular bodybuilders of the late nineteenth century and was photographed striking athletic poses by numerous photographers. While these images were not made for the purpose of homoerotic arousal, they have long been embraced in gay culture. Mapplethorpe, for example, owned an album of forty-seven photographs of Sandow. See Sotheby's auction of Monday, May 24, 1982.

45. See Waugh, *Hard to Imagine*, pp. 176–205.

46. *Physique Pictorial* was one of the best-known of these magazines. It was published by the Los Angeles–based Athletic Model Guild and edited by Bob Mizer, beginning in October 1953.

47. See Waugh, *Hard to Imagine*, pp. 176–253; Vince Aletti, "Let's Get Physical," *The Village Voice Literary Supplement*, July 1986, pp. 8–9; and Aletti, "Boys on Film," *The Village Voice*, August 11, 1992, p. 95.

48. Waugh, *Hard to Imagine*, p. 217.

49. Also known as *The Incredible Torture Show*, directed by Joel M. Reed.

50. Born in Germany as Arnulf Dykman, Peter Berlin was the great-nephew of the photographer George Hoyningen-Huene. He moved to San Francisco in the early 1970s and became known for cruising in clothes he made to enhance his physique.

51. Kenneth Clark, *The Nude: A Study in Ideal Form* (Princeton: Princeton University Press, 1956), pp. 2–29.

52. Mapplethorpe, quoted in Morrisroe, *A Biography*, p. 193.

53. See Susan Sontag, "The Pornographic Imagination," in *Styles of Radical Will* (New York: Farrar, Straus and Giroux, 1969), p. 58.

54. Also in 1963, Warhol made the film *Blow Job*, in which a stationary camera tightly frames the head of a young hustler, recording his facial reactions to oral sex. Because the action remains off-camera, the movie is not explicitly sexual, but the erotic charge is all the stronger for the mystery. See Stephen Koch, *Stargazer: The Life, World and Films of Andy Warhol* (New York: Marion Boyars, 2002).

55. There is no checklist or review of the show on record, according to e-mail correspondence between the author and Harold Jones, director of Light Gallery at the time, and Irene Berger, his assistant, August 1 and 21, 2006.

56. See Marla Prather, *Unrepentant Ego: The Self-Portraits of Lucas Samaras* (New York: Whitney Museum of American Art, 2003), p. 30.

57. See Peter Galassi, *American Photography 1890–1965 from The Museum of Modern Art, New York* (New York: The Museum of Modern Art, 1995), p. 37.

58. These works were auctioned as part of Mapplethorpe's estate in 1989. See The *Collection of Robert Mapplethorpe*.

59. I am grateful to Larry Davis of the SoHo Photo Gallery for confirming the date and content of the Tress exhibition. See *Duane Michals: Photographs, Sequences, Texts 1958–1984* (Oxford: Museum of Modern Art, 1984), n.p.

60. See Stephen Koch's chronology in Urs Stahel and Hripsimé Visser, eds., *Peter Hujar: A Retrospective* (Zurich, Berlin, and New York: Scalo, 1994), p. 198.

61. Philippe Garner, conversation with the author, July 5, 2006. Garner is now International Specialist Head, Photographs and 20th Century Decorative Art and Design, Christie's.

62. "New Documents" also featured work by Lee Friedlander and Garry Winogrand.

63. Mapplethorpe also made sculptural works with these images by encasing a Polaroid of the bottle of champagne in a decorative wooden box and giving it as a gift to friends along with a chilled bottle of the champagne.

64. With this kind of Polaroid film, each sheet of film had to be pulled out of the camera and timed during its development. The negative was then pulled from the positive and placed in a fixing solution. After washing and drying the negative, it could be used to make further prints and enlargements.

65. Smith, conversation with the author.

66. The articles Susan Sontag collected in *On Photography* (New York: Picador, 1977) were written between 1973 and 1977.

67. Walter Benjamin, "The Work of Art in the Age of Mechanical Reproduction," *Illuminations*, ed. Hannah Arendt, trans. Harry Zohn (New York: Shocken Books, 1968). Originally published as *Illuminationen* (Frankfurt: Suhrkamp Verlag, 1955), p. 218.

68. Mapplethorpe began to hire darkroom assistants, including Marcus Leatherdale, Adal Maldonado, and Tom Baril, in 1979.

69. I am grateful to Matthew Lyons, Assistant Curator at The Kitchen, for his archival research on this show, and to Thomas Solomon, who consulted the Holly Solomon Gallery archives.

70. See Morrisroe, *A Biography*, p. 217.

71. Mapplethorpe, postcard to Croland, October 27, 1971, in the collection of Croland. Homem, conversation with the author, January 5, 2007.

Plate List

Because Mapplethorpe's Polaroids are not dated or signed, it is impossible to securely position each and every one along an accurate timeline. The format of the pictures, however, provides a rough guide to when they were made. Mapplethorpe worked from 1970 to 1973 with a Model 360 Polaroid camera, which took black-and-white or color film that yielded a 2⅞ x 3¾–inch image on a 3¼ x 4¼–inch sheet. In 1973 he acquired a Graflex, which produced a larger image, 3½ x 4½ inches on a 4⅛ x 5⅛–inch sheet. Mapplethorpe's friends and associates remember that he stopped using the Model 360 camera in any regular way after that, so I am proposing that the smaller prints were made from 1970 to 1973 and the larger prints from 1973 to 1975. In some cases, more exact dating is made possible by additional facts, such as when Mapplethorpe met a subject, or by information gathered through interviews with those who were present around the time an image was made. Because a Polaroid print is unique and not an enlargement, the dimensions below refer to the whole sheet; for framed objects, height precedes width precedes depth. —SW

1. *Untitled (self-portrait)*. 1971
Three monochromatic dye diffusion transfer prints (Polaroids) and spray paint on paper potato sack in wood frame
25⅜ x 16¼ x 1½ in. (64.5 x 41.3 x 3.8 cm)
Collection Charles Cowles (UC024)

2. *Untitled (Patti Smith)*. 1970
Four monochromatic dye diffusion transfer prints (Polaroids) with pigment in painted plastic mounts and Plexiglas frame
5½ x 15 x 1 in. (14 x 38.1 x 2.5 cm)
Robert Mapplethorpe Foundation (U191)

3. *Patti Smith (Don't Touch Here)*. 1973
Four monochromatic dye diffusion transfer prints (Polaroids) and paper in painted plastic mounts and Plexiglas frame
5½ x 18¾ x 1 in. (14 x 47.6 x 2.5 cm)
Private collection (U309)

4. *Untitled (Patti Smith)*. 1971
Internal dye diffusion transfer print (Polaroid)
4¼ x 3¼ in. (10.8 x 8.3 cm)
Robert Mapplethorpe Foundation (PD468)

5. *Untitled (Patti Smith)*. 1971/73
Internal dye diffusion transfer print (Polaroid)
4¼ x 3¼ in. (10.8 x 8.3 cm)
Private collection (PD132)

6. *Candy Darling*. 1973
Four monochromatic dye diffusion transfer prints (Polaroids) in painted plastic mounts and Plexiglas frame
5½ x 15 x 1⅝ in. (14 x 38.1 x 2.5 cm)
Solomon R. Guggenheim Museum, Gift, Robert Mapplethorpe Foundation (95.4306; U155)

7. *Untitled (Candy Darling)*. 1971/73
Internal dye diffusion transfer print (Polaroid)
3¼ x 4¼ in. (8.3 x 10.8 cm)
Private collection (PD430)

8. *Untitled (Sam Wagstaff)*. 1972/73
Internal dye diffusion transfer print (Polaroid)
3¼ x 4¼ in. (8.3 x 10.8 cm)
Private collection, courtesy Xavier Hufkens, Brussels (PD149)

9. *Untitled (Sam Wagstaff)*. 1973/75
Internal dye diffusion transfer print (Polaroid)
5⅛ x 4⅛ in. (13 x 10.5 cm)
Robert Mapplethorpe Foundation (PD196)

10. *Untitled (self-portrait)*. 1970/73
Three monochromatic dye diffusion transfer prints (Polaroids) with pigment in plastic sleeve
3¼ x 4¼ in. (8.3 x 10.8 cm) each
Private collection (PD438)

11. *Untitled*. 1970/73
Three internal dye diffusion transfer prints (Polaroids) in plastic sleeve
4¼ x 3¼ in. (10.8 x 8.3 cm) each
Private collection (PD504)

12. *Untitled*. 1970/73
Internal dye diffusion transfer print (Polaroid)
4¼ x 3¼ in. (10.8 x 8.3 cm)
Collection Tony Bonakdar (PD261)

13. *Untitled*. 1970/73
Internal dye diffusion transfer print (Polaroid)
4¼ x 3¼ in. (10.8 x 8.3 cm)
Private collection (PD188)

14. *Untitled*. 1975
Internal dye diffusion transfer print (Polaroid)
4¼ x 3½ in. (10.8 x 8.9 cm)
Robert Mapplethorpe Foundation (PD432)

15. *Untitled*. 1975
Internal dye diffusion transfer print (Polaroid)
4¼ x 3½ in. (10.8 x 8.9 cm)
Robert Mapplethorpe Foundation (PD467)

16. *Untitled*. 1970/73
Monochromatic dye diffusion transfer print (Polaroid)
3¼ x 4¼ in. (8.3 x 10.8 cm)
Robert Mapplethorpe Foundation (PD539)

17. *Untitled.* 1971/73
Monochromatic dye diffusion transfer print (Polaroid)
3¼ x 4¼ in. (8.3 x 10.8 cm)
Robert Mapplethorpe Foundation (PD554)

18. *Untitled.* 1971/73
Monochromatic dye diffusion transfer print (Polaroid)
3¼ x 4¼ in. (8.3 x 10.8 cm)
Robert Mapplethorpe Foundation (PD526)

19. *Untitled.* 1971/73
Monochromatic dye diffusion transfer print (Polaroid)
3¼ x 4¼ in. (8.3 x 10.8 cm)
Robert Mapplethorpe Foundation (PD177)

20. *Untitled.* 1970/73
Monochromatic dye diffusion transfer print (Polaroid)
3¼ x 4¼ in. (8.3 x 10.8 cm)
Robert Mapplethorpe Foundation (PD547)

21. *Untitled.* 1970/73
Monochromatic dye diffusion transfer print (Polaroid)
3¼ x 4¼ in. (8.3 x 10.8 cm)
Robert Mapplethorpe Foundation (PD546)

22. *Untitled (Catherine Tennant's House, London).* 1973
Monochromatic dye diffusion transfer print (Polaroid)
3¼ x 4¼ in. (8.3 x 10.8 cm)
Private collection (PD251)

23. *Untitled (Catherine Tennant's House, London).* 1973
Monochromatic dye diffusion transfer print (Polaroid)
4¼ x 3¼ in. (10.8 x 8.3 cm)
Collection Galerie Stefan Röpke, Cologne (PD33)

24. *Untitled (Catherine Tennant's House, London).* 1973
Monochromatic dye diffusion transfer print (Polaroid)
3¼ x 4¼ in. (8.3 x 10.8 cm)
Robert Mapplethorpe Foundation (PD265)

25. *Untitled.* 1973
Monochromatic dye diffusion transfer print (Polaroid)
3¼ x 4¼ in. (8.3 x 10.8 cm)
Robert Mapplethorpe Foundation (PD552)

26. *Untitled.* 1970/73
Monochromatic dye diffusion transfer print (Polaroid)
3¼ x 4¼ in. (8.3 x 10.8 cm)
Robert Mapplethorpe Foundation (PD564)

27. *Untitled.* 1973/75
Monochromatic dye diffusion transfer print (Polaroid)
5⅛ x 4⅛ in. (13 x 10.5 cm)
Robert Mapplethorpe Foundation (PD599)

28. *Untitled.* 1970/73
Monochromatic dye diffusion transfer print (Polaroid)
4¼ x 3¼ in. (10.8 x 8.3 cm)
Robert Mapplethorpe Foundation (PD42)

29. *Untitled.* 1970/73
Monochromatic dye diffusion transfer print (Polaroid)
4¼ x 3¼ in. (10.8 x 8.3 cm)
Robert Mapplethorpe Foundation (PD48)

30. *Untitled (Patti Smith).* 1973
Monochromatic dye diffusion transfer print (Polaroid)
3¼ x 4¼ in. (8.3 x 10.8 cm)
Robert Mapplethorpe Foundation (PD359)

31. *Untitled (Patti Smith).* 1973
Monochromatic dye diffusion transfer print (Polaroid)
3¼ x 4¼ in. (8.3 x 10.8 cm)
Robert Mapplethorpe Foundation (PD363)

32. *Untitled (Patti Smith).* 1973/75
Monochromatic dye diffusion transfer print (Polaroid)
5⅛ x 4⅛ in. (13 x 10.5 cm)
Private collection (PD63)

33. *Untitled (Patti Smith).* 1973/75
Monochromatic dye diffusion transfer print (Polaroid)
5⅛ x 4⅛ in. (13 x 10.5 cm)
Private collection (PD398)

34. *Untitled (Patti Smith).* 1973/75
Monochromatic dye diffusion transfer print (Polaroid)
5⅛ x 4⅛ in. (13 x 10.5 cm)
Collection James Lahey (PD194)

35. *Untitled (Patti Smith).* 1973/75
Monochromatic dye diffusion transfer print (Polaroid)
5⅛ x 4⅛ in. (13 x 10.5 cm)
Private collection, Switzerland (PD16)

36. *Untitled (Patti Smith).* 1970/73
Monochromatic dye diffusion transfer print (Polaroid)
4¼ x 3¼ in. (10.8 x 8.3 cm)
Robert Mapplethorpe Foundation (PD407)

37. *Untitled (Patti Smith).* 1973/75
Monochromatic dye diffusion transfer print (Polaroid)
5⅛ x 4⅛ in. (13 x 10.5 cm)
Collection Michael Bentele (PD1)

38. *Untitled (Patti Smith).* 1973/75
Monochromatic dye diffusion transfer print (Polaroid)
5⅛ x 4⅛ in. (13 x 10.5 cm)
Private collection (PD392)

39. *Untitled (Patti Smith).* 1973/75
Monochromatic dye diffusion transfer print (Polaroid)
5⅛ x 4⅛ in. (13 x 10.5 cm)
Collection Dmitri Levas

40. *Untitled (Patti Smith).* 1970/73
Monochromatic dye diffusion transfer print (Polaroid)
4¼ x 3¼ in. (10.8 x 8.3 cm)
Private collection (PD364)

41. *Untitled (Patti Smith)*. 1970/73
Monochromatic dye diffusion transfer print (Polaroid)
4¼ x 3¼ in. (10.8 x 8.3 cm)
Private collection (PD380)

42. *Untitled (self-portrait)*. 1970/73
Monochromatic dye diffusion transfer print (Polaroid)
4¼ x 3¼ in. (10.8 x 8.3 cm)
Robert Mapplethorpe Foundation (PD325)

43. *Untitled (self-portrait)*. 1970/73
Monochromatic dye diffusion transfer print (Polaroid)
4¼ x 3¼ in. (10.8 x 8.3 cm)
Private collection (PD117)

44. *Untitled (self-portrait)*. 1970/73
Monochromatic dye diffusion transfer print (Polaroid)
4¼ x 3¼ in. (10.8 x 8.3 cm)
Private collection (PD315)

45. *Untitled (self-portrait)*. 1972/73
Monochromatic dye diffusion transfer print (Polaroid)
4¼ x 3¼ in. (10.8 x 8.3 cm)
Private collection (PD104)

46. *Untitled*. 1971/72
Monochromatic dye diffusion transfer print (Polaroid)
4¼ x 3¼ in. (10.8 x 8.3 cm)
Robert Mapplethorpe Foundation (PD538)

47. *Untitled*. 1970/73
Monochromatic dye diffusion transfer print (Polaroid)
4¼ x 3¼ in. (10.8 x 8.3 cm)
Private collection (PD14)

48. *Untitled (self-portrait)*. 1972
Monochromatic dye diffusion transfer print (Polaroid)
3¼ x 4¼ in. (8.3 x 10.8 cm)
Solomon R. Guggenheim Museum, Gift, Robert Mapplethorpe Foundation (93.4268; PD44)

49. *Untitled (self-portrait)*. 1970/73
Monochromatic dye diffusion transfer print (Polaroid)
3¼ x 4¼ in. (8.3 x 10.8 cm)
Whitney Museum of American Art, Purchase, with funds from Elizabeth Kabler and Raymond W. Merritt (2001.10; PD344)

50. *Untitled*. 1973
Monochromatic dye diffusion transfer print (Polaroid)
5⅛ x 4⅛ in. (13 x 10.5 cm)
Private collection (PD227)

51. *Untitled*. 1973
Monochromatic dye diffusion transfer print (Polaroid)
5⅛ x 4⅛ in. (13 x 10.5 cm)
Private collection, courtesy Baudoin Lebon, Paris (PD129)

52. *Untitled (self-portrait)*. 1973
Monochromatic dye diffusion transfer print (Polaroid)
5⅛ x 4⅛ in. (13 x 10.5 cm)
Private collection (PD342)

53. *Untitled (self-portrait)*. 1973
Monochromatic dye diffusion transfer print (Polaroid)
5⅛ x 4⅛ in. (13 x 10.5 cm)
Private collection (PD192)

54. *Untitled (self-portrait)*. 1973
Monochromatic dye diffusion transfer print (Polaroid)
5⅛ x 4⅛ in. (13 x 10.5 cm)
Private collection, courtesy Baudoin Lebon, Paris (PD39)

55. *Untitled (self-portrait)*. 1973
Monochromatic dye diffusion transfer print (Polaroid)
5⅛ x 4⅛ in. (13 x 10.5 cm)
Private collection (PD146)

56. *Untitled (Sam Wagstaff)*. 1973/75
Monochromatic dye diffusion transfer print (Polaroid PolaPan 4x5 film Type 52)
4¼ x 5¼ in. (10.5 x 13 cm). Courtesy of the Polaroid Collections (79:591:14)

57. *Untitled (Sam Wagstaff)*. 1973
Monochromatic dye diffusion transfer print (Polaroid)
4⅛ x 5⅛ in. (10.5 x 13 cm)
Collection Bruce Weber (PD25)

58. *Untitled (Sam Wagstaff)*. 1972/73
Monochromatic dye diffusion transfer print (Polaroid)
4¼ x 3¼ in. (10.8 x 8.3 cm)
Robert Mapplethorpe Foundation (PD178)

59. *Untitled (Sam Wagstaff)*. 1973/75
Monochromatic dye diffusion transfer print (Polaroid)
5⅛ x 4⅛ in. (13 x 10.5 cm)
Robert Mapplethorpe Foundation (PD197)

60. *Untitled*. 1973/75
Monochromatic dye diffusion transfer print (Polaroid)
4⅛ x 5⅛ in. (10.5 x 13 cm)
Collection Judy Linn

61. *Untitled*. 1973/75
Monochromatic dye diffusion transfer print (Polaroid)
4⅛ x 5⅛ in. (10.5 x 13 cm)
Robert Mapplethorpe Foundation (PD464)

62. *Untitled*. 1973/75
Monochromatic dye diffusion transfer print (Polaroid)
5⅛ x 4⅛ in. (13 x 10.5 cm)
Private collection, courtesy Gallery Xavier Hufkens, Brussels (PD280)

63. *Untitled (Constantine Hotel)*. 1973/75
Monochromatic dye diffusion transfer print (Polaroid)
5⅛ x 4⅛ in. (13 x 10.5 cm)
The Paul Rusconi Collection, Los Angeles (PD12)

64. *Untitled*. 1970/73
Monochromatic dye diffusion transfer print (Polaroid)
3¼ x 4¼ in. (8.3 x 10.8 cm)
Robert Mapplethorpe Foundation (PD563)

65. *Untitled (Helen Marden's Bats)*. 1973/75
Monochromatic dye diffusion transfer print (Polaroid)
5⅛ x 4⅛ in. (13 x 10.5 cm)
Robert Mapplethorpe Foundation (PD485)

66. *Untitled*. 1970/73
Monochromatic dye diffusion transfer print (Polaroid)
3¼ x 4¼ in. (8.3 x 10.8 cm)
Robert Mapplethorpe Foundation (PD429)

67. *Untitled*. 1970/73
Monochromatic dye diffusion transfer print (Polaroid)
3¼ x 4¼ in. (8.3 x 10.8 cm)
Robert Mapplethorpe Foundation (PD275)

68. *Untitled*. 1973/75
Monochromatic dye diffusion transfer print (Polaroid)
5⅛ x 4⅛ in. (13 x 10.5 cm)
Solomon R. Guggenheim Museum, Gift, Robert Mapplethorpe Foundation (93.4270; PD3)

69. *Untitled*. 1973/75
Monochromatic dye diffusion transfer print (Polaroid)
5⅛ x 4⅛ in. (13 x 10.5 cm)
Robert Mapplethorpe Foundation (PD568)

70. *Untitled*. 1973/75
Monochromatic dye diffusion transfer print (Polaroid)
4⅛ x 5⅛ in. (10.5 x 13 cm)
Collection Joan and Michael Salke (PD34)

71. *Untitled (self-portrait)*. 1973/75
Monochromatic dye diffusion transfer print (Polaroid)
4⅛ x 5⅛ in. (10.5 x 13 cm)
Robert Mapplethorpe Foundation (PD328)

72. *Untitled*. 1973/75
Monochromatic dye diffusion transfer print (Polaroid)
5⅛ x 4⅛ in. (13 x 10.5 cm)
Robert Mapplethorpe Foundation (PD215)

73. *Untitled*. 1970/73
Monochromatic dye diffusion transfer print (Polaroid)
4¼ x 3¼ in. (10.8 x 8.3 cm)
Robert Mapplethorpe Foundation (PD426)

74. *Untitled (Jamie)*. 1970/73
Monochromatic dye diffusion transfer print (Polaroid)
4¼ x 3¼ in. (10.8 x 8.3 cm)
Robert Mapplethorpe Foundation (PD56)

75. *Untitled (Jamie)*. 1970/73
Monochromatic dye diffusion transfer print (Polaroid)
4¼ x 3¼ in. (10.8 x 8.3 cm)
Robert Mapplethorpe Foundation (PD453)

76. *Untitled (Michael)*. 1973/75
Monochromatic dye diffusion transfer print (Polaroid)
5⅛ x 4⅛ in. (13 x 10.5 cm)
Robert Mapplethorpe Foundation (PD41)

77. *Untitled*. 1970/73
Monochromatic dye diffusion transfer print (Polaroid)
4¼ x 3¼ in. (10.8 x 8.3 cm)
Robert Mapplethorpe Foundation (PD57)

78. *Untitled (Jay Johnson, London)*. 1973
Monochromatic dye diffusion transfer print (Polaroid)
4¼ x 3¼ in. (10.8 x 8.3 cm)
Robert Mapplethorpe Foundation (PD80)

79. *Untitled (Nicholas Black, London)*. 1973
Monochromatic dye diffusion transfer print (Polaroid)
4¼ x 3¼ in. (10.8 x 8.3 cm)
Robert Mapplethorpe Foundation (PD490)

80. *Untitled (Randy)*. 1973/75
Monochromatic dye diffusion transfer print (Polaroid)
5⅛ x 4⅛ in. (13 x 10.5 cm)
Robert Mapplethorpe Foundation (PD72)

81. *Untitled (Randy)*. 1973/75
Monochromatic dye diffusion transfer print (Polaroid)
5⅛ x 4⅛ in. (13 x 10.5 cm)
Robert Mapplethorpe Foundation (PD609)

82. *Untitled (Jay Johnson)*. 1970
Monochromatic dye diffusion transfer print (Polaroid)
3¼ x 4¼ in. (8.3 x 10.8 cm)
Private collection (PD448)

83. *Untitled (François)*. 1973/75
Monochromatic dye diffusion transfer print (Polaroid)
4⅛ x 5⅛ in. (10.5 x 13 cm)
Robert Mapplethorpe Foundation (PD604)

84. *Untitled (Stewart Foster)*. 1973/75
Monochromatic dye diffusion transfer print (Polaroid)
5⅛ x 4⅛ in. (13 x 10.5 cm)
Private collection, courtesy Xavier Hufkens, Brussels (PD245)

85. *Untitled (Stewart Foster)*. 1973/75
Monochromatic dye diffusion transfer print (Polaroid)
5⅛ x 4⅛ in. (13 x 10.5 cm)
Robert Mapplethorpe Foundation (PD610)

86. *Untitled (Nicholas, London)*. 1973
Monochromatic dye diffusion transfer print (Polaroid)
3¼ x 4¼ in. (8.3 x 10.8 cm)
Robert Mapplethorpe Foundation (PD551)

87. *Untitled*. 1973/75
Monochromatic dye diffusion transfer print (Polaroid)
5⅛ x 4⅛ in. (13 x 10.5 cm)
Private collection (PD11)

88. *Untitled*. 1973/75
Gelatin-silver print from Polaroid negative
4¼ x 3¼ in. (10.8 x 8.3 cm)
Robert Mapplethorpe Foundation (U406)

89. *Untitled (Boaz Mazor)*. 1973/75
Monochromatic dye diffusion transfer print (Polaroid)
5⅛ x 4⅛ in. (13 x 10.5 cm)
Collection James Magni and Todd Williamson (PD213)

90. *Untitled*. 1973/75
Monochromatic dye diffusion transfer print (Polaroid)
5⅛ x 4⅛ in. (13 x 10.5 cm)
Private collection (PD253)

91. *Untitled*. 1973/75
Monochromatic dye diffusion transfer print (Polaroid)
5⅛ x 4⅛ in. (13 x 10.5 cm)
Private collection (PD143)

92. *Untitled*. 1970/73
Monochromatic dye diffusion transfer print (Polaroid)
4¼ x 3¼ in. (10.8 x 8.3 cm)
Private collection (PD36)

93. *Untitled*. 1973/75
Monochromatic dye diffusion transfer print (Polaroid)
5⅛ x 4⅛ in. (13 x 10.5 cm)
Robert Mapplethorpe Foundation (PD174)

94. *Untitled*. 1970/73
Monochromatic dye diffusion transfer print (Polaroid)
3¼ x 4¼ in. (8.3 x 10.8 cm)
Private collection (PD172)

95. *Untitled (Jamie)*. 1973/75
Monochromatic dye diffusion transfer print (Polaroid)
4⅛ x 5⅛ in. (10.5 x 13 cm)
Robert Mapplethorpe Foundation (PD592)

96. *Untitled (Enrique Maza)*. 1970/73
Monochromatic dye diffusion transfer print (Polaroid)
3¼ x 4¼ in. (8.3 x 10.8 cm)
Robert Mapplethorpe Foundation (PD81)

97. *Untitled*. 1970/73
Monochromatic dye diffusion transfer print (Polaroid)
3¼ x 4¼ in. (8.3 x 10.8 cm)
Robert Mapplethorpe Foundation (PD84)

98. *Untitled (Eddie)*. 1973
Monochromatic dye diffusion transfer print (Polaroid)
4¼ x 3¼ in. (10.8 x 8.3 cm)
Robert Mapplethorpe Foundation (PD566)

99. *Untitled (Eddie)*. 1973
Monochromatic dye diffusion transfer print (Polaroid)
4¼ x 3¼ in. (10.8 x 8.3 cm)
Robert Mapplethorpe Foundation (PD567)

100. *Untitled*. 1973
Monochromatic dye diffusion transfer print (Polaroid)
5⅛ x 4⅛ in. (13 x 10.5 cm)
Robert Mapplethorpe Foundation (PD591)

101. *Untitled*. 1973
Monochromatic dye diffusion transfer print (Polaroid)
5⅛ x 4⅛ in. (13 x 10.5 cm)
Robert Mapplethorpe Foundation (PD572)

102. Untitled. 1973/75
Monochromatic dye diffusion transfer print (Polaroid)
5⅛ x 4⅛ in. (13 x 10.5 cm)
Robert Mapplethorpe Foundation (PD542)

103. *Untitled*. 1973/75
Monochromatic dye diffusion transfer print (Polaroid)
5⅛ x 4⅛ in. (13 x 10.5 cm)
Robert Mapplethorpe Foundation (PD469)

104. *Untitled*. 1970/73
Monochromatic dye diffusion transfer print (Polaroid)
3¼ x 4¼ in. (8.3 x 10.8 cm)
Robert Mapplethorpe Foundation (PD529)

105. *Untitled (Diane)*. 1973/75
Monochromatic dye diffusion transfer print (Polaroid)
5⅛ x 4⅛ in. (13 x 10.5 cm)
Robert Mapplethorpe Foundation (PD2)

106. *Untitled (Diane)*. 1973/75
Monochromatic dye diffusion transfer print (Polaroid)
5⅛ x 4⅛ in. (13 x 10.5 cm)
Robert Mapplethorpe Foundation (PD541)

107. *Untitled (Lucy, Paris)*. 1971/73
Monochromatic dye diffusion transfer print (Polaroid)
3¼ x 4¼ in. (8.3 x 10.8 cm)
Private collection (PD58)

108. *Untitled (Lucy, Paris)*. 1971/73
Monochromatic dye diffusion transfer print (Polaroid)
4¼ x 3¼ in. (10.8 x 8.3 cm)
Robert Mapplethorpe Foundation (PD550)

109. *Untitled*. 1970
Monochromatic dye diffusion transfer print (Polaroid)
4¼ x 3¼ in. (10.8 x 8.3 cm)
Private collection, courtesy Gallery Xavier Hufkens, Brussels (PD374)

110. *Untitled*. 1970/73
Monochromatic dye diffusion transfer print (Polaroid)
4¼ x 3¼ in. (10.8 x 8.3 cm)
Robert Mapplethorpe Foundation (Detail, PD534.3)

111. Untitled. 1973-75
Monochromatic dye diffusion transfer print
(Polaroid PolaPan 4x5 film Type 52)
5¾ x 4¼ in. (14.6 x 10.8 cm). Courtesy of the Polaroid Collections (79:591:16)

112. *Untitled (Lucy, Paris)*. 1971/73
Monochromatic dye diffusion transfer print (Polaroid)
4¼ x 3¼ in. (10.8 x 8.3 cm)
Private collection (PD224)

113. *Untitled (Lucy, Paris)*. 1971/73
Monochromatic dye diffusion transfer print (Polaroid)
4¼ x 3¼ in. (10.8 x 8.3 cm)
Private collection, courtesy Gallery Xavier Hufkens, Brussels (PD225)

114. *Untitled (Lucy, Paris)*. 1971/73
Monochromatic dye diffusion transfer print (Polaroid)
3¼ x 4¼ in. (8.3 x 10.8 cm)
Robert Mapplethorpe Foundation (PD218)

115. *Untitled (Lucy and Fred, Paris)*. 1971/73
Monochromatic dye diffusion transfer print (Polaroid)
4¼ x 3¼ in. (10.8 x 8.3 cm)
Robert Mapplethorpe Foundation (PD540)

116. *Untitled (The Dancer)*. 1974
Monochromatic dye diffusion transfer print (Polaroid)
5⅛ x 4⅛ in. (13 x 10.5 cm)
Robert Mapplethorpe Foundation (Detail, U313)

117. *Untitled (The Dancer)*. 1974
Monochromatic dye diffusion transfer print (Polaroid)
5⅛ x 4⅛ in. (13 x 10.5 cm)
Robert Mapplethorpe Foundation (PD484)

118. *Untitled (The Dancer)*. 1974
Monochromatic dye diffusion transfer print (Polaroid)
5⅛ x 4 ⅛ in. (13 x 10.5 cm)
Private collection (PD148)

119. *Untitled (The Dancer)*. 1974
Monochromatic dye diffusion transfer print (Polaroid)
5⅛ x 4⅛ in. (13 x 10.5 cm)
Private collection (PD483)

120. *Untitled (The Dancer)*. 1974
Monochromatic dye diffusion transfer print (Polaroid)
5⅛ x 4⅛ in. (13 x 10.5 cm)
Collection James Lahey (PD336)

121. *Untitled (The Dancer)*. 1974
Monochromatic dye diffusion transfer print (Polaroid)
5⅛ x 4⅛ in. (13 x 10.5 cm)
Robert Mapplethorpe Foundation (PD341)

122. *Untitled (Gyles Fontaine)*. 1974
Monochromatic dye diffusion transfer print (Polaroid)
5⅛ x 4⅛ in. (13 x 10.5 cm)
Robert Mapplethorpe Foundation (PD531)

123. *Untitled (Gyles Fontaine)*. 1974
Monochromatic dye diffusion transfer print (Polaroid)
5⅛ x 4⅛ in. (13 x 10.5 cm)
Robert Mapplethorpe Foundation (PD533)

124. *Untitled (Peter Berlin)*. 1974
Monochromatic dye diffusion transfer print (Polaroid)
5⅛ x 4⅛ in. (13 x 10.5 cm)
Robert Mapplethorpe Foundation (PD524)

125. *Untitled (Peter Berlin)*. 1974
Monochromatic dye diffusion transfer print (Polaroid)
5⅛ x 4⅛ in. (13 x 10.5 cm)
Private collection (PD254)

126. *Untitled*. 1970/73
Monochromatic dye diffusion transfer print (Polaroid)
3¼ x 4¼ in. (8.3 x 10.8 cm)
Robert Mapplethorpe Foundation (PD459)

127. *Untitled*. 1973/75
Monochromatic dye diffusion transfer print (Polaroid)
5⅛ x 4⅛ in. (13 x 10.5 cm)
Robert Mapplethorpe Foundation (PD53)

128. *Untitled (Manfred)*. 1974
Monochromatic dye diffusion transfer print (Polaroid)
5⅛ x 4⅛ in. (13 x 10.5 cm)
Robert Mapplethorpe Foundation (PD530)

129. *Untitled (Manfred)*. 1974
Monochromatic dye diffusion transfer print (Polaroid)
5⅛ x 4⅛ in. (13 x 10.5 cm)
Robert Mapplethorpe Foundation (PD211)

130. *Untitled*. 1970/73
Monochromatic dye diffusion transfer print (Polaroid)
3¼ x 4¼ in. (8.3 x 10.8 cm)
Private collection, courtesy Gallery Xavier Hufkens, Brussels (PD51)

131. *Untitled (La Serpentine)*. 1971
Monochromatic dye diffusion transfer print (Polaroid)
4¼ x 3¼ in. (10.8 x 8.3 cm)
Private collection, courtesy Gallery Xavier Hufkens, Brussels (PD173)

132. *Untitled*. 1970/73
Monochromatic dye diffusion transfer print (Polaroid)
4¼ x 3¼ in. (10.8 x 8.3 cm)
Robert Mapplethorpe Foundation (PD136)

133. *Untitled*. 1970/73
Monochromatic dye diffusion transfer print (Polaroid)
3¼ x 4¼ in. (8.3 x 10.8 x 8.3 cm)
Collection A. G. Rosen (PD444)

134. *Untitled*. 1973/75
Monochromatic dye diffusion transfer print (Polaroid)
5⅛ x 4⅛ in. (13 x 10.5 cm)
Robert Mapplethorpe Foundation (PD10)

135. *Untitled*. 1973/75
Monochromatic dye diffusion transfer print (Polaroid)
5⅛ x 4⅛ in. (13 x 10.5 cm)
Robert Mapplethorpe Foundation (PD290)

136. *Untitled*. 1970/73
Monochromatic dye diffusion transfer print (Polaroid)
3¼ x 4¼ in. (8.3 x 10.8 cm)
Robert Mapplethorpe Foundation (PD545)

137. *Untitled (Peter Berlin)*. 1973/75
Monochromatic dye diffusion transfer print (Polaroid)
5⅛ x 4⅛ in. (13 x 10.5 cm)
Private collection (PD210)

138. *Untitled (self-portrait)*. 1970/73
Monochromatic dye diffusion transfer print (Polaroid)
4¼ x 3¼ in. (10.8 x 8.3 cm)
Solomon R. Guggenheim Museum, Gift, Robert Mapplethorpe Foundation (93.4272; PD116)

139. *Untitled. 1973/75*
Monochromatic dye diffusion transfer print (Polaroid)
5⅛ x 4⅛ in. (13 x 10.5 cm)
Private collection (PD208)

140. *Untitled*. 1973
Monochromatic dye diffusion transfer print (Polaroid)
3¼ x 4¼ in. (8.3 x 10.8 cm)
Robert Mapplethorpe Foundation (PD168)

141. *Untitled*. 1973
Monochromatic dye diffusion transfer print (Polaroid)
3¼ x 4¼ in. (8.3 x 10.8 cm)
Robert Mapplethorpe Foundation (PD167)

142. *Untitled*. 1973
Monochromatic dye diffusion transfer print (Polaroid)
3¼ x 4¼ in. (8.3 x 10.8 cm)
Private collection (PD165)

143. *Untitled*. 1973
Monochromatic dye diffusion transfer print (Polaroid)
3¼ x 4¼ in. (8.3 x 10.8 cm)
Collection James White (PD38)

144. *Untitled (self-portrait)*. 1972
Monochromatic dye diffusion transfer print (Polaroid)
4¼ x 3¼ in. (10.8 x 8.3 cm)
Solomon R. Guggenheim Museum, Gift, Robert Mapplethorpe Foundation (93.4269; PD101)

145. *Untitled*. 1973/75
Monochromatic dye diffusion transfer print (Polaroid)
5⅛ x 4⅛ in. (13 x 10.5 cm)
Robert Mapplethorpe Foundation (PD19)

146. *Untitled (Charles and Jim)*. 1973
Monochromatic dye diffusion transfer print (Polaroid)
4⅛ x 5⅛ in. (10.5 x 13 cm)
Robert Mapplethorpe Foundation (PD155)

147. *Untitled (Charles and Jim)*. 1973
Monochromatic dye diffusion transfer print (Polaroid)
4⅛ x 5⅛ in. (10.5 x 13 cm)
Robert Mapplethorpe Foundation (PD158)

148. *Untitled (Charles and Jim)*. 1973
Monochromatic dye diffusion transfer print (Polaroid)
4⅛ x 5⅛ in. (10.5 x 13 cm)
Robert Mapplethorpe Foundation (PD149.2)

149. *Untitled (Charles and Jim)*. 1973
Monochromatic dye diffusion transfer print (Polaroid)
4¼ x 3¼ in. (10.8 x 8.3 cm)
Robert Mapplethorpe Foundation (PD458)

150. *Untitled (Gyles Fontaine)*. 1973/75
Monochromatic dye diffusion transfer print (Polaroid)
5⅛ x 4⅛ in. (13 x 10.5 cm)
Robert Mapplethorpe Foundation (PD596)

151. *Untitled*. 1973/75
Monochromatic dye diffusion transfer print (Polaroid)
4⅛ x 5⅛ in. (10.5 x 13 cm)
Robert Mapplethorpe Foundation (PD598)

152. *Untitled (Judy Linn)*. 1973/75
Monochromatic dye diffusion transfer print (Polaroid)
5⅛ x 4⅛ in. (13 x 10.5 cm)
Robert Mapplethorpe Foundation (PD594)

153. *Untitled (David Croland)*. 1973
Monochromatic dye diffusion transfer print (Polaroid)
5⅛ x 4⅛ in. (13 x 10.5 cm)
Robert Mapplethorpe Foundation (PD597)

154. *Untitled (David Croland)*. 1973
Monochromatic dye diffusion transfer print (Polaroid)
5⅛ x 4⅛ in. (13 x 10.5 cm)
Private collection, courtesy Gallery Xavier Hufkens, Brussels (PD246)

155. *Untitled (Henry Geldzahler)*. 1973
Monochromatic dye diffusion transfer print (Polaroid)
4⅛ x 5⅛ in. (10.5 x 13 cm)
Robert Mapplethorpe Foundation (PD571)

156. *Untitled (Helen Marden)*. 1973/75
Monochromatic dye diffusion transfer print (Polaroid)
5⅛ x 4⅛ in. (13 x 10.5 cm)
Robert Mapplethorpe Foundation (PD523)

157. *Untitled (Clarissa Dalrymple)*. 1973/75
Monochromatic dye diffusion transfer print (Polaroid)
4⅛ x 5⅛ in. (10.5 x 13 cm)
Robert Mapplethorpe Foundation (PD603)

158. *Untitled (Ozzie Clark)*. 1973/75
Monochromatic dye diffusion transfer print (Polaroid)
4⅛ x 5⅛ in. (10.5 x 13 cm)
Robert Mapplethorpe Foundation (PD613)

159. *Untitled (Marianne Faithfull)*. 1974
Monochromatic dye diffusion transfer print (Polaroid)
5⅛ x 4⅛ in. (13 x 10.5 cm)
Robert Mapplethorpe Foundation (PD521)

160. *Untitled (Christopher Gibbs).* 1974
Monochromatic dye diffusion transfer print (Polaroid)
5⅛ x 4⅛ in. (13 x 10.5 cm)
Robert Mapplethorpe Foundation (PD611)

161. *Untitled (Michael Ranney).* 1973/75
Monochromatic dye diffusion transfer print (Polaroid)
5⅛ x 4⅛ in. (13 x 10.5 cm)
Robert Mapplethorpe Foundation (PD612)

162. *Untitled (Nicky Weymouth).* 1973
Monochromatic dye diffusion transfer print (Polaroid
4¼ x 3¼ in. (10.8 x 8.3 cm)
Robert Mapplethorpe Foundation (PD6)

163. *Untitled (Nigel Weymouth).* 1973/75
Monochromatic dye diffusion transfer print (Polaroid)
5⅛ x 4⅛ in. (13 x 10.5 cm)
Robert Mapplethorpe Foundation (PD460)

164. *Untitled (David Croland).* 1973
Monochromatic dye diffusion transfer print (Polaroid)
5⅛ x 4⅛ in. (13 x 10.5 cm)
Robert Mapplethorpe Foundation (PD593)

165. *Untitled (Nancy Nortia).* 1973/75
Monochromatic dye diffusion transfer print (Polaroid)
5⅛ x 4⅛ in. (13 x 10.5 cm)
Robert Mapplethorpe Foundation (PD463)

166. *Untitled.* 1973/75
Monochromatic dye diffusion transfer print (Polaroid)
5⅛ x 4⅛ in. (13 x 10.5 cm)
Robert Mapplethorpe Foundation (PD601)

167. *Untitled (Lars Kampmann).* 1973/75
Monochromatic dye diffusion transfer print (Polaroid)
5⅛ x 4⅛ in. (13 x 10.5 cm)
Robert Mapplethorpe Foundation (PD600)

168. *Untitled.* 1973/75
Monochromatic dye diffusion transfer print (Polaroid)
5⅛ x 4⅛ in. (13 x 10.5 cm)
Robert Mapplethorpe Foundation (PD232)

169. *Untitled.* 1970/73
Monochromatic dye diffusion transfer print (Polaroid)
3¼ x 4¼ in. (8.3 x 10.8 cm)
Robert Mapplethorpe Foundation (PD549)

170. *Untitled.* 1973/75
Monochromatic dye diffusion transfer print (Polaroid)
4⅛ x 5⅛ in. (10.5 x 13 cm)
Robert Mapplethorpe Foundation (PD575)

171. *Untitled.* 1970/73
Monochromatic dye diffusion transfer print (Polaroid)
4¼ x 3¼ in. (10.8 x 8.3 cm)
The Paul Rusconi Collection, Los Angeles (PD5)

172. *Untitled.* 1975
Monochromatic dye diffusion transfer print (Polaroid)
4⅛ x 5⅛ in. (10.5 x 13 cm)
Robert Mapplethorpe Foundation (PD543)

173. *Untitled.* 1973/75
Monochromatic dye diffusion transfer print (Polaroid)
5⅛ x 4⅛ in. (13 x 10.5 cm)
Robert Mapplethorpe Foundation (PD75)

174. *Untitled.* 1974
Monochromatic dye diffusion transfer print (Polaroid)
5⅛ x 4⅛ in. (13 x 10.5 cm)
Robert Mapplethorpe Foundation (PD565)

175. *Untitled.* 1974
Monochromatic dye diffusion transfer print (Polaroid)
5⅛ x 4⅛ in. (13 x 10.5 cm)
Collection David Croland

176. *Untitled (Bond Street).* 1973/75
Monochromatic dye diffusion transfer print (Polaroid)
5⅛ x 4⅛ in. (13 x 10.5 cm)
Robert Mapplethorpe Foundation (PD522)

177. *Untitled.* 1973/75
Monochromatic dye diffusion transfer print (Polaroid)
4⅛ x 5⅛ in. (10.5 x 13 cm)
Robert Mapplethorpe Foundation (PD544)

178. *Untitled (self-portrait).* 1973/75
Monochromatic dye diffusion transfer print (Polaroid)
4⅛ x 5⅛ in. (10.5 x 13 cm)
Private collection (PD125)

179. *Untitled (self-portrait).* 1973/75
Monochromatic dye diffusion transfer print (Polaroid)
4⅛ x 5⅛ in. (10.5 x 13 cm)
Private collection (PD68)

180. *Untitled.* 1973/75
Monochromatic dye diffusion transfer print (Polaroid)
5⅛ x 4⅛ in. (13 x 10.5 cm)
Robert Mapplethorpe Foundation (PD477)

181. *Untitled.* 1973/75
Monochromatic dye diffusion transfer print (Polaroid)
5⅛ x 4⅛ in. (13 x 10.5 cm)
Robert Mapplethorpe Foundation (PD569)

182. *Untitled (self-portrait).* 1973
Monochromatic dye diffusion transfer print (Polaroid)
4⅛ x 5⅛ in. (10.5 x 13 cm)
Private collection

183. Invitation to Light Gallery opening, January 6, 1973
Embossed gelatin silver print from Polaroid negative
with adhesive dot
4⅛ x 5⅛ in. (10.5 x 13 cm)
Robert Mapplethorpe Foundation

Selected Exhibition History

The exhibitions below featured or included Polaroid photographs by Robert Mapplethorpe.

Solo Exhibitions

1973
"Polaroids." Light Gallery, New York. January 6–February 3.

1979
"Robert Mapplethorpe: 1970–1975." Robert Samuel Gallery, New York.

1983
"Robert Mapplethorpe: 1970–1983." Institute of Contemporary Art, London. November 4–December 19. Traveled: Stills, Edinburgh, August 19–September 17; Arnolfini, Bristol, September 24–October 23; Midland Group, Nottingham, January 7–February 4, 1984; Museum of Modern Art, Oxford, England, April 1–May 27, 1984.

1988
"Robert Mapplethorpe: The Perfect Moment." Institute of Contemporary Art, University of Pennsylvania, Philadelphia. December 9, 1988–January 29, 1989. Traveled: Museum of Contemporary Art, Chicago, February 25–April 9, 1989; Washington Project for the Arts, Washington, D.C., July 21–August 31, 1989; Wadsworth Atheneum, Hartford, Conn., October 21–December 31, 1989; University Art Museum, University of California, Berkeley, January 17–March 18, 1990; Contemporary Art Center, Cincinnati, Ohio, April 8–May 21, 1990; Institute of Contemporary Art, Boston, Mass., June 14–August 31, 1990.

"Robert Mapplethorpe." Whitney Museum of American Art, New York. July 28–October 23.

1991
"Robert Mapplethorpe: Early Works." Robert Miller Gallery, New York. April 23–May 18.

1992
"Robert Mapplethorpe." Louisiana Museum, Humlebaek, Denmark. February 8–May 24. Traveled: Centro di Documentazione di Palazzo di Rivoli Museo d'Arte Contemporanea, Turin; Moderna Museet, Stockholm, January 30–March 21, 1993; Residence of Embassador Negroponte, Manila, 1993; Taidemuseo, Turku, Finland, 1993; Palais des Beaux Arts, Brussels, 1993; Centro per l'Arte Contemporanea Luigi Pecci, Prato, September 25, 1993–January 7, 1994; Tel Aviv Museum of Art, Israel, 1994; Fundació Joan Miró, Barcelona, 1994; Kunsthaus Wein, Vienna, 1994; Museum of Contemporary Art, Sydney, 1995; Art Gallery of Western Australia, Perth, 1995; City Gallery Wellington, New Zealand, 1995; Hayward Gallery, London, 1996; Gallery of Photography, Dublin, 1996; Museo de Art Moderna, São Paulo, 1997; Staatsgalerie, Stuttgart, 1997.
"Robert Mapplethorpe." Tokyo Metropolitan Teien Art Museum. June 2–July 2. Traveled: ATM Contemporary Art Gallery, Mito, July 18–November 3; The Museum of Modern Art, Kamakura, January 9–February 7, 1993; Nagoya City Art Museum, February 13–April 4, 1993; The Museum of Modern Art, Shiga, April 10–May 23, 1993.

1993
"Black and White Polaroids: 1971–1975." Robert Miller Gallery, New York. May 11–June 25.

1996
"Les Autoportraits de Mapplethorpe." Galerie Baudoin Lebon, Paris. March 21–May 4.

"Robert Mapplethorpe Polaroids." Roslyn Oxley9 Gallery, Sydney. May 8–June 1.

"Photosommer: Robert Mapplethorpe—Polaroids." Galerie Stefan Röpke, Cologne. July 5–September 10.

"Robert Mapplethorpe." Mitsukosi Museum of Art, Shinjuku. December 5–January 19, 1997. Traveled: Takashimaya Grand Hall, Osaka,

March 20–April 1, 1997; Fukushima Prefectural Museum of Art, April 19–June 1, 1997; Hokkaido Asahikawa Museum of Art, June 7–July 6, 1997; Sogo Museum of Art, Yokohama, July 31–August 24, 1997; Marugame Genichiro Inokuma Museum of Art, Marugame, September 6–October 19, 1997.

1999
"Robert Mapplethorpe." Sala Parpalló, Centre Cultural de la Beneficència, Valéncia. September 16–November 28.

2000
"Robert Mapplethorpe Polaroids 1971–1974." Asprey Jacques, London. September 15–November 18.

"Robert Mapplethorpe: Autoportrait Polaroids 1972–74." Cheim & Read Gallery, New York. April 28–June 10.

"Robert Mapplethorpe: Polaroids." Blum & Poe Gallery, Los Angeles. September 14–October 14.

2001
"Robert, Patti and Sam." Asprey Jacques Gallery, London.

2002
"Robert Mapplethorpe Retrospective." Museum of Contemporary Art, Sapporo. August 24–September 25. Traveled: Daimaru Museum, Tokyo, October 17–29; Daimaru Museum, Shinsiabashi-Osaka, January 30–February 11, 2003.

"Polaroids 1971–1975 Robert Mapplethorpe." Galerie Thomas Schulte, Berlin. September 27– November 30.

2005
"Robert Mapplethorpe: Tra Antico e Moderno. Un'antalogia." Promotrice delle Belle Arti, Turin. October 8–January 1, 2006.

2006
"Robert Mapplethorpe: Still Moving & Lady." With photographs by Judy Linn. Alison Jacques Gallery, London. September 8–October 7.

Group Exhibitions

1973
"Polaroids: Robert Mapplethorpe, Brigid Polk, Andy Warhol." Gotham Book Mart, New York.

1978
"Seven Artists' View of the Male Image." Robert Samuel Gallery, New York.

1981
"Instant Fotografie." Stedelijk Museum, Amsterdam. December 4–January 17, 1982.

1998
"Robert Mapplethorpe Portraits, Patti Smith Dessins." Galerie Baudoin Lebon, Paris. June 3–July 4.

"Mapplethorpe–Warhol, Celebrity Portraits." Marc Selwyn Fine Arts, Los Angeles. April 22–May 27. Sean Kelly Gallery, New York, June 9–July 28.

Selected Bibliography

The publications below discuss or contain reproductions of Polaroids by Robert Mapplethorpe.

Les Autoportraits de Mapplethorpe. With essays by Jean-Michel Ribettes and Jean-Louis Déotte. Paris: Baudoin Lebon/ Jean-Pierre Faur, 1996.

Celant, Germano. *Mapplethorpe.* Milan: Electa, 1992.

——. *Robert Mapplethorpe: Tra Antico e Moderno. Un'antalogia.* With an essay by Robert Rosenblum. Florence: Artificio Skira, 2005.

Cheim, John, ed. *Robert Mapplethorpe: Early Works.* New York: Robert Miller Gallery, 1991.

Danto, Arthur C. "Instant Gratification: Robert Mapplethorpe's Polaroids 1970–1976." *Aperture* no. 163 (spring 2001): 44–53.

Hayakawa, Hiroaki, Hidehito Shinmyo, Akira Tomita, and Tomoko Ogita, eds. *Robert Mapplethorpe.* With essays by Noriko Fuku, Marco Livingstone, and Richard D. Marshall. Japan: Art Life, Ltd., 1996.

Holborn, Mark, and Dimitri Levas, eds. *Mapplethorpe.* With an essay by Arthur C. Danto. New York: Random House, 1992.

——. *Mapplethorpe: Altars.* With an essay by Edmund White. New York: Random House, 1995.

Kardon, Janet. *Robert Mapplethorpe: The Perfect Moment.* With essays by David Joselit and Kay Larson. Philadelphia: Institute of Contemporary Art, University of Pennsylvania, 1988.

Levas, Dimitri, ed. *Mapplethorpe: The Complete Flowers.* With an essay by Herbert Muschamp. Dusseldorf: teNeues Publishing Group, 2006.

Marshall, Richard D. *Robert Mapplethorpe.* With essays by Richard Howard and Ingrid Sischy. New York: Whitney Museum of American Art and New York Graphic Society Books, 1988.

——. *Robert Mapplethorpe: Autoportrait Polaroids, 1972–74.* New York: Cheim and Read, 2000. Exhibition brochure.

——. *Robert Mapplethorpe: Autoportraits.* Santa Fe: Arena Editions, 2001.

Nomura, Chinobu, and Taku Shibuya, eds. *Robert Mapplethorpe Retrospective.* With essays by Toshio Smiizu and Kohtaro Iizawa. Tokyo: Tetsuya Kotani, APT International, 2002.

Robert Mapplethorpe. With essays by Christian Caujolle and Luis Revenga Valéncia: Sala Parpalló, 1999.

Robert Mapplethorpe: 1970–1983. With essays by Stuart Morgan and Alan Hollinghurst. London: Institute of Contemporary Art, 1983.

Robert Mapplethorpe: 1992–1993. With essays by Lydia Cheng, Ken Moody, Noriyoshi Sawamoto, Toshio Shimizu, and Mutsuo Takahashi. Tokyo: Asahi Shimbun, 1992.

Robert Mapplethorpe Portraits, Patti Smith Dessins. With an essay by Baudoin Lebon and Patti Smith. Paris: Baudoin Lebon, 1998.

Sokolowski, Thomas. *Right from the Start: The Early Polaroids of Robert Mapplethorpe.* Sydney: Roslyn Oxley9 Gallery, 1996. Exhibition brochure.

Index of Names

Page numbers in italics refer to illustrations

Acknowledgments

This book arose out of an invitation to visit the Robert Mapplethorpe Foundation archive from Michael Ward Stout, the artist's longtime friend and legal counsel and President of the organization. On my first visit, in 2003, I asked to view lesser-known works. What I saw took me thoroughly by surprise: the archive includes notebooks filled with black and white Polaroid photographs that Mapplethorpe made between 1970 and 1975, most of them never before exhibited or published. Many of the pictures seemed so intimate in their revelation of Mapplethorpe's curiosity about seeing with the camera that I felt I was peering into the photographer's diary. The themes that would later define his career were all there—flowers, nudes, self-portraits, sex pictures—but these small, silvery images were disarming in their revelation of Mapplethorpe's early fascination with the medium and pleasure in light, composition, and design.

It is therefore Michael Stout, and the trustees and staff of the Robert Mapplethorpe Foundation, that I must first thank for the opportunity to study this exceptional body of work. Joree Adilman, Foundation Manager, has won my unending appreciation for her attentiveness and keen detective skills during my research. I am also grateful to Jennifer Fiore and David Zuckerman, Foundation Assistants, who tirelessly attended to my visits to the archive. Diana Hagerbaumer, Assistant to the Foundation Manager, provided much-needed assistance and John Charles Thomas offered wise legal counsel. I owe a particular debt of gratitude to Marisa Cardinale, Consultant, for consistently greeting my questions and needs with prompt attention and good humor. Her patience, extraordinary efforts, and knowledge of the artist's career have gained her a place in my mind and heart as the project's guardian angel.

The study of this material now, over three decades after it was made, comes with its own difficulties and concerns. Few of the photographs are annotated with titles or dates and Mapplethorpe did little record-keeping at this point in his career. The identification of sitters and approximate dates has been challenging and many questions remain unanswered. To the extent that events and relationships in Mapplethorpe's early years affected the formation of his work, this book supplies biographical information as it relates to the Polaroids or to the artist's creative development. In researching his life and career, I have benefited immeasurably from the writings of those who have previously studied Mapplethorpe's art, in particular Germano Celant, Arthur C. Danto, Janet Kardon, Richard Marshall, Ingrid Sischy, and Thomas Sokolowski. I am also indebted to Mapplethorpe's biographer, Patricia Morrisroe, for her extensive account of the artist's life.

Many colleagues and collectors contributed to my understanding of this material by sharing their knowledge of the period or by opening their archives for my review. Among them I am particularly grateful to Philip and Shelley Fox Aarons, Vince Aletti, Irene Berger, Andreas Brown, Richard Calvocoressi, George Chauncey, Stuart Comer, Charles Cowles, Philippe Garner, Ron Gregg, Antonio Homem, Harold Jones,

Rick Karr, and Ryan McGinley. Many individuals at institutions, corporations, and artists' estates provided important information or research assistance, including Ted Mann at the Solomon R. Guggenheim Museum; Matthias Harder at the Helmut Newton Foundation; Thomas Solomon at the Holly Solomon Gallery archives; Barbara Hitchcock at Polaroid Corporation, and Matthew Lyons at The Kitchen. Special thanks go to Maxwell L. Anderson, Willard Holmes, Adam D. Weinberg, and Elisabeth Sussman for embracing this project at different stages of its evolution. Elvine Topac is greatfully acknowledged for her assistance and support.

I would like to thank Publisher Jürgen Krieger, Curt Holtz, and the staff of Prestel Verlag for undertaking this venture. I am deeply indebted to Christopher Lyon, who guided every aspect of the book's production with a sure hand and a keen eye for artistic excellence, and to Amanda Freymann, who applied her exceptional skills and experience to the translation of Mapplethorpe's photographs to the printed page. David Frankel edited the essay with intelligence, insight, and rigor. For the vision, sensitivity, and handsome design of the book I extend sincere appreciation to Dimitri Levas. Yukiko Yamagata provided crucial and timely assistance with the back matter of the book. Reegan Finger is gratefully acknowledged for creating a useful index. Thanks go to all of the artists and their representatives who provided reproduction for this publication.

A salute goes to the gallerists who have recognized the value of Mapplethorpe's Polaroids, particularly John Cheim, Howard Read and Sean Kelly. Alison Jacques warrants special notice as a long-standing champion of the idea of researching and exhibiting Mapplethorpe's Polaroids; this project would surely not have come to fruition without her commitment to the artist's career. As I pursued the subject of the Polaroids, many of Robert's photographic subjects and friends were generous with their time and recollections, including Tom Cashin, Clarissa Dalrymple, Jay Johnson, Judy Linn, and Jack Walls. I am especially indebted to David Croland, Edward Mapplethorpe, and Patti Smith, who tirelessly addressed my many queries and concerns. Special thanks go to them for their warmth and responsiveness, and for sharing their knowledge about the artist's life and work.

On a more personal note, I would like to thank those who provided invaluable support and served as crucial sounding boards during this project, in particular Greg Cameron, Rita Frankiel, Madeleine Grynsztejn, Jodie Ireland, and Susan Meiselas. The effect of Duane Schuler's perceptive comments and vital encouragement is reflected on every page. Last but most important, I owe a debt of gratitude to the artist who made the photographs that have captivated and challenged me for the past four years. It has been a pleasure and a privilege to attempt to decode this complicated body of work. It is my hope that this study will be the beginning of a dialogue about Mapplethorpe's Polaroids that will shed new light on the artist's career and invite a deeper appreciation for his special gifts.

—SW

Copyright

This catalogue was published in conjunction with the exhibition *Polaroids: Mapplethorpe* at the Whitney Museum of American Art, New York, in 2008.

Front and back covers: from an invitation to the opening of Robert Mapplethorpe's exhibition at Light Gallery, January 6, 1973:
Robert Mapplethorpe. *Untitled (self-portrait)*. 1973. Embossed gelatin silver print, adhesive dot, and protective film sleeve, 3 1/4 x 4 1/4 in. (8.3 x 10.8 cm) overall. Robert Mapplethorpe Foundation

Frontispiece: Robert Mapplethorpe. *Untitled (Graflex Camera)*. 1973/75. Monochromatic dye diffusion transfer print (Polaroid), 4 1/8 x 5 1/8 in. (10.5 x 13 cm). Robert Mapplethorpe Foundation

Reprinted 2023

Published by Prestel Verlag, Munich · London · New York,
A member of Penguin Random House Verlagsgruppe GmbH,
Neumarkter Str. 28, 81673, Munich, Germany

Library of Congress Control Number is available.

British Library Cataloguing-in-Publication Data: a catalogue record for this book is available from the British Library.

The Deutsche Bibliothek holds a record of this publication in the Deutsche Nationalbibliografie; detailed bibliographical data can be found under: http://dnb.ddb.de

ISBN 978-3-7913-4870-4
www.prestel.com

Design by Dimitri Levas
Design Layout by Abbey Fortney / Inspiri24 Design Studio
Editorial direction by Christopher Lyon
Edited by David Frankel
Production of original edition by Amanda Freymann
Production of this edition by Corinna Pickart
Separations by Prographics, Rockford, Illinois
Printed and bound by Passavia GmbH & Co. KG, Passau, Germany
Paper: Condat matt Périgord

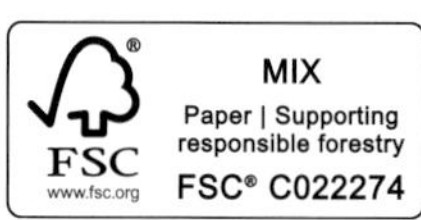

Penguin Random House Verlagsgruppe FSC® N001967
Printed in Germany